EDIBLE ACTION

EDIBLE ACTION

Food Activism and Alternative Economics

Sally Miller

Fernwood Publishing • Halifax & Winnipeg

Editing: Robert Clarke
Text Design: Brenda Conroy
Cover Design: John van der Woude
Printed and bound in Canada by Hignell Book Printing
This book is printed on paper containing 100% post-consumer fibre.

Published in Canada by Fernwood Publishing
Site 2A, Box 5, 32 Oceanvista Lane
Black Point, Nova Scotia, B0J 1B0
and #8 - 222 Osborne Street, Winnipeg, Manitoba, R3L 1Z3
www.fernwoodpublishing.ca

Fernwood Publishing Company Limited gratefully acknowledges the financial support
of the Government of Canada through the Book Publishing Industry Development
Program (BPIDP), the Canada Council for the Arts and the Nova Scotia
Department of Tourism and Culture for our publishing program.

Library and Archives Canada Cataloguing in Publication

Miller, Sally, 1962-
Edible action: food activism and alternative economics / Sally Miller.

Includes bibliographical references.
ISBN 978-1-55266-280-9

1. Agriculture--Economic aspects. 2. Food supply. 3. Agriculture--Social
aspects. 4. Food industry and trade. I. Title.

HD9000.5.M49 2008   338.19   C2008-903224-1

Contents

In the spirit of a gift economy, Edible Action *is dedicated to all those who have inspired me over the years, in the hopes that this may begin to return the favour.* Edible Action *is especially dedicated to Carol Stull of Finger Lakes Organic. The world of sustainable agriculture is not the same without her.*

Acknowledgements

Thanks are due to the educators, co-operators, friends, and activists too numerous to mention who have taught me, listened to me, and accompanied me in the quest for a better world. I am grateful to the people I have worked with in food initiatives both in Canada and the United States. I appreciate the chance I had to teach, write, and learn through York University's extraordinary Faculty of Environmental Studies. Special thanks are due to professors Deborah Barndt and Patricia (Ellie) Perkins for support and timely criticism while I worked on the manuscript. And profound thanks go to my professors at Cornell, though I have wandered far afield from my doctoral work in Nepal. Nonetheless, their footprints are evident in the journey to *Edible Action*. I am very grateful to the Catalyst Centre for general support and also for providing space for the pilot of the Popular Economics Course, which eventually became part of their curriculum.

The people I interviewed for this book cannot be thanked enough for their incredible generosity with their time and thoughts. I was touched by their willingness to try to help me get it right, and apologize for any errors I have made (which are of course my own).

Immense thanks go to Matthew Adams for his support and faith. Thanks are also due to my parents, for teaching me to love language and writing, and to Anne, Chris, Corvin, Geri, Melinda, and Peter for listening patiently when I needed to rant about my ideas. Thanks also to the wonderful people at Fernwood who have supported my efforts to get those ideas out in public.

Immense thanks also go to the Ontario Arts Council and Carrot Cache for support for portions of this work.

Introduction

Beautiful Tomatoes
and the Dance for Land

A friend and her little brother were left alone one day to eat their bowls of tomato soup. They soon discovered that although the soup looked pretty neat just sitting in the bowl, it looked even better splattered on the wall. Spoons, it turned out, made excellent catapults. Choosing beauty over appetite, they launched great dollops of the stuff onto the white walls. They admired the beautiful red splotches, no two alike. They enjoyed the tomato soup thoroughly until their mother came back to the room and they saw her face. Food is so much more than sustenance.

Food gathers meaning like an insatiable sponge. To paraphrase Claude Lévi-Strauss, food is good to think with. Many listeners have delighted in my friend's story because, like spoons filled with soup, it is brimming over with meaning. The story ruminates about North American eating practices, the origins of rebellion, the beauty of food, alliances, and misunderstanding. From annual family gatherings to daily concerns over hunger, from anxiety over hidden ingredients in food to innovative co-operative businesses, from the fight for land to the fight for nature-friendly agriculture, food becomes not just the key to how we live our lives in this world, but a way in which we talk about the world. Food is an idiom that, like a language full of puns, is useful for talking about certain things because it is so hospitable to the multiplication of meaning. Food is also a catalyst for social change — as both an inspiration and ally. In the case of this book, food provides an especially useful tool for discussing the ambivalence and shifting communication invoked by the work of social change. Food dogs the progress of social change. Like a puppy it runs eagerly ahead, leads the way, then falls back again, distracted by a bug.

The ways in which people and societies change through food are myriad. The examples of this change are equally mind-boggling in their extent and colour. Food inspires actions in Canada and across the world — actions that redress inequities between North and South, between rich and poor. Whether through food banks and community kitchens, or consumer movements or agrarian reform, the ways in which people try to change the world through food are plentiful and diverse. Sometimes they celebrate together while at other times they seem to be shouting each other down.

Food protests were vivid and enthusiastic within the widespread movement that stopped the World Trade Organization (WTO) talks on free trade in Seattle in 1999, hurled itself against the massive fence during the Free Trade of the Americas (FTAA) talks in Quebec City in 2001, and once again demonstrated and celebrated as world trade talks disintegrated in Cancun in 2003.[1] Reports from Cancun gave witness to the breakdown of a world trade plan controlled by a wealthy few. A key issue was agricultural subsidies: unfair subsidies united Southern nations against the selective protectionism that makes the transported product of U.S. farming cheaper than locally grown Mexican (or Canadian) products.[2]

Edible Action is concerned with two aspects of the relation of food and social change. First, what are the numerous ways in which food has inspired social change? And second, why is food such a successful catalyst for social change? These questions open the door for continued thoughtful practice and reflection. The answers will indicate which key issues are mobilized by food and agriculture, and provide a map for the alternatives that food engages.

That something is wrong with the food system is patently, heartbreakingly, true. Every day almost 16,000 children die from hunger-related causes (one every five seconds) (Bread for the World 2007). Across the globe small farmers fight to keep their land, to grow food for their communities, to keep their heads above the rising tide of debt. And, lest one associates these figures only with the images of famine in Africa that the media is addicted to, we must remember that 14.7 percent of Canadians live in food-insecure households (Pegg 2007), and about 7 percent are chronically hungry. In the United States the number is even higher: 11 percent of households each year experience or are at risk of hunger (Bread for the World 2007). This occurs in a country with immense food surpluses discarded by supermarkets, restaurants, agribusinesses, and institutions such as schools, or dumped as supercheap food on poor Southern nations, thereby destroying local food systems.

In Canada many farmers just don't see the point of continuing to work the land; they are at the losing end of a mathematical calculation about debt and economics that will never balance in their favour. As Brian Halweil (2000) points out, "Since 1950, the number of people employed in agriculture has plummeted in all industrial nations, in some regions by more than 80 percent." The National Farmers Union in Canada calculates that almost two out of three family farms have folded since World War II (National Farmers Union 2003). Many farmers decide to sell their land to developers because they can earn much more that way than they can make farming it. The developers remove and resell the topsoil, and plant homes made of ticky-tacky on the resulting desert. In an unspeakable tragedy in a wealthy country like Canada, growing numbers of farmers every year commit suicide rather than live through the experience of losing their land and livelihood. As researcher Christine Ahn (2003) notes, in Britain and Canada farmers commit suicide at double the rate of the general population. It is a trend south of the border as well. Farmers in the United States — who are now relatively small in number — are five times more likely to commit suicide than they are to die from farm accidents. Ahn quotes Brian Halweil of World Watch: "The true number may be even higher, as suicide hotlines report that they often receive calls from farmers who want to know which sorts of accidents are least likely to be investigated by insurance companies that don't pay claims for suicides." Other countries show the same pattern. Between 1998 and 1999 in India, over 1,000 farmers committed suicide: "Three hundred of them killed themselves by swallowing the very same costly pesticides that they had gone into debt to purchase" (Ahn 2003).

Across a great divide from these deaths, immense profits are being made, raked in by corporate food giants such as Cargill, McDonald's, and George Weston (Schlosser 2002; Kneen 1995). Around the globe the culture of globalization mangles and remakes economies everywhere. According to Halweil (2000), "In the United States, the share of the consumer's food dollar that trickles back to the farmer has plunged from nearly 40 cents in 1910 to just above 7 cents in 1997." In Mexico in the 1990s, the prices that farmers got for their corn and beans plummeted while the price of tortillas rose by 179 per cent (Desmarais 2007: 63). This story is retold in all corners of the globe. It is a tale fashioned by globe-trotting multinational corporations, and it ends in local hunger and despair.[3]

Talking with Your Mouth Full

> If there's something wrong with the food system, there's something wrong with the economic system. (Lucien Royer, People's Food Commission, 1979)

> Whether from despair or anger, farmers seem increasingly ready to rise up, sometimes violently, against government, wealthy landholders, or agribusiness giants. (Halweil 2000)

All over the world, people are using food to change how they live: their society, politics, and economies. For instance, every week the farmers of Plan B Organic Farm near Toronto bring their organic produce to farmers' markets all over the region. They also supply food to members of their Community-Supported Agriculture (CSA) program, in which people pay early in the spring to receive a weekly share of the season's harvest. One market that Plan B helped to start is the Dufferin Grove market, where farmers, bakers, and organic meat purveyors rub elbows with the community pizza oven and park community garden.

On Salt Spring Island, British Columbia, the first Canadian multistakeholder co-op, Growing Circle, buys local foods to supply local people and puts everyone on the board. At the other end of Canada, over 200,000 people are members of the Co-op Atlantic network of food co-ops, co-op farm stores, nd funeral and housing co-ops. Over the border in Maine, 50,000 to 60,000 people show up every year at the Common Ground Fair, a celebration of rural living put on by the Maine Organic Farmers and Gardeners Association. The Community Food Security Coalition in Venice, California, has taken its community food mapping process on the road across the United States, offering local people a way of viewing their community through food access and of taking charge of their food security. Consumer actions and boycotts have forced Starbucks, a giant coffee corporation, to offer fair trade coffee in its cafés. Dunkin' Donuts quickly followed suit.

In Canada, the United Kingdom, Japan, Europe, Africa, Mexico, and beyond, community organizers, activists, farmers, environmentalists, scientists, and Southern producers have joined forces to keep genetically modified foods out of the fields and off the shelves. In the global South, landless people have begun to occupy and win unused land back from wealthy landowners. Across the world, rural producers have joined forces in La Vía Campesina, an international movement of peasants and small farmers that fights for more just and sustainable food and agriculture systems. As the people at SunRoot Organic Farm in Kennetcook, Nova Scotia, told me, food is a medium that people use to talk about politics and to take action. Steve Law, one of SunRoot's three farmer-activists, told me, "What we are doing here on the farm is part of trying to model a different world." Across North America and the world, people have joined together to create diverse food initiatives. They are using food to talk about politics, economic justice, and social change.

Edible Action explores the cultural responses that arise when the principles of globalization, structural adjustment, and consolidation are applied to food and agriculture. These principles include: consolidate production under huge transnational corporations, slash public spending, consolidate land-holdings, increase efficiency, reduce small-scale industry, open all doors to free trade, constrict the movement of organized labour, and curtail the protection of local production. How do cultures erupt in creative and popular protest around food and agriculture issues? Why do food issues bring people out to the streets, to their city councils, and even (in Brazil) to their national governments? Why do they also result in an extraordinary feast of workable alternatives — that is, edible action? Polls show widespread concern about food and environmental issues, but how does the step from knowledge or concern to action take place? Why does food have a significant ability to mobilize people, moving them readily from information to political action for change?

Food Is Good to Think With

> We can understand, too, that natural species are chosen [as totems] not because they are "good to eat" but because they are "good to think." (Lévi-Strauss 1962)

When we fight about food we are also fighting about social change. *Edible Action* explores this thesis through the stories of various key movements in food and agriculture. The book investigates the ways in which the narratives of change overlap and build to a realistic conversation about social change. Throughout the book, this conversation exemplifies the growth of food democracy, in the sense not of pure agreement (coincidence of thought) but of negotiated agreement (consensus). Such a democracy in Canada builds on the legacy of the People's Food Commission (PFC) in the late 1970s, which set a historical context in Canada for the unfolding of social change through food. Like the "totemic species" that Lévi-Strauss describes, food is good to think with. The question that impels this book is: if food is good to think *with*, what do we use it to think *about*?

The answer to this question lies in the resistance that food activists, innovators, farmers, and store owners pose to the logic of conventional food economics. For instance, in the Maritime provinces, managers of the 200,000-member co-op network actively consider ways of building social capital. They have created an economic system in which the concatenation of overlapping interests guarantees that the standard rift between producers and consumers, which has built to crisis proportions in the food system, is almost impossible to maintain in all seriousness. Elsewhere, natural food stores have developed highly successful strategies based on a non-conventional understanding of customer behaviour. Price takes a back seat to the negotiations of needs, desires, plans for the planet, and care for other people. Food security organizations, such as the Stop Community Food Centre, FoodShare in Toronto, and the Food Project in Boston, focus on fairness and a right for all to feed themselves before profit. Fair trade organizations and localization initiatives seek to reduce the dangerous distance between producer and consumer that infects our food system. Out of this welter of alternatives, practices, and hope, the elements of true democracy become visible: participatory, constantly negotiated, constantly in process. These organizations have redefined financial success. They have eschewed the single-minded pursuit of growth and profit for the subtler goals of environmental health, democracy, and a world without hunger. An alternative economics rises from the stories of their everyday strategies, visions, and practical solutions.

Alternative Economics

> From the viewpoint of human reality that which is restored by the disestablishment of the commodity fiction [which separates the economic from the social] lies in all directions of the social compass (Polanyi 1944).

The practice of these food innovators is not just something dreamed up from a distance, but is clearly an elaborated working model for operation. On the way to changing the food system, food initiatives have necessarily created alternative economic systems, which are not mere parasites on systems of capitalism but are whole and internally consistent. Contrary to popular belief, these innovative organizations succeed at least as well as do conventional organizations. In the case of co-ops, they can even boast on average greater longevity and a much improved quality of working life. They have given people who might otherwise consider themselves unqualified to talk about economics an idiom in which to resist the depredations of the dominant economic system.

Edible Action builds on my own experience: over ten years of work experience in the natural and organic food sectors, with organic farmers, processors, and consumers, in retail, wholesale, and co-ops. The analysis and research strategies have developed partly from my work for the Ph.D. in anthropology on storytelling in Nepal (Cornell University, 1992). The approach I take relies on a journalistic approach to the interviews, although it is certainly informed by my readings of ethnographic method; and I have offered considerable opportunity for interviewees to change or adjust the direction of the research, to tell me what they consider most important for the book and to steer me towards other key people to interview.

My approach to stories derives from a conviction that our approach to the world, as part of the function of a culture, is rhetorical; that is, we are constantly shaping our experience and determining our actions by the way in which we narrate events to ourselves and to each other. To look at widespread actions around food (in some cases global action) is to explore functioning mythologies. In this analysis, a cultural mythology is a patterned construction of reality that is shared and laboured over by numerous participants. This "mythology" is not fiction but the cultural work that we use to make sense of the world and to establish beliefs and rules for action and change. The progress in social movements is a study in a dialogue among storytellers, as each of us offers up our realities, and compares and discusses them. The resulting cacophony is both chaotic and purposeful. As we begin to repeat each other's stories, or to tell them together in a counterpoint, cultures begin to take new shapes, and different directions are taken by members of a society.

Part of the challenge in writing this book has been the enormous number of stories about people using food to change the world. The choice of which stories to tell in-depth has been a little like living with a baby monitor, trying to decipher the point at which the babbling becomes pointed and moves uniformly towards a clear demand for change.

The final chapter explores the next step: what kind of food education and organizing would bring all of these stories and idioms of food into one conversation? How can food, with which we delight to talk about economics, give people everywhere strategies for challenging an economic system that is increasingly failing larger and larger sectors of society, as the gap between rich and poor widens every day and more people, both North and South, gaze into a hungry and poisoned future?

My hope is that the landscape and vision of social change offered in this book will be both an inspiration and a kind of mnemonic device that will trigger memories and thoughts of personal experience and action that will further people the landscape with extraordinary moments and initiatives.

I was once told during my doctoral research in Nepal that there was part of a religious holiday when women could keep all the land they could dance across that day. The earth is starting to shake with the spirit and the strength of dancers and food protesters everywhere, and the land they are reclaiming is enough to feed us all.

Notes

1. The food issues that brought people to these anti-globalization protests are numerous. Some prominent ones include local food and agriculture, genetically engineered food, and corporate control of food and trade regulations.
2. The resistance to genetically engineered corn was also instrumental in the disintegration of the talks (Deborah Barndt, personal communication).
3. The details of this growing global inequity (which I will return to in chapter 4) have been carefully documented by numerous scholars and journalists. For progressive economists, the gap is a given, a product of social change since about 1970 in North America. For Canada, see Yalnizyan (1998); for a global perspective see the work of Susan George (1984), David Korten (2001), and others.

Chapter 1

Lessons from History

I don't know who's really responsible for the rising price of food. Everyone denies responsibility. The small farmers say they're not responsible, and I believe them. Agribusiness say it's not responsible, and I don't believe them. Government says it's not responsible, and I believe them least of all. (Gus Long, People's Food Commission, 1978)

Footsteps fill the air of the small room, a room like numerous others roped into service for Canada's People's Food Commission (PFC). The air may be slightly stale, the smell of a local high-school gymnasium perhaps, or a recreation centre; chairs scrape across a concrete floor to shape a half-circle or lines; people face front expectantly. A session of the 1978–80 People's Food Commission hearings is about to begin. The PFC was a series of informal hearings on food that inspired new ways of thinking about social change in Canada (see People's Food Commission [PFC] 1980).

In the late 1970s in North America, word of food safety crises, environmental crises, military coups in Latin America, and courageous responses bellowed from newspapers and other media. A boycott against Nestlé's infant formula was in full swing. Nestlé was selling powdered milk to mothers in developing countries, teaching them to stop breast-feeding and instead to take their often impure water, mix it with the Nestlé product, and feed it to their children. Fear of pesticides in food and soil was rising rapidly. The organic food movement and a new wave of food co-ops were inaugurated. Meanwhile the food industry was increasing its imports from the South, making a smooth transition from the exploitation of colonialism to exploitation through unbearable debt load, shifting agricultural lands to cash crops for export, and wreaking havoc on subsistence in the South.

The issues of three decades ago are painfully familiar. The speakers at the PFC hearings were concerned about toxins in the food, the effects of unsustainable agriculture, the impact of refined sugar on children. Today around the world we hear reports of mad cow disease, appearing now both in cattle and occasionally in humans; recalls for different food disasters, often in the dangerous forms of E. coli, are frequent. The story of the PFC allows us to consider what makes us stand up and speak out. In 2007 several scientists found adverse results from tests on bovine growth hormone and were pressured by industry lobbying to conceal their results. In the late 1970s, according to the testimonies at the hearings, people were concerned that corporations might be acquiring too much power over the food system. How were small farms to survive?

Farmers big and small in this first decade of the new century make very little more now per tonne of food than they did then, and they receive a great deal less of your food dollar. Raj Patel (2007: 64) points out that, contrary to market theory, the more that U.S. farmers sold, the less they got; by 1980 U.S. farmers received 97 cents for every dollar they spent on growing their crops. If farmers in the 1970s found the situation unsustainable, how can we describe the current situation except as a disaster or a tragedy?

Likewise, in either 1979 or perhaps last year, your son or daughter might have become a vegetarian, perhaps citing a course that made them re-examine their food choices. Your search for food that would be acceptable to them leads you from limited displays in the corporate supermarket into the friendly aisles of local natural food stores, co-ops, or the farmers' market. At some point in your past or future, you might have made the decision to tell someone about this, perhaps defending or explaining your children's food choices, describing new allergies a friend had developed, maybe working through a parent's cancer or a neighbour's food or water poisoning. What tipped your concern over the edge into speaking to others about it? What led or would lead you to speak up in front of a larger group, putting into public record your anger, your concerns, your analysis of food problems?

In 1978 and 1979 thousands of Canadians, in small and large venues across Canada, from northern British Columbia to Labrador, gathered to speak and put on record their concerns about the food system. The People's Food Commission was loosely organized — as Jean Christie, the PFC national co-ordinator (interview 2002) said, it was run on "a wing and a prayer" — and spectacularly diverse. The people who testified at the hearings spoke about food safety, breastfeeding, animal husbandry. Some (consumers) decried high food prices. Others (producers) decried the desire for cheap food. They gave witness to the collapse of small farms and agriculture in Canada. They spoke up for co-operation in co-ops. Politicians from the New Democratic Party of Canada (NDP) — a progressive political party that grew originally from the co-operative movement in the Prairies — showed up, as did many union representatives, including members of the National Farmers Union. High-school students wrote and performed plays; the activity in each region led to parallel initiatives. For instance, in one town a giant chicken picketed a supermarket.

Anyone could present their views — and do it in various forms — at the hearings. The Commission, unlike the government commissions it reflected, was largely decentralized. Although there was a small national staff, each region and municipality was self-organized. Each local working group received a kit with suggestions for community research methods and media outreach.

The initial impetus for the PFC is best described by a series of questions asked anonymously by the Local Working Group (LWG) kit (sent to communities that had decided to organize a hearing). The Local Working Group kit named four goals that local members could use to explain the PFC to people: "1) Give a wide range of Canadians a platform to express their concerns about food...; 2) generate new information and greater awareness about food and food issues...; 3) Build coalition...; 4) Initiate follow-up action."

Always lightly funded, the PFC was an extraordinary and mostly volunteer effort that saw hundreds of people standing up to make statements, show slides, enact puppet shows, and generally speak out on the state of the food system and what should be done. In addition to producers, consumers, unions, and politicians, the food industry was represented — both the Grocery Manufacturers Association (representatives of the corporations) and the United Food and Commercial Workers union. The people from the nascent Land Trust movement showed up; Pollution Probe spoke out as well. The ecumenical group GATT-Fly and other similar organizations, precursors to the anti-globalization movement of today, were all there. Small grants paid the way for a few representatives to come from the South. They spoke at meetings and provided insight into how imported food was produced, the unsustainability of the export economy in the South, and strategies for improvement. Many people were also not there: First Nations peoples were underrepresented; and Quebec ran a parallel but independent commission. An equally important issue is why some people abstained from the PFC process.

To read the briefs of the People's Food Commission is inspiring because so many people had the courage to speak, took time to prepare carefully (the eloquence, creativity, and thoughtfulness of many of the testimonies is striking). People gave up time to organize meetings, get the word out, and attend and facilitate meetings. There is also, in reading the many pages of testimony that Christie carefully filed, the bittersweet sense of familiarity. That recognition of sameness should not slide into despair — the recurrence of food issues means that we are in the grip of a powerful movement of history, and an incredible shifting and concentration of power. It was this conjuncture of pressures and recognitions that brought the People's Food Commission to fruition in the late 1970s; since then many activists who cut their teeth on the Commission have continued through union activism, food activism, and poverty actions to fight for economic and food justice. Eventually the initiative itself ran out of money and energy. At the final stage the Commissioners (mostly volunteers) collated and sorted the submissions. The project was written up in *The Land of Milk and Money*, a book that stands as a testament to the variety of opinions and stances at the PFC.

The PFC was part of a peculiarly Canadian tradition of commissions. These commissions, sometimes called royal commissions in honour of the

British monarchy's continuing lurking presence, are struck in Canada in order to allow the participants to assess the feelings, opinions, and ideas of people across the nation about a particular issue. Often the commissions are clearly and firmly under government auspices, held in Ottawa by invitation only (ensuring, of course, that only particular voices will be heard, although organizers will insist on their attempts to have all interests represented). Historically, commissions have often represented a turning point in Canada's policies on important issues. The Royal Commission on Women (1970) helped in the fight for greater equality for women in Canada; the Romanow Commission (2002) confirmed Canadians' powerful adherence to the principle of the right to health care regardless of ability to pay. In 1977 the Mackenzie Valley Pipeline Inquiry under Justice Thomas Berger impressed many with its committed attempts to reach all concerned. The Inquiry focused on land use and the local attitudes towards the proposed pipeline in the Northwest Territories. Justice Berger travelled from one isolated town to another and sat in local hearings at which experts and local people alike spoke.

The Berger Inquiry paved the way for the People's Food Commission, although the PFC took the concept much further. The marvelous kits sent out to regional and local organizers were a primer on popular education and community organizing. They exhorted the organizers to reach a full diversity of interests in their communities, and suggested creative and striking ways of using food (about which everyone has an opinion) to bring everyone out to speak their minds. As Mark Langevin and Peter Rosset (1997: 335) state, "Food is a window which allows us to look into any society, anywhere in the world, and determine critically important things about its structure, especially with regard to social justice and the distribution of power and wealth."

The People's Food Commission represents a key moment in Canada's social history, when all of the most generative themes of social change through food came together in thousands of testimonies across Canada. All the pressures that have made our food system the inequitable and unsustainable behemoth that it is were already well in play, enshrined in government policies, new trade relations, and the agricultural economy. From the PFC moment the threads of everything we seek to change about the food system weave down through the decades to the present day. "It was no accident that the People's Food Commission was organized in 1977. By that year, Canada's food system was showing signs of severe strain" (PFC 1980: 7).

The time of the PFC hearings was marked by extraordinary upheavals in food systems, with disastrous results both North and South. The willingness of ordinary Canadians to speak out about whatever chunk of the iceberg they could see from their vantage points attests to the growing urgency of the global problems. Local agriculture was collapsing in the North and South.

The gap between rich and poor was rapidly expanding. Consumers were angry and uncertain as to where to place the blame. Hunger in developed countries was rising, while hunger in developing countries was not proving amenable to easy technological solutions such as hybrid seeds and other Green Revolution magic. The PFC allows us to conduct a retrospective conjunctural analysis,[1] identifying the historical moment, the actors and projects that culminated in this crucial period.

Crises and turning points mark this whole historical period, beyond the world of food. Reviewing a timeline for the period from the point of view of the less powerful is like trying to read an old history book that mice have nibbled. Despite the holes, we can still piece together a picture of momentous events for the poor, for grassroots organizing, and for ordinary people everywhere. Here is the middle class, beginning its long slide towards lower incomes, debt, and high risk. Over there are the Vietnamese, fighting a jungle war against impossible odds. Closer to home, oil prices are up; inflation, unemployment, and housing prices, all up. Food prices rose by 50 percent between 1973 and 1977 (PFC 1980: 7–8).

In Canada not only was the economy struggling, but the issue of Quebec's sovereignty had brought the Canadian government to a moral low as it called out troops and suspended civil liberties in Quebec. The referendum on separation was in 1980. Earlier, the hugely popular Prime Minister Trudeau had lost popularity over the Quebec issue, only returning to power in 1980. Trudeau eventually got the Canadian Constitution out of the hands of Britain (giving Canada the right to change its own laws) and inaugurated the Canadian Charter of Rights and Freedoms in 1982, protecting many key Canadian rights, including speech and the right to vote. For the first time, too, the youth of that generation could peer into a future in which it was no longer a foregone conclusion that they would make higher incomes than their parents did.

Like the U.S.-supported military interventions in the South, these events were often hidden in mainstream news and education. They were concealed to some extent by an aspect of the Christian or cultural ethics of individualism that assumes your problems must be above all your fault, the result of a failure to work hard enough, perhaps. These ethics plague us today, translating in times of trouble into, "You have no one to blame but yourself." It is nonetheless hard to understand how military turmoil in the South went largely unnoticed in the Northern mainstream culture. There were democratic and socialist revolutionary movements in numerous sites of colonialisms past. These were followed (within the decade before the PFC) by military coups, frequently supported by the U.S. government. Brazil went in 1964; Bolivia in 1971; Uruguay in 1973; Chile with Allende's assassination in 1973; Argentina in 1976 (Berryman 1987: 97). The coups were followed by the installation of right-wing governments: full-scale democracy or socialism receded into the realm of wishful thinking.

Meanwhile, liberation theology and popular education were taking a grassroots, participatory approach to relieving the suffering of the poor and returning power to the oppressed. The communities organized by these models of direct democracy were sometimes called base communities. A 1978 congress of base communities in Brazil proclaimed: "1) the main root of the oppression they suffer is the elitist, exclusive, capitalist system; and 2) people resist and are liberated to the extent that they become united and create a network of popular movements" (Berryman 1987: 76). Liberation theologian Archbishop Oscar Romero began to address the violent oppression in El Salvador in his sermons, and pursued the goals of social justice by organizing community and religious groups. He was assassinated in 1980.

Revolutionary groups preaching justice and social equity that did gain power showed a dangerous tendency to try to feed everyone; witness, for instance, the radical programs of the Sandinista government of Nicaragua in the early 1980s, which redistributed land and established farming co-operatives. They were eventually undermined by the right-wing, U.S.-backed contras. Removing food from the free market was already unacceptable. It would only lead, perhaps, to other "socialist" tendencies such as ensuring water for everyone (another struggle that today has joined the fight for food). In Tanzania the popular president Julius Nyerere also instituted radical social programs with the goal of ensuring that everyone's basic needs were met. In South Africa the struggles against apartheid were eclipsing other considerations, and the issue reached global prominence with the murder of activist Steven Biko in 1977. At the same time, the aid organization Oxfam gamely continued to try to maintain neutrality and continue its agricultural development projects in South Africa (Black 1992: 246). Would the answer to hunger and toxic food be reached through politics or through justice?

Agricultural Crisis in the 1970s

> We delude ourselves that our agriculture is efficient, while all along the capital of the land is decreasing: capital in the soil, capital in diversity, capital in rural social systems. (Ecology Action Centre of Halifax, PFC, April 1979)

A bit earlier, the publication of Rachel Carson's *Silent Spring* (1962) had galvanized the environmental movement. The organic and sustainable food movement was gathering momentum around the time of the PFC, and received some mention across the country. As well, development circles were pondering the growing awareness that the Green Revolution had not quite been the magic bullet that everyone had been hoping for. During the Green Revolution of the 1960s and onwards, ecologist Jules Pretty (1995: 27) points out, scientists "widely believed... that they would be able to transform agricultural systems without affecting social systems." But this widely touted attempt to impose North American forms of agriculture on developing countries fell short dramatically, both technically (failing over the long-term to produce the expected higher yields) and socially (failing to convince highly knowledgeable local farmers that such a massive change in technique and expenditure was really necessary). Export agriculture (cash crops such as bananas, chocolate, and coffee) did not feed anything but the foreign debt; and the snazzy new hybrid seeds that were introduced turned out to be water-hungry and fragile. Worse, the new techniques seemed to increase yields only at first, and only with the addition of other expensive inputs such as chemical fertilizer and pesticides.

These problems, immediately apparent to the indigenous farmers who had put their life savings and more into the new technologies, percolated back to awareness among activists in the North. The beautiful agricultural revolution was in shambles overseas, and the squeeze used by the United States to increase Southern reliance on cheap imported food (dumping) had begun to be practised in Canada. Food was still cheap here, but for the most part it wasn't our food, and it wasn't our farmers profiting from it. The Agriculture Committee of the Ecology Action Centre testified on April 21, 1979: "The food does not seem to taste quite as good as it used to. But many people have more or less accepted that this is the 'modern world,' and that this is the price we must pay to feed so many people at reasonable monetary cost."

The PFC did more than trumpet a moment of urgency in food economics and justice. As a unique exercise in direct democracy, a counterpoint to the Canadian tradition of royal commissions, the PFC also marked a turning point in thought about food systems and food justice. Before the late 1970s, the conventional response to famine and hunger (elsewhere) was food aid or attempts to correct the assumed naiveté and backwardness of non-Northern farmers. By the late 1970s many organizations, including Oxfam-Canada and Food First in San Francisco, were reporting that the ex-colonies of the so-called Third World were in worse shape than ever, that promising democratic and socialist revolutionary movements for equity, justice, and autonomy in Latin America had been met with U.S.-backed assassinations, coups, and repression. The growing awareness of injustice meant that many non-governmental organizations (NGOs) were experimenting with more and more sophisticated notions of participatory development. "Give a person a fish, he'll eat for a day, teach the person to fish and he will eat for the rest of his life" had not yet become a cliché.

The organizers of and participants in the PFC were part of a hugely ambitious, national experiment in bottom-up democracy. While the PFC itself faltered in taking the steps from reflection to action, the drive behind it inspired local community organizing and new approaches across Canada, including a new generation of food and poverty activists. Activists were beginning to look to the inspiration of participatory democracy organizing in Latin America, learning from Paulo Freire's popular education projects in Brazil. These communities also were the sites in which liberation theology was taking Vatican II to unheard of heights of social justice and grassroots organizing. In Freire's Recife area of Brazil, Oxfam (recently converted momentarily to the practice of popular education) was experimenting with participatory development modelled on Freire's work. The determination of that earlier movement persists in the activist work of labour and popular education, and in organizations such as the B.C. Food Systems Network.

While food aid was steadily increasing, and becoming a tool of U.S.-subsidized agriculture (see Friedmann 1993a, 1993b), the recognition that hunger was a systemic problem, a matter of unequal distribution and access rather than scarcity, was taking hold of food activism circles. In her history of Oxfam, Maggie Black (1992: 71) writes that in the international Food and Agriculture Organization (FAO) and other circles of food change it was gradually becoming clear that "hunger was much more deep-rooted and its elimination required a longer-term and more considered approach."

How to Tell a Story

When a journalist sits down to recount an event, the writer weighs and compares a number of possible frames. The writer's choice of how to tell the story determines what is remembered and what is forgotten. Does Jack the Giant Killer scale the vine, alone and foolhardy and brave, to bring the giant to his knees? Or is it another Jack (or more often in this case, Jill) who, cast out from her home on some bogus excuse, only succeeds in gaining the treasure through the support of a series of characters she befriends along the way? Occasionally the friends are miraculously more powerful than they seemed at first. Among my favourite tales are the ones that tell about how Jill's friend has an innate ability, like a humble frog's loud croak or a mosquito's incessant whine, that turns out to be useful after all, and turns the tide of the narrative in her favour.

In a true democracy (that is, one in which people are not just represented but have equal voices and power in events), who would be the heroes? What story frames would be favoured to describe political events? The material gathered by the People's Food Commission resists the Jack the Giant Killer story; it is unusually difficult to identify a key organizer or even a group of movers and shakers behind that material. The people I spoke to about it had quite different stories about how it got started. History books tend to tell mainstream history as a series of actions/decisions/commands by key figures such as the prime minister of Canada. I wondered as a child why the only actors on this barren stage seemed to be white middle-aged men. Often in my history books (in the United States), they and their photographs received commemorative little boxes all to themselves. I searched these books in vain for someone who looked like me. In a democracy, perhaps the hidden miraculous powers in each of us would be allowed to bubble to the surface.

The People's Food Commission was conducted and reported on in a way that resists the conventional story frame. To write about it is to challenge the heroic version of history, and it is to think of narratives driven by democracy — of narratives propelled by the movement of organizations and a widespread attention to new models of development, by resistance to nationwide pressures of corporatization and food poverty. The PFC process represents an incredible moment of participatory democracy that reverberates in the history of social change in Canada. Not only were the Commission's objectives somewhat various, but once the hooting and hollering were all over, the judgments of its efficacy were also various.[2]

Witnesses for Change

> The egg producers who were present had a meeting with the PFC staff and commissioners sitting in at various points. They decided to take common action to stop shipping to the Creamery and sell direct instead. (Callen, PFC, Shadow Lake, Saskatchewan)

The egg producers who took action together after the PFC represent the exception rather than the rule. Although the PFC was criticized for a lack of tangible outcomes on a national scale, the process of witnessing, attending to the voice of the other, has a power for change not to be underestimated. To witness partakes of a particular relationship to action. Witnessing has a long history in North America both politically (in government inquiries and commissions) and in various religious practices, particularly Quakerism. To bear witness is in itself effective. It can reaffirm a faith in belief, offer confirmation of shared values, or even teach shared values. It also can imagine a future in which the occurrence of events or miracles has enacted a change in people's lives. However, the outcome of witnessing is unpredictable and not carved in stone; the PFC shone with hope rather than commitment. As Neva Hassanein (2003: 81) points out in a discussion of food democracy, stating a grievance is not always enough: "Grievances do not automatically translate into action."

In the context of Quakerism, witnessing is part of a movement for social justice, a movement that includes community action and organized movements for peace and other issues. In the case of a movement like the People's Food Commission, many people wondered why the process rarely led to action.[3] Once the hearings ended, where could it have gone from there?

Since the days of the PFC, various actions for social change have taken place: the movement against genetically modified organisms (GMO), the organic movement, co-operative development, the food security movement, the fair trade movement, and food democracy. As in the PFC, these actions have led to the rise of many voices, some in harmony, some jangling and discordant. Here, as readers, we bear witness to the extraordinary resilience, creativity, and determination that food actions reveal across time and around the world.

Notes

1. Conjunctural analysis, developed from Paulo Freire's popular education work in Brazil, teases out the various threads of a historical moment and their interconnections and mutual pressures.
2. I originally presented some of this material on the People's Food Commission at the Joint Annual Meetings of Agriculture, Food and Human Values Society and Association for the Study of Food and Society, May 2003.
3. From interviews and also informal conversations with various actors in the PFC.

Chapter 2

Frankenfoods and
the Fight to Define Nature

From 1998 to 1999 my work as a sales representative with the Organic Meadow organic dairy co-op found me doing demos in various stores and supermarkets with organic milks and cheeses and other foods. Organic Meadow is a subsidiary of OntarBio, a southwestern Ontario farmers' co-op. As I stood there in stores surrounded by healthy, pesticide-free, and antibiotic-free dairy stuffs, I often talked to people who already knew the products. They came by the table to tell me how much they liked them, or to ask the co-op to make new products, chocolate milk, perhaps. I was fascinated with what made people switch to organic milk. My interest was only partly in learning more about marketing the products; for me it was also a sociological question. I began to realize (as customers kept telling me these stories) that many households had switched to organic milk before even considering the organic approach to other categories of food. Often the first organic product that crosses a household's threshold is organic milk for the kids. As I continued to offer bits of organic cheese, and little cups of milk, I began to weave the ideas here: that food is a catalyst for social change, and that stories about food can be used to shape social change.

Frankenfoods Inspire New Coalitions of Activists

The Big Carrot Natural Food Market was established in 1983 on Danforth Avenue in Toronto, and provides a wide range of organic and natural foods. But it is no ordinary food store. After a long period of investigation and verification, the staff removed all food products containing genetically modified organisms from their store. For our interview at the Big Carrot, Asa Copithorne and I sat in the store's busy deli while staff rushed around and customers intent on finding safer, better food worked their way along the aisles.

The Big Carrot is a worker-owned co-op. Copithorne argues that it was their co-op structure that made it possible for them become the only retail store in Canada to remove GMOs from their shelves, a huge decision that was expected to hurt the bottom line (see chapter 9 for more on this case). Still, the Big Carrot is not alone in the battle to keep GMO foods out of our fields and our kitchens.

In December 2000, to tremendous media attention, the Big Carrot opened its doors on their GMO-free food aisles. Copithorne was somewhat surprised at all the media interest; after all, any natural food store has a purchasing policy and constantly reassesses what it carries. It rejects some products and replaces others in an ongoing research project to offer safe food to consumers. Why did the GMO move grab media and public attention in a way in which organic and natural food never had?

The broad social relevance of the GMO issue, and its ability to mobilize people around multiple issues, may provide an answer. Over the past thirty years, corresponding to some extent with the rise of environmentalism, the world of food politics has moved rapidly to encompass many different issues. In cases of GMO protests in the North, consumer health concerns have tended to predominate over issues of ecosystem health.[1] Many people first begin to question the conventional food system when they become aware of food safety issues. To avoid pesticides, for instance, consumers will turn to organic food, especially for their children. Copithorne of the Big Carrot reported that it was health concerns that originally made the store address the issue of GMOs. Other factors of concern included the danger of increased food allergies and the antibiotic resisters in the new seeds. In the end the store removed GMOs from its shelves because the staff firmly believed there was just not enough conclusive evidence about the effects of GMOs, and that genetically engineered (GE) food was in no way "natural."

Across Canada, despite the assurances of the grocery associations and BIOTECanada, an industry-funded association that represents biotechnology companies, people generally mistrust the safety of genetically engineered food, and have successfully resisted both bovine growth hormone (BGH) and, more recently, the genetically engineered wheat that the U.S.-led biotech industry was hoping to test on Canadian soil. The issue of GE food provided a social cross-cutting mobilization that had eluded the generally mid- to upper-class-based organic movement. The concern over GMOs is widespread and deep (95 percent of Canadians support mandatory labelling). The desirability of genetically engineered food is in doubt across classes and income levels, including both farmers and eaters. The jury is still out on many of the factors, but consumers, increasingly worried over food safety, tend to invoke the precautionary principle: that we should not be the guinea pigs for an experiment that is being conducted on eaters around the world.

Given that corn, wheat, and soy products are extensively used in packaged foods, even if you don't munch down on an ear of GMO corn this week, you are undoubtedly getting your daily dose of GMOs in your breakfast cereal or cereal bar, your can of soup, your crispy salted snack of choice, or your drink. For suppliers that want to avoid GMOs, the test for the organisms in a harvested crop is quite simple, and certainly available (despite claims by the grocery industry). The only question that holds up the proceedings is exactly how accurate the results should be for the public; the test is capable of accuracy to an extremely small amount (for instance, the company Genetic ID offers tests that are good to .01 percent detection of GMOs). The grocery industry in the United States and Canada has steadfastly refused to allow labelling except voluntarily — and "voluntarily" means that it is not happening. Elsewhere (Japan, the European Union), testing and labelling are in place. Organic or conventional non-GMO farmers whose crops are contaminated by nearby GMO crops risk losing their crops and income from them after testing is done. Some countries, including Zimbabwe and Zambia, have refused GMO products as food aid. Supermarkets in the European Union, such as Sainsbury, Co-op, Tesco, and Iceland, have for years placed various bans on GMO products (usually in the processing of their own branded products if not on a wider selection of their shelves) (Organic Consumers Association 2003).[2]

Cowboy Science

Genetically engineered food is not the result of traditional plant breeding of the sort practised by farmers for centuries, including, for instance, indigenous Andean potato farmers, with their hundreds of different varieties (Hansen 2000). Genetic engineering involves completely novel scientific techniques that involve shooting (literally) novel genes (of a fish, for instance) into another gene (such as a tomato) in the hopes that a new (and patentable) plant will thereby result. GMO researchers may also insert a bacterial "truck" with a viral promoter that turns off the plant cell's natural immune system. This prevents the cell from rejecting the foreign material (Hansen 2000). The techniques of this work are so slapdash and unpredictable as to debase the name of science. As Brewster Kneen points out, the theory behind genetic engineering seems to hearken back to some outdated notions of science (Kneen 1999; conversation with Food Group, Toronto, Feb. 13, 2004; Suzuki 2004).

The power that industry has had to shape and control GMO research also renders it suspect. One whistle-blowing scientist lost his job and his reputation in the scientific community. As that story unfolded it became clear that Dr. Arpad Pusztai had proceeded in his work following more or less good scientific principles, but unfortunately did it under the auspices of an industry-supported project. Some of his conclusions were thoroughly unwelcome to his sponsors. According to one report:

> Twenty international scientists have signed an unprecedented memorandum supporting the controversial findings of suppressed research which found that rats fed on genetically modified potatoes suffered a weakened immune system and damage to vital organs. In a report published for the first time today, the scientists from 13 countries also demand the immediate professional rehabilitation

of the British scientist, Dr. Arpad Pusztai, who discovered these preliminary findings last year and was forced to retire after speaking out about his concern. (Gillard, Flynn, and Rowell 1999)

Kneen asks, "What were we trying to solve in the first place?" He argues that part of the reason for the bad science in most of the GMO research may be the commercial motivations behind this science. The reason for plant genetic engineering is not really to solve world hunger, as the bio-technology companies like Monsanto and their advocacy front groups, such as the Council for Biotechnology Information, would have you believe. As recent studies have shown, biotech seeds rarely lead to improved yields over the long term. In the first place, poor farmers and hungry people can't afford the seeds — but even if they could afford them they would do better with non-GMO seeds (see Kneen 1999). GMO seeds can provide better yields under the perfect circumstances that nature and impoverished farmers can rarely provide: irrigation, strategic use of expensive chemicals, and no drought, among other factors.

One reason that companies have addressed all this energy and attention to selling the public on GE food has been that the existing traditionally bred plant and its fruits are, from their point of view, recalcitrant to the needs of the market economy. The fruit may ripen and squish unsatisfactorily; it develops brown spots or other signs of rotting when shipped thousands of miles in a very cold truck; it produces a riot of shapes and sizes that weigh out inconsistently and don't fit very well into a square packing case. North America has been largely deprived, for instance, of the extraordinary beefsteak tomato, which grows in wonderful haphazard globules of juicy and sweet tomato-ness that lap all over the place like a sloppy friend. The varieties of the beefsteak tomato, existing now mostly as heritage varieties preserved by organic farmers, home gardeners, and diehard seed-savers, are plentiful. They have mouth-watering and inventive names like Mr. Stripey, Purple Cherokee, and Black Brandywine. They are not all red and stubbornly not square.

As Deborah Barndt (2002) demonstrates in her study of tomatoes, globalization, and the market economy, tomatoes nowadays have been bred for uniformity and shelf life. Flavour and variety have been jettisoned in the interests of creating a more effective commodity. Even before scientists began shooting non-tomato genes into tomatoes, seed companies were coaxing farmers into using the hybrid varieties, which were aimed at a lucrative market to the detriment of flavour and biodiversity. The hybrids also tend not to breed true from seed, which means that the farmer is forced to purchase the seeds anew each year rather than save them from the previous crop. Kenny Ausubel (1994: 113), of Seeds of Change, writes, "To add deficiency to injury, however, breeding F1 hybrid plants for the typical industrial traits

— tensile strength for shipping, uniform ripening, and cosmetic appearance — generally lowers the plant's nutritional values." He reports that since 1900, 97 percent of "reliably cultivated food plants" have vanished. They are the victims of markets based on uniformity, centralization, and long-distance transport (Ausubel 1994: 64).

Among the patentable inventions that food scientists came up with, they inserted flounder genes into tomatoes to make the fruit last longer in cold conditions. This innovation made the tomato amenable to shipping and provided access to distant markets. The resulting tomato, which tasted like a dog's chew toy, was eventually withdrawn.[3] This breeding is not something tomatoes would have come up with on their own, even with gentle nudging from traditional farmers.

One technique of genetic engineering applied to corn involved inserting a pesticide into the plant to fight the corn borer pest. Corn pollinates areas as far as four kilometres away, well beyond the confines of one farm. Since organic products are prohibited from containing GMOs, BT corn with its built-in pesticide can render nearby organic farms useless for corn. Organic farmers have lost their entire crop due to this cross-fertilization.

Uniquely the Same: The Path to Patent and Profit

Bio-tech companies can sue farmers who accidentally plant contaminated seed because the corporations have been allowed to patent their pesticide-infected corn, their pesticide-resistant soybeans (now you can spray the chemicals right on the plants, instead of just on the ground). For the purposes of patent law, these new foods are now defined as "novel" and are therefore subject to ownership by the inventor. The control and profits that result from this arrangement are precisely why these corporations want you to eat more GMOs. However, for the purposes of food safety, companies have succeeded in bamboozling the U.S. Food and Drug Administration (FDA) and the Canadian Food Inspection Agency (CFIA) into accepting the argument that the new food product resulting from these novel seeds is "substantially equivalent" (and therefore presumably not so novel) to existing tomatoes, corn, and wheat, and therefore no special tests are required to see if it is safe to eat. We must really admire the rhetorical ingenuity and legal legerdemain that delivers food to us that is both completely novel and basically the same.

Why is it so important to create patentable seeds? As George Monbiot (1997) points out, the world's most popular herbicide is Roundup, which in 1997 earned Monsanto almost $1.5 billion. When the patent ran out in 2000, Monsanto stood to lose a healthy chunk of profit, because imitators could now launch an identical product and charge less. Enter Roundup Ready soybeans. Touted to need less pesticide input, but to be resistant to

Roundup, the new seed would save farmers money and guarantee Monsanto continued sales of its showcase pesticide.

Todd Leake, a conventional farmer who pioneered the initiatives in North Dakota to keep GMOs out of the state, says the new GE products seemed attractive when they came out in the mid-1990s. The marketing included "heady promises that new biotech crops capable of producing industrial chemicals and even pharmaceuticals would expand agricultural markets and thereby raise farm incomes. 'But when they finally came out with actual product,' he said, 'it was all about selling more Roundup'" (Nace 2006: 2). Studies done after the introduction of Roundup Ready soybeans and other similar products indicate that their usage does not seem to have stemmed the application of chemicals (SEJUP 2004). In fact, since farmers know the plant will not be damaged, they can administer doses of pesticides throughout the season. The chemicals can be sprayed directly on the plants and their beans, thereby avoiding the moderation required with a normal soybean.

Seed Stocks under Siege

More iniquitous than our increased chemical intake, however, is the devastating effect of the loss of commonly owned seed stock to a private company. Traditionally, farmers can save their seeds from year to year; they can trade them around, try out each other's versions, and accomplish a slow, locally based breeding process over generations. This patience rewards farmers with seeds that suit local climate and tastes. For instance, indigenous South Asian rice varieties are resistant to drought, and they produce food in bad and good years alike. GMO seeds, like the hybrid seeds of the earlier Green Revolution, tend to produce the advertised higher yields only under ideal conditions — for instance, in the laboratory where they were designed.

GMO seeds, because they are patented, and are the intellectual property of Monsanto (or Novartis, or another of the handful of companies that control the development of biotech; see Kneen 1999), cannot be saved but must be purchased anew each growing season. That necessity not only adds considerable cost to the work of a farmer, but also, over the years, shatters the practice and culture of traditional breeding and seed supply management. Seed-saving depends on networks of farmers and extensive communication, knowledge, and dialogue, all of which breaks down if the seeds come each year direct from Monsanto. Biotech companies like Monsanto, recognizing the resilience and importance of these networks, often launch their GMO seeds by giving them out for at least one season as freebies. Woe to the farmer who tries to replant the next year from the seeds of the resulting plants; they may face lawsuits for "stealing" Monsanto's property.

Patents raise a whole new dynamic between farmers, or perhaps reinforce old lines of conflict. Monsanto has already instituted (and won) lawsuits

against hapless farmers who, because corn pollinates on the wind, accidentally grew and harvested plants that were in effect GMOs, contaminated
from nearby biotech fields. Once pollinated, the plant technically belongs
to Monsanto or some other corporation, and a farmer can only use it by
signing a contract with the corporation. The contract certifies Monsanto's
financial and legal right in their harvest. Without this agreement, farmers
cannot save the seeds and replant them.

Percy Schmeiser, a Canadian farmer, planted GE canola after it had
drifted in on the wind the year before and contaminated his regular seed.
Like most traditional farmers, he saved and replanted his own seed, rather
than buying it each year. Monsanto, deciding to make an example of him,
sued him for patent infraction. The company neglected to find out that he
was a well-known local politician who had also developed seed specifically for
Saskatchewan growing conditions. The case went all the way to the Supreme
Court of Canada, where the judges waveringly (in a split decision) ruled in
favour of the corporation, but contrary to Monsanto's demands protected
Schmeiser's ownership of his land and livelihood.

In 2007 the Schmeisers won the Right Livelihood award, Sweden's "alternative Nobel." Writer Ted Nace (2006: 1) reports that Leake, the farmer
from North Dakota, pointed to Monsanto's 800 number on a fridge magnet
and said, "They call it customer support…. It's actually a snitch line, where
you report that your neighbor is brown-bagging [saving seed]. Or where
somebody reports you, and a week or two later you find a couple of big guys
in black Monsanto leather jackets standing in your driveway." The farmers
of North Dakota also succeeded in thwarting Monsanto's development of
GM wheat. After a long battle, Monsanto withdrew all pending regulatory
applications, citing "a lack of widespread wheat industry alignment" (Nace
2006: 7).

GMOs raise a host of legal, political, and trade issues, and invoke the
new conflicts over intellectual property that have erupted between North
(where the seed companies are) and South (where the seed stocks are and
traditional breeding persists) (Shiva 1993). The GMO issue invokes discourses
of power and trust around scientific knowledge, and similar discourses about
technology.

As writer Marion Nestle (2003: 219) points out, "The inequitable distribution of political power… is at the root of public distrust of genetically
engineered foods." Similarly, the assumption that a scientific solution must be
better than more place-specific, indigenous solutions, Vandana Shiva (1993:
137) says, derives from a cultural and intellectual arrogance. She describes
the intellectual imperialism that has accompanied more physical incursions
of colonialism: "Biodiversity-based technologies of tribal and peasant societies have been viewed as backward and primitive and have been displaced by

technologies which use biological resources in such a way that they destroy diversity and people's livelihoods."

The Rural Advancement Foundation International (RAFI), now the ETC Group (Action Group on Erosion, Technology and Concentration), reports that contamination of corn stocks in Mexico by GMOs has already become a serious problem (Carlsen 2004). Some of the stocks have been contaminated with StarLink, a GM corn not approved for human consumption. Mexico provides the stewardship for an extensive variety of the corn stock of the world. Aside from the health issues of eating StarLink corn by accident, contamination of such a key bank of biodiversity represents a serious ecological threat. The reduction of biodiversity increases the fragility of the food system, as many communities have learned to their despair. A food culture based on single varieties can be that much more easily wiped out by blights or viruses, or even by one year of bad climate luck. The Irish potato famine, for instance, is often attributed to single-variety monocropping. A diversity of varieties means that drought years can still provide perfect environments for drought-friendly, usually indigenous, crops, while the others languish. Conserving diverse varieties during normal years is a hedge against disaster.

Resistance Is Fertile

The distaste for and resistance to the scientific or technological solution to tomatoes that don't travel well have resulted in numerous victories across the world. As Jules Pretty (1995) and John Pottier (1999) have pointed out, people do not respond passively to intellectual imperialism, whether in the fields of Bangladesh or the food stores of Ohio. People read the story in ways that are consistent with their understanding of the world, and resistance is bred from this narrative work.

The face of resistance is multiplicitous and powerful. As sociologists have noted, concern does not always translate into action, but the GMO issue has mobilized food activists across the world. The countries willing to plant and eat GMOs were rapidly isolated — the United States, Canada in part (although Canada rejected GE wheat), and Argentina. Even in these stubbornly pro-biotech strongholds, the cracks of resistance began to show. McDonald's, the king of profits from food, had by 2000 quietly instructed its farmers (who for the most part grow exclusively for McDonald's) not to grow GMO potatoes (Barboza 2000).

The anti-GMO movement has been successful in many ways, and began to have an impact on Monsanto's bottom line. In 2003 Monsanto's stock dropped like a stone. According to one report, "Monsanto, which in June sharply cut its earnings outlook through 2003, has been beleaguered of late by troubles in Latin America, increasing competition for its top-selling

Roundup herbicide product, and problems gaining global acceptance of its genetically modified seed technology" (Gillam 2003). Monsanto's net loss increased to $210 million in its fourth quarter of 2007, over a $144 million loss from the year before (Kaskey 2007).

Several creations from Monsanto crashed and burned, taking a great deal of wasted research money with them. The most outrageous examples were the Terminator and Junkie seeds (so-called by popular press and activists). The Terminator seeds produced plants with sterile seeds that could not be reused. That was an extraordinary step, tantamount to stepping out over a cliff at night because some guy told you there was a bridge there. It destroys one essential factor of most plants, which is that they can keep reproducing themselves ad infinitum. What if that characteristic spread from Monsanto's petri dishes to the broader planetary ecosystem? How would we get that genie back in the bottle? As the years rolled on, Monsanto also tried the Junkie Gene, so dubbed because they were bred to be addicted to pesticides. Without frequent chemical doses, they would wither away. This story of hubris and corporate short-sightedness is not science fiction. It is only a corporation devoting its power and creative energy to shore up the sacred goal of profit-taking.

Promoters of biotech also began to bleat plaintively about their deeply caring attitude to the poor and the obstacles that bankruptcy would place before their core goal of feeding the hungry.[4] In aid of this remade self-image, Aventis (another biotech mammoth) introduced (or tried to introduce) vitamin A-enriched rice (Golden Rice) to combat vitamin A deficiency (which can lead to blindness) in the developing world. As Shiva (1993: 26) pointed out, the only reason there was a problem at all was because traditional diets, normally high in vitamin A, had been threatened by commercial agriculture methods (growing food for profit) that have colonized developing countries as surely as the old imperialists had moved in on the same territory. Subsistence agriculture, often but not always the prerogative of women in Asia, Africa, and Latin America, suffers from the incursions of agribusiness and cultural shifts towards consolidated (non-common or public) land and monocrops produced for cash rather than for food (see Pottier 1999). Raj Patel (2007: 137) writes that vitamin A deficiency is a result of "problems of income and food distribution" and that "it is absurd to ask a crop to solve" these problems. "The danger of crops such as Golden Rice is not merely that they are ineffective publicity stunts. They actively prevent the serious discussion of ways to tackle systemic poverty."

The reaction in India and abroad against the rice has been strong, prompting Greenpeace Canada to file a false advertising complaint with Advertising Standards Canada. The Rockefeller Foundation, which funded the original research, agreed that in the quantities that anyone would normally eat it the so-called Golden Rice would not cure blindness. A person would have to eat nine kilograms per day to benefit from the effects. A pregnant woman would have to eat twice as much, said another report (Brown 2001). By 2003 the BBC had interviewed a biotech scientist who pointed out that the beta carotene already exists in rice and could be enhanced by normal means, without resorting to GMOs. In addition, the BBC exposé pointed out that people on poor diets already were unlikely to be able to absorb beta carotene properly. To benefit from additional beta carotene they would require more green, leafy vegetables (Kirby 2003).

Got Hormones?

Resistance to GMOs and resistance to the use of hormones tend to go hand in hand, perhaps because the corporations that bring these solutions forward are the same. The logic that searches for technological solutions through injections of hormones or by messing with the genes is similar. In each case the intention is to make nature more uniform and less stubbornly unpredictable and variable; and the tendency of pharmaceutical companies to engage in this work is increasing (see Charman 2003).

Many countries have successfully kept bovine growth hormone (BGH), also brought to us by Monsanto, out of their milk. This hormone, approved by the FDA in 1993, was developed to increase the yield from dairy cows. Bizarrely, its introduction occurred in the context of an existing dairy surplus. Again, what problem was being solved here? The answer is that it solved the problem that large agribusinesses were having with competition. The additional surpluses created by the use of BGH drove dairy prices so low that many small producers went under and access to the marketplace was improved for a few big players.

Various opposition groups rapidly mobilized around the problem, citing studies showing increased health problems and earlier mortality in BGH-fed cows, as well as the increased dangers of antibiotics in the milk as sick cows were medicated.[5] Since cows have similar biologies to humans (BGH is almost identical to a hormone in human milk), there was a well-founded concern about the effect that the inevitable presence of increased hormones in cow milk would have on growing children. In Canada, researchers who came out against the hormone were harassed and pressured by the government, which was being pressured by Monsanto (Sierra Club 1998), to sign their approval for the hormone (Cummins 1998). Amid this brouhaha, however, Canada indeed finally did refuse approval for the use of BGH in the country, to the considerable disgruntlement of biotech companies.

With extensive public support, the European Union has also been able at various times to institute bans on experimental GE plots on its land, on GE in the food, and against hormones in beef. In a Byzantine series of moves the EU hormone ban (and the GMO ban to a lesser extent) became a source of acrimonious free-trade conflict with the United States, which seemed determined both to continue its increasingly isolated practice of injecting growth hormones into beef cattle to speed them to market and to force other countries to accept the hormone-laden meat. The United States instituted various trade sanctions (including one on Roquefort cheese, which comes only from the Millau region), and attempted thereby to force the European Union to rescind its ban. Eventually, the U.S. government threatened to take the issue to the World Trade Organization (WTO), where in a (no doubt) fair and neutral "trial" (by unelected officials representing various industry and state interests) the WTO would debate whether refusing to buy U.S. beef because it is laced with hormones represents a restraint of free trade. By the delightful logic of free trade, almost anything will fall under the rubric of restraint, including refusing to feed your citizens something you think is bad for them. By this logic, if a customer has chosen one product over another because of any noted difference, including pricing, quality, place of origin, presence of hormones, or religious preference, the rejected seller can claim restraint of trade. Could the success of such a suit mean that the United States could sue Islamic states for refusing to eat pork?

The struggle reached new heights when U.S. trade officials used the threat of a WTO suit on hormones to try to persuade France to join the "Coalition of the Willing" in the U.S. War on Iraq, Part 2 — or as Michael Moore (2003: 73) calls it, the "Coalition of the Coerced, Bribed and Intimidated." After France stated its national lack of willingness, despite these persuasive arguments, the U.S. trade officials announced that they would go ahead with the suit, and instituted the lengthy proceedings. After that, they took their toys and went home.

Events took a new turn later on as the GMO ban in the European Union ended and new terms had to be renegotiated.

> Politicians have been slowly hammering out the details of the plan, amid fierce public protests. But many member states — including Italy, France, Greece, Austria and Denmark — remain dubious. Their demands for maximum protection have delayed action. Now, America plans to administer a force-feeding. The United States — peeved by the loss of $300 million in agricultural sales each year — is threatening to spark a trade war over GMOs. (Castleman 2003)

Through the Story We Relate

The news stories roll easily off the tongue and can instil a kind of horror in the listener or reader. We gasp, and wonder how people can behave this way. This particular kind of shock leads quickly from "Who is to blame?" to "What can I do, just one lone person?"

These two questions erupt simultaneously from a certain telling of the tale, and together they can easily immobilize resistance. Note the contradictory logical assumptions: the search for a singular perpetrator or two, to blame and bring to justice, conjures up a complementary feeling that as an individual (without the drive of the evildoer) we can do nothing. This rhetorical move serves above all to distance the individual (each of us, ourselves) from ghastly acts (those of others), first identifying the actors as monsters and then denying one's own ability to act with such single-minded and isolated purpose. More challenging to our self-conception is the analysis of writers, like Joel Kovel, who argue that the individual capitalists may be driven by profit and growth above all else, but that their actions and choices are determined in a systemic framework of capitalism that prevents them from acting in any other way. Similarly, Harry Glasbeek's careful legal analysis of the place and motivations of corporate chief executive officers emphasizes the insidious effect of the place of the manager in society. They are responsible only to a group of faceless shareholders, and unrewarded for any attempts to protect the workers, the environment, or future generations (Glasbeek 2002). "The core myth of today's aristocracy — that shareholder returns must be maximized — is considered unchallengeable, nearly sacred. It is a myth with the force of law. We might call it our modern version of the divine right of kings" (Kelly 2000).

Your storyteller, including myself, is no neutral reporter. Every storyteller has an axe to grind. The choice of tenor and shape foretells the storytellers' intentions, the dialogue they would like to have with readers, the trajectory of the ideas and details of their stories. The ways of telling the story offer up the elements in a certain way. The writers hope for a certain gleam in the reader's eye here, perhaps a certain sad tear shed there. Here, to call this a story is not to imply that what has happened with GMOs is in any way fictional, but to indicate that a report on events, a timeline, and the history of a movement are innately rhetorical. The actual journey of the reader beyond the text is of course eminently unpredictable and surprising; nonetheless, the rhetoric of the story must still be unhinged and challenged.

For instance, a food story told to shock and create horror at the awful things that those in power (corporations and their leaders, presidents of powerful nations) can do may immobilize us, but it might also inspire people to action. An initial positive reaction is likely to be individual action, paralleling a tale of individual villains. There is no reason to assume that acts of resistance will not re-create some of the narrative oppression from which they seek to escape. Perhaps the relentless focus on individual action explains the need in social justice movements for organizers to remind people that they are stronger together. A cartoon that has circulated among activists shows a big fish eating a much smaller fish, while behind the big fish hundreds of smaller fish are converging to eat the big fish first.

In the case of social change around food, certain issues do seem to catalyze individual response more than collective action. Such issues lead to changes in personal choice and preference. The moment of change may come as the individual shopper lifts the organic peanut butter off the shelf and leaves the highly processed sugar-laden conventional spread behind, or reaches out towards the organic milk, or perhaps lets her parents know that she has become a vegetarian. Much analytical energy has been devoted to figuring out how the personal and the global intersect. We are exhorted to "think globally and act locally." The decisions to change personal actions, to refuse to eat GMO soybeans in soy milk (many are now labelled) or in cereal, are all important to the issue of food.[6]

In general, North American and European consumer concern around GMOs tends to be impelled by doubts about food safety. Fears about food safety are often shaped around a mistrust in science; a sense that scientists may not be concerned enough about protecting our health, or that the relation between regulation and science is uncertain (Nestle 2003).

Food safety concerns often lead to predominantly individual action — changing buying habits, protecting yourself and your family. Food safety issues come to the fore in a context of crises like the Alar events of the late 1980s, when the health dangers of Alar, a common apple pesticide, were revealed to the public (several years after science had reported the problem) and people reacted with panic and turned to organics in droves. The Alar example is revealing because, while people turned to organic in a kind of hysteria (to the point that supply was insufficient to deal with the sudden demand), the anxiety did not last. Organic farmers told me that the scare did them no favours. It created a demand spike that they couldn't fill, and then left them with extra inventories and rotting produce when the panic subsided (see Montague 1997).

Food without Trust

As Ulrich Beck (1992) points out in his influential book *The Risk Society*, Western culture is characterized by a loss of *recreancy*, that is, a loss of trust in institutions that have supposedly been established to protect our interests. The Canadian Food Inspection Agency (CFIA) has failed miserably to be a neutral body, and many people decried the 1999 devolution of regulatory responsibility from Health Canada into its hands. As a FoodShare (1999: 59) report made clear, "The CFIA's conflicting mandate is to promote biotechnology, food production, and trade." In addition, the very expensive research required to confirm the safety of these new products is conducted by the companies themselves. This lack of scientific neutrality exacerbates the concern around GMOs. Consumers have realistic doubts about Monsanto's claims that their new, patented products are safe. A question recurs in research on food: does the culture of food necessarily engage questions of trust by its very nature?

Although it is important to consider our food choices and to read labels, we also need to consider the relation between individual action and broader institutional or societal change. If we choose to buy only local tomatoes, will that choice make a difference to the Mexican migrant workers who toil in Ontario's greenhouses? How does our choice relate to the unsustainable levels of energy use in year-round greenhouse operations? Will our choices help to change the approach of wholesalers who make their living on well-travelled, absolutely uniform fruits and vegetables? The beautiful organic carrots from Israel are certainly GMO-free — but does buying them really change the food system?

The emphasis on consumer refusals to eat GMOs, based usually on the precautionary principle (we don't know what they do to us yet), and on personal health concerns, can obscure environmental and agricultural issues that are already beyond doubt. For example, GE crops with inserted pesticides have already begun to create "superweeds" that are resistant to the herbicide in the plant (Brown 2005).

A key to the success of the anti-GMO movement has been coalitions of affected groups: producer groups outside North America, farmers' groups within North America who have customers abroad, NGOs such as Greenpeace and the Council of Canadians, consumer groups, natural food associations, and prominent scientists. In contrast to the health fears over Alar, the GMO concern persisted and survived beyond individual actions to produce coalitions of people and organizations that formed around the issue. The Alar events (and many other similar crises) did create a climate of awareness, even though most people returned to buying conventional food after the scare was over. Likewise, as the environmental movement grew, the mistrust in science grew, as did the suspicion in the mainstream culture that science — and corporations that depend on science — do not have everyone's best interests in mind. The events multiply and create a climate and a framework for understanding.

Of Rhetoric and Roquefort

In an analysis of any food issue, one must ask: who became concerned about the issue? And why and how did their concern lead to social change? An emphasis on personal choice was an inevitable result of the initial progress and tenor of the GMO narratives. The emphasis on personal choice leads to consumer boycotts as a strategy. These can be extraordinarily successful. For instance, a carefully orchestrated consumer approach to Starbucks' refusal to carry fair trade coffee finally led the coffee giant to add fair trade coffee to its lineup. For a long time the company refused to brew it in its daily coffee, however, though they would make it for you specially if you asked and were willing to wait.

The emphasis on individual choice and action (even in the context of a boycott) invokes images of heroes and singular actors making personal choices. This narrative may be peculiar to or especially exaggerated in North America. It can lead to particular ways of describing actions for social change that may erase or conceal the existence of coalitions and mutual support. The focus on individual action may underestimate the extent of agreement over the need for social change. For instance, the Ontario government exhorts residents to buy energy-efficient light bulbs to fight the climate crisis. People would perhaps accomplish more if they united to demand fines for owners of commercial buildings who leave the lights on all night long (and in the process we would save the lives of the birds that tend to crash into the bright buildings at night).

Consider, for example, the case of Jose Bove, who shot to eminence as an activist through a combination of social action, media hysteria, and narrative choice. On August 12, 1999, in Millau, a small town in Southwest France, a group of farmers and others "ransacked" a McDonald's that was under construction. The action took place during a demonstration against the U.S. trade sanctions imposed on French products (including the local Roquefort cheese) in response to the refusal by France to accept U.S. hormone-treated beef. Bove has since become a highly visible and effective symbol of courage and determination for anti-globalization protesters and a hero to many food activists. In 2007 he announced that he was running for president in France.

How did a minor protest become an international rallying point? That is, what happened, but also, what narrative choices were made as the story was told and retold? News reports said that the McDonald's was "ransacked," or "wrecked," and my personal favourite, "pillaged" — that Bove and the barbarian hordes had united in unreasoning violence. Other reports, though, made it clear that the McDonald's was not ransacked but dismantled (it was only partly built), and that this was done not just by Bove but by a group of two hundred farmers and other people, including children, who carefully unscrewed boards, took the nails out of roof tiles, and deposited the whole pile at the door of the local government. How one tells the story depends on the point of view, and the teller's interests (in the denser meaning of "stakes") in the proceedings. It also depends on narrative preferences, which are nothing if not politically informed. Mainstream media coverage of protests, for instance, consistently underestimates the number in attendance at a protest and overestimates the occurrence of violence. Many versions of the events that day at Millau erase the two hundred people who were with Bove, just as photos of black-hooded protesters breaking windows are believed to make the best media.

Bove and his compatriots did not ransack or disassemble the building in a cultural vacuum, nor did "readers" and "listeners" come to understand the events in a vacuum. The events at McDonald's that day took place during the global trade conflict over hormones. Over the next few years food eventually became a pawn in President George W. Bush's attempts to rally the troops. Food was used by Americans and French alike to express their mutual displeasure. The actions of the French farmers took place in the context of other events, including a "proud" American moment when a North Carolina restaurant decided to rename their french fries "freedom fries," or when other patriots poured French wine in the gutter to signify their displeasure with France's refusal to go to war. The context for the Bove story also includes widespread direct actions in which activists and farmers burned experimental GMO plots (thereby instantly solving the cross-pollination and superweed problems). The context also includes the ongoing free-trade battles and conflict over WTO regulations.

Still, even though the farmers' action in Millau was embedded in general agricultural resistance and protest across the European Union, in the way the story was told Bove himself was reconstructed as a farmer-hero. When he attended the massive demonstrations in Seattle and Quebec City, he was greeted with the fanfare befitting a hero. His story became a rallying point and inspiration for other activists; portrayals of Bove emphasize that he is a farmer, and sympathetic reporters enthusiastically weave the mythology of a folk hero, an innocent and ignorant commoner who was pushed too far. What stake does a social movement have in being led by an unintentional leader, one who, untrained and unprepared, is thrust into the spotlight? Does this naive authenticity somehow stamp the issues with a seal of approval and truth? Is this the story of the village idiot who speaks truth, the boy who saw the emperor's nakedness for what it was? Is it the tale of the innocent peasant against the titans, the common man against the scientists?

Bove is indeed a thoughtful and well-read activist with a personal history of involvement in various social movements. He is also a "real" farmer. His activist history is sometimes used against him, as if it made his actions less "authentic." The farmer activist is an identity fraught with meaning for how we see food and food production. An invidious example of this shows up in the case of Rosa Parks: the story of the woman who mobilized a whole civil rights effort by refusing to sit at the back of the bus. Most people don't realize that she had been a participant at the Highlander School in Tennessee, a popular education centre that teaches political consciousness and strategizing, and that she was part of a group embedded in the growing civil rights movement. A coalition came up with the strategy that she, in her great courage, carried out. This alternative reading suggests that activists are experienced, think strategically, and are embedded in coalitions. It detracts from the innocent hero story and can be even a little less comforting — if she was trained and was one of many, it becomes harder to excuse an individual's own lack of action. "We are a very naive public about the processes of social change," writes bell hooks (1996: 230), "and that naiveté is not accidental. This culture doesn't encourage us to think about transformation as a process. Instead, we are addicted to notions of radical revolutionary moments that transform everything overnight" (quoted in Trend 1996).

The conventional approach to the story obscures the learning and expertise of activists. This omission is particularly ideological and dangerous in the case of oppressed groups such as small farmers or women of colour. The rhetorical tendency to posit a naive hero obscures the farmers' knowledge, and tells instead the story of an ordinary person pushed to the breaking point. The shape of the story denies history to people who act; it releases ordinary people, if they want, from the obligation of thinking or acting. In this version of the story, the ability to act and change will hit the ordinary person like a bolt of lightning. When they get pushed too far, they will suddenly know what to do, like a medieval nun suddenly hit with sainthood (or demonic possession). The identity of the activist is rhetorically shifted well outside everyday identity and is hence removed for the most part from the choices of ordinary people. Thus even if we have gone so far as to choose, say, to drink organic soy milk, we may still not think that we can participate in collective action. The shifting of actor responsibility and strategic, knowledge-able action plays through this narrative tapestry that is woven with villains who have too much power and are solely responsible for the devastation we deplore; and with ordinary people who are stung suddenly to effective action. Between these two constructions of action and identity lies a community of action and understanding that does not make good press.

As we sit by our own rhetorical firesides, let us note the occurrence of alternative stories. Note, for instance, that the fair trade movement has yet to cough up a well-known example of mobilized personhood. Although many people have done extraordinary things (farmers in the South trying to form fair trade co-operatives have been harassed and murdered), as a movement it has so far tended to be a tale of numerous minor heroes, co-operative action, and consumer groups.

The analysis of the narrative devices and the chosen rhetoric of a story does not mean that we must discount the events or the importance of the issue; it allows us to analyze how a collective movement emerged, how it progressed, who was mobilized by it, and why the change it has achieved takes the shape it does. There is no underlying "truth" to a story; the truth is always already narrated — that is, there is no event without narrative choice. The events that Saturday at the Millau McDonald's site helped to mobilize people with numerous and multiple interests and led to the creation of coalitions. It helped to link food issues with the anti-globalization movement. Other events will remobilize some of these groups, while failing to inspire others.

The Cultural Construction of Meaning

> I understand culture, then, to encompass the struggle to control and contribute to the social circulation and uses of meaning, knowledges, pleasures and values. (Fiske 1993)

What we have looked at is culture defined as a struggle to control the meanings of an event through the way in which the story is told. The story of Bove and the farmers' action at Millau touches and challenges people, offering them diverse positions in relation to capitalism and globalization. These positions are reflected in how they choose to tell the story. As commonly told in the mainstream media, the story strategically eliminates other ways of telling it, such as collective action, non-violent action, and the individual's embeddedness in wider movements, the least of which is probably the attacks on McDonald's restaurants around the world.

Antonio Gramsci, a political theorist who resisted Fascism in Italy, emphasized that the gradual development of a collective will, leading to social action, depends on the negotiation of multiple interests and multiple points of consent. Gramsci stated:

> It is vital that there should not be passive and indirect consent but active and direct consent, the participation of individual members, even if this provokes an appearance of breakup and tumult.... An orchestra in rehearsal, each instrument playing for itself, gives the impression of the most dreadful cacophony. And yet these rehearsals are necessary for the orchestra to live as a single "instrument." (Gramsci, in Forgacs 2000: 244–45)

Thus a social movement and social change can be defined amongst large groups of people who may have very different reasons for taking a stand in the same place, or marching in the same march, perhaps not the absence of heroes but lots of heroic moments for everyone.

Other recent food movements — organics, vegetarianism — emphasize changing the products of our food system, and they draw on elements and motivations to action reflected in the GMO material. Each tells a slightly different story, overlapping, answering, and forgetting other movements and thus engaging in an ongoing dialogue that achieves action and change.

Notes

1. In the South the issues focus more on agriculture: for instance, preserving biodiversity or protecting the indigenous control of seed stocks.

2. In 2004 the European Union lifted a five-year ban on GMOs and put stricter labelling regulations in place. Numerous European Union countries then began to work to ban GE crops on their farmland (Bebb 2004).

3. As produce manager of GreenStar Co-op in Ithaca, New York, I believed it important to understand the products I was putting on the shelves. One quiet evening another staff person and I, after exclaiming over the strange texture of the non-organic tomatoes we had received from a supplier, decided to do a test (in the interests of science). We dropped one on the floor to see what would happen. It bounced. Retail is hard work, but it can be fun too.

4. Tremendous resources have gone into persuading people that GMOs are good for them and good for the planet. In the United States in 1999, for instance, pro-biotech groups, including retailers, processors, and the biotech companies, initiated a $50-million-dollar pro-GE campaign. They put over $676,000 into lobbying, hoping to stop the mandatory labelling initiatives (Halweil 2000).

5. Groups working against the introduction of BGH include Organic Consumers Association, Food and Water Inc., Consumers Union, and in Canada the Council of Canadians, Sierra Club of Canada, and the National Farmers Union.

6. Canadian grocery stores argue that there is no way of testing for GMOs and have required natural food suppliers to black out the GMO-free labels. There are a range of accurate testing options for GMOs.

Chapter 3

Lunch with Alternative Economics

We think if we can tell you where your potatoes were grown and by whom and why and for whom and deliver a superior quality product... we have a story to tell, instead of just selling a commodity, a potato, we're selling a story, a really interesting story. (John Harvie, CEO, Co-op Atlantic, 2003)

As we settled into lunch at Bob's, around the corner from our various workplaces, one of my friends asked Bob, the owner/operator of an excellent Indian restaurant in Toronto, why he doesn't advertise more on the sidewalk or in local papers. Despite frequent praise in various restaurant reviews as being both cheap and good, the restaurant quietly chugs along without a lot of fanfare. Bob explained that he was not trying to grow big and successful; he said he just runs it so he won't have to get a job.

As my research expanded for this book, I found that stories about food are a delight to discover, easy to entice from informants, and a joy to share with friends. Food stories can get a workshop started with laughter and a sense of common concerns; they can allow us to dig deep into common cultures and heritages, or to face and learn the diversity of our surroundings. As Richard Manning (2004: 163) remarks in his history of the ecological and economic disasters of agriculture, "Food tells a people's collective story in the same way that the molecules we eat assemble the body." Deborah Barndt (2002: 85) points out that food is one site of the cultural work of producing meaning. The stories we tell about food, the way we tell them — the elements we include and the ones that slip through the cracks — are an extended work of culture, shaping the world in an ongoing construction of reality. Such a process is, of course, a dialogue. You tell me a story and I hear it in the context of my own beliefs, and pass it on with my own spin. This process is the essence of culture, and occurs everywhere, not just in food.

If, as Lévi-Strauss observes, food is good to think with, what do we use food to think about? Not only does food offer a rich landscape of social change and innovation, but it also can speak easily about redressing the ills of the economic system. It becomes increasingly important to share a way of addressing the economy as the global economic system, failing more and more people every day, creates a poverty that is witnessed in hunger, obesity, and food dangers everywhere.

Economics itself is typically the purview of the experts; the ability to talk about economics is highly protected by the elite and regulated along strict guidelines.[1] As numerous scholars have pointed out, the taboos and elitism surrounding the practice of economics reflect its position as a religion rather than a mathematical theory in our culture. Most ordinary people (lacking a Ph.D. in economics) feel unqualified to discuss this widespread cultural system that impinges on them throughout their lives, from the moment they receive their shrinking paycheques to the shame they feel refusing expensive treats to their children. As Alexa McDonough writes in the foreword to *Just Making Change*, "It is very much in the interests of the financial sector to maintain the illusion that the financial system is beyond the comprehension or influence of the ordinary Canadian citizen" (Nystrom 1999: 12).

Economics as Culture

> I and Fritz Schumacher… both agreed that economics had become a form of brain damage. (Henderson 1991: 51)

The result of the control of economics in the hands of a few is drastic and provocative for those who would prefer a better, more equitable world: for those, for instance, who would like to see the rich not so rich and the poor a little less hungry and homeless (or home insecure), who might like to see workers with livable minimum wages, perhaps a maximum wage for top-earners, who would like to see universal subsidized day care (as in Quebec). Around the world wonderful work has been done to offer a people's economic education and to give people some power over their economic relations, from the Coady movement in Atlantic Canada, which spawned the extensive co-operative system there, to the Center for Popular Economics in Massachusetts, to the recent development by the Catalyst Centre in Toronto of a popular economics curriculum for Canada. As J.K. Gibson-Graham (1996: 3) mentions, the hegemony of a uniform approach to economics makes it difficult to imagine anything else, "to discover or create a world of economic difference." It is essential to provide the tools, both in education and in practice, to imagine another economics.

In the case of food, these tools become much more accessible, because food is good to think (about economics) with. Each type of food story not only talks about economics and how to change the economic system for the better, but sinks its teeth into a particular aspect of the problem. The anti-GMO movement addresses the rampant hegemonies of consumer preference and choice and challenges the orthodox tenet of consumer behaviour that is willingness to pay (WTP) theory. As a foundation of neo-classical economics, WTP theory assumes that the price of any good is established by the consumer's willingness to pay for that good. If consumers report that they are not willing to pay more for a clean environment, then cleaning up the environment is said to have little value. If consumers report that they cannot afford solar panels to heat hot water for their homes, although they might say they believe that is the right way to build new homes, nonetheless the analysis will say that there is no market for solar hot-water systems (see, for instance, Olewiler and Field 1995). Willingness to pay theory, a somewhat bizarre invention of theoretical economists, has become a cornerstone of our economic culture and of our belief in how the world works.[2] The GMO-free movement, among others, throws these assumptions into confusion and begins to posit new ideas and new models for our economic exchanges.

The Empty Pockets of Consumer Power

> The link between economy (including forms of exchange and trade) and personhood has excited anthropologists ever since fieldwork began. (Pottier 1999: 103)

I am approaching the North American economic culture as an anthropologist, which I am, rather than as an economist. From an anthropological perspective, the economy, like any other cultural production, represents the site of important rituals, rules, and assumptions that are significant cultural expressions and speak of who we think we are and how we think we should act within a culturally defined identity. I begin therefore from cultural artifacts in search of clues to cultural patterns and beliefs.

In a recent and endlessly repeated commercial for some dough wrapped around tomato sauce and cheap cheese, a young man sits and watches the TV, conveniently located in the exact line of sight of you, the viewer. As you/the TV watches, a horrendous crash comes from somewhere back inside the house, and an older man, presumably the boy's father, starts calling him. Dad, clearly already cognizant of a deficit of caring in his young offspring, yells for him to call Mom, apparently thinking that Mom is more likely to leave work or wherever she is, drive home, and extricate Dad than Junior is likely to get up off the sofa and rescue him. The boy ignores the pleas for help. But wait! Now his stomach is rumbling. He leaps up, goes to the fridge, gets the advertised product, and settles back into the chair. Dad's cries become increasingly plaintive. The commercial echoes many others, including one in which a young lover waters down her partner's cola because it is the last one and she wants most of it for herself. Some might say that these tales are ironic, not meant to be taken literally. Irony, however, while not literal, is eminently serious. These kinds of advertisements contain important statements about who we are.

The place of identity and our relations with each other have taken truly bizarre turns over the past few years, to the point that the stories told would be incomprehensible to someone outside our culture. One professional woman comes home to a man ("Herbert") who is pretending to be a cat; he won't talk to her because she won't give him the cat food he craves. She gives it to him, and all is well. At the very end the puzzled viewer might notice that the restoration of good relations has also turned the man back into a cat; clearly the best human relation is none at all. This ideal is mediated by the purchase of the right food.

Another recent commercial has a couple standing amongst the overbearing plenty of an electronics store. A young man and woman (the salespeople; or perhaps one should say matchmakers in this case) are making helpful suggestions, directed at rationalizing the purchase of large and larger systems. The couple is increasingly delighted that both of them agree to each suggested purchase. The marriage brokers smirk knowingly at each other. The consumer couple gets more and more ecstatic as the items pile up, gazing adoringly each other as each one says, "Yes, yes!" more and more vigorously. The man is so overwrought with emotion that he plunges to one knee in the middle of the store; he is going to beg for something — probably her hand? She is distracted, however, by another enormous piece of technology and skips away; their relationship thrives on the thrill of their agreement in the purchase of thousands of dollars of equipment and has no time for little things like standard commitment ceremonies. He is left alone on his knee, looking foolish. We know that as long as they keep buying things their relationship will be just fine.

These acts of identity construction engage us in a dialogue in which we may or may not identify with the key character. We may indeed be as selfish as the young man eating dough pockets; or we may be considering acts of selfishness that are bolstered by the extremity of these visions. We may sometimes feel as if our identities are only truly embodied when we are shopping, that interactions with goods are more real than any human relationship we have. The construction of identity engages a complex dialogue with stories offered by media, friends and teachers, and even, perhaps, with our internal mythologies, wherever they derive from. In Gramscian terms, and echoing Michel Foucault, the relation of an individual to hegemony and dominant ideologies is complex and shifting, a matter of multiple positions and identifications.

The everyday economic life of a North American person echoes with images of personhood that may or may not resonate with who we think we are. These images haunt our dreams and actions, telling us who we are, declaring the lines of new moralities, challenging preconceptions about right behaviour. The stories of consumer power weave one particular vision of individual identity — a peculiarly North American work of identity construction, brought to a sort of fever pitch in the mythologies of consumer power, choice, and market democracy. As in the relation between ritual practice and esoteric religious texts, notions of consumer power are popular versions of the willingness to pay doctrine — and have complex and interdependent relations with that theory.

First, in the tropes of consumerism, what does the culture tell us about who we are? One ad[3] starts like one of those Canadian heritage moments in which all the reasons that white European-descended Canadians have to be proud are celebrated in romantic historical snippets. In this ad, a hellish war is winding down. One soldier rescues a wounded buddy from the battlefield, carrying his unconscious form to safety. They head back to the local pub to celebrate their victory, still swathed in bandages and tattered clothes. First the barkeeper pours out some wine of local vintage, but the rescued soldier brushes it away, demanding the advertised beer. After a pint is poured for him, however, he loves the beer so much that he places one heavy foot on the beer-tube, cutting off the flow. His buddy (who saved his life) is told the beer is gone, and he has to drink the wine. Such extreme visions tell us that we have a right to everything we want (all of it), regardless of little annoyances such as trust, personal debt, familial demands of caring, and support. Of course, like most mythologies, the story exaggerates for effect and is overdetermined with indirect and wayward meaning. Dracula stories don't teach us that tall dark strangers might suck our blood (unlikely), but that young nubile women are in danger (somewhat more likely, if oppressive, restricting the lives of young women through threat and fear).

The story represents a kind of riffing on the essential selfishness of consumer images. In advertising, the words of consumer activist associations, and even progressive initiatives such as boycotts, consumers are encouraged to believe that they have a right to have whatever they want (whether it is fast food or fair trade coffee). Consumers are also imagined to be powerful, smart, and rational. The story of the consumer is encapsulated in the often repeated slogan to "vote with your dollar." As one excellent website on fighting corporate concentration enthusiastically concludes: "Shopping is voting!" The trouble with this inspiring bedtime story ("Daddy, tell me the one about how the leftists shopped 'til they dropped"?) is that you can only shop and avoid certain brands in favour of others if you have dollars to fork over. Shopping seems to instil a sense of power, as we sort out the best bargains and exercise our hard-earned knowledge of prices and quality.[4] A powerful story like this is complexly translated into popular action and life.

Consumers do wield certain kinds of power, particularly when they act together. To recognize the dangers of the consumer trope is not to belittle the spectacular effects of consumer actions such as the boycott against Nestlé to end its promotion of breast-milk substitutes in developing countries.[5] It is important to celebrate our successes while exploring the inevitable consequences of the philosophies behind them. Such an examination allows us to consider additional strategies in tandem with consumer strategies.

You Know You Want It?

One fallout in daily life from economic theory is an assumption that consumers know exactly what they want, that what they want is obvious. Ads imply that we are all going on a jolly ride together, checking out things that you, the transparent consumer, already know you want. "You know you want it" whines one annoying ad. The infamous "Just do it!" ads similarly suggest a completely inhuman lack of complexity in our desires, which would be perhaps a welcome relief but is obviously absurd. Lisa Hamilton (2003) writes that Americans are so trained to expect consumption to be simplistic that Community-Supported Agriculture projects confuse them. "The benefits of belonging to a CSA are less quantifiable than Americans are used to. We are conditioned to ask 'How much does it cost? What will it do for me? What is its immediate value?'" The problem is that we actually come to identify ourselves as people who care only for the answers to those questions, and not for the ones answered by CSAs. The rationality that is shaped around us like a second skin in this consumer culture is simple-minded; it brooks no double entendres, no shaded meanings, and allows only an unambiguous, determined, and immediate grasp of what we want.

The work of the cultural construction of identity is always overdetermined. Those who deviate from the standard model are pressured to reform and ridiculed. We are shamed by others for making "stupid" or irrational purchases (for missing a sale on the item that we purchased at full price, for instance). We are teased for not acting in our own interests. We are called "bleeding hearts," as if to say that to show compassion for others means that our core life-blood will leak out, risking our very mortality. This constant pressure results in a kind of global anxiety in which we can only insist on our successful identity in the culture by constant, frantic shopping. "Buy Nothing Day," an important day of protest against consumerism, strikes at the heart of our culture and poses a significant challenge.

Economic culture relies in this democratic culture on key inequities, particularly between the economics expert or insider and the average person. Not only is the status of economics experts highly elevated (even mystified, as a priesthood would be), but consumers are then cynically offered insider knowledge. Loblaw's in-store newsletter is called "Insider's Report," echoing the canny economic practice of insider trading. The newsletter, available to all, makes everyone into an "expert" the minute they walk in the door. Consumers are taught to think that they can become smart investors; the Internet reeks with tip sheets to make consumers feel like they have the scoop on investments, that they have the power to amass wealth and capital when in fact small investors accumulate very little, except a determinate sense of their identity in the world of economics (see Frank 2001; Stanford 1999). The construction of the smart consumer is particularly bemusing in light of growing problems around food safety and the loss of nutritional value in our food. The knowledge that the "smart" consumer is vouchsafed is considerably circumscribed and controlled. Consumers are encouraged to find the cheapest chips, or perhaps the best for dipping, but not to consider forgoing chips altogether.

One natural food store owner calls consumers "destructive," and decries the tendency of customers to show their cleverness by complaining about price comparisons ("Loblaw's has it five cents cheaper"). Consumer knowledge is very much constructed, and constructed with a particular bias. Consumers are not encouraged to retain knowledge about how the cattle industry destroys the environment or about the effects of pesticide and hormone runoff on our water supply. The kind of knowledge that the smart consumer holds is narrow and specific. It includes the price of milk (regardless of where it comes from, the level of hormones and antibiotics in it, and the state of the environment in which the dairy operates); it includes a false notion of free choice. The mythology of the consumer going off to market is like Puss in Boots, the clever cat that can figure anything out, get whatever he needs. The reality is more like Jack and the beanstalk, the charming dolt who trades his mother's cow for a bean. Not all of us can count on a magical beanstalk to get us out of a mess.

Concomitant with the notion of consumer power is an even deeper belief that choice is a right. Activists and corporations are often in unison in this belief, or at least harmony, although the results they seek are different. Supermarkets trumpet the choice and variety they offer, and many of us who seek to change the food system will also say the consumer has a right to choose. For instance, as a produce manager of GreenStar Cooperative Market in Ithaca, New York, I expanded our offerings to include many conventionally grown basic products if they were much cheaper than the current organic offerings and especially if they were local. I juggled price, origin, and production method to create a display that I hoped would entice low-income customers back to a store that was rapidly becoming focused on upscale clientele. This strategy is common to many but not all natural food stores. Generally such stores will accompany a broad selection with education in the hopes that consumers will more often choose sustainable products.

This issue is so important that most purveyors of natural food will have decided where they stand, and perhaps suffered through periods of acrimony and conflict over whether they should carry everything and let the customers decide, or refuse to carry some things out of principle, and explain their decisions when the customer asks. The conflict for natural food stores has in the past tended to centre on refined sugar, various stimulants, and meat, but now may focus more on the store's position on the latest diet craze and GMOs.

There is tremendous power in choice, particularly when bolstered by knowledge. But it is not necessarily a right in the way that food is a right. Our culture's imagined consumer is defined by her or his ability to choose: to make smart, rational, fully informed and self-interested choices. Activists and corporations merely disagree on what "fully informed" means. The identity that is hypothesized, in fact required, in standard willingness to pay theory is this fully informed character, whether it is the wise purchaser of organic milk or the discriminating buyer of new flavour colas. Nothing, presumably, prevents a wise purchaser from driving the extra ten blocks to the supermarket if the organic milk is cheaper there.

The range of knowledge that the food activists insist upon is quite different from the knowledge offered by the supermarkets, which offer an array of products but conceal a range of information that would help consumers understand the food system better. This difference, unfortunately, is necessarily thinner than most activists would like. Time and again in interviews I was told by co-ops and natural food stores that due to lack of time and money they are doing much less education than they would like, that they often leave the research to their consumers. The result is an extraordinary culture that I have marvelled at since I began to work in the organic and natural food sector. The owners and operators of small food co-ops and natural food stores are attuned to customer demands, and they spot trends largely from customer conversations. As Linda Tuijtel, the grocery manager of Foodsmiths in Perth, Ontario, told me, "One of the secrets is listening to the customer, listening to their ideas, what they prefer and trying to go with that." That practice folds back into consumer power, which operates strongly in small stores, where people's voices really are listened to with a fair amount of concern and attention.

This principle (listening to customers' words) is significantly different from the manifestations of consumer preference theory (WTP), where the seller tabulates what the consumer buys, as if that represented the only expression of what they want (it ignores what they want but can't find represented on the shelf, or want but can't fit in their backpacks, as well as complex dialogic questions of consumption). Cashiers at supermarkets are often trained now, in a kind of parody of customer service, to ask customers, "Did you find everything you need?" Most of us at this point have waded through the endless lonely aisles of the mass market, fended off the blandishments of what we want but shouldn't have, and are now standing at the head of a long line, rooting for our money. Did I find what I need? Where to begin? "Yes," we mumble, offering a non-answer to go with the non-question.

The trajectory of choice in supermarkets or big box stores like Wal-Mart tells a different story from that told in the aisles of a natural food store.[6] The huge aisles of the big supermarkets dwindle into the distance with endless different types of cereal, chips, soda, and "ready-to-eat" meals. Yet a careful inspection of a supermarket's offerings reveals a hidden uniformity. Despite all the different names, for instance, many of the cereals are owned by one company. In addition, the key ingredients (like the astonishing variety of things that can be made from corn, from the array of chips to syrup, starch, and oil) tend to come from a very few low-profile processing companies like Archer Daniels Midland and Cargill (see Kneen 1995). The choice seems wide, but the recipes are narrow, and they echo the fast food emphasis on salt and sugar (see Schlosser 2002). The uniformity in our fantasy of choice leads to a uniformity of dietary problems in North Americans, who are getting fatter and fatter, and (recent studies show) also shorter and shorter (Bilger 2004).

The dangers of being driven by the chimera of choice are emblazoned in the strategic use of choice as a right by the powerful in the food sector. Paul Krugman, in "Girth of a Nation" (2005), reports:

> The Center for Consumer Freedom, an advocacy group financed by Coca-Cola, Wendy's and Tyson Foods, among others, has a Fourth of July message for you: worrying about the rapid rise of obesity is unpatriotic. "Far too few Americans," declares the center's Web site, "remember that the Founding Fathers, authors of modern liberty, greatly enjoyed their food and drink…. Now it seems that food liberty — just one of the many important areas of personal choice fought for by the original American patriots — is constantly under attack.

A Plea for Jack the Giant-Killer

> Thanks to hyperactive corporate consolidation, combined with the patenting of plants and the genetic engineering of food, a very small group of people now exerts enormous influence over the global food system. This is bad news for millions of farmers and the six billion of us who must eat every day. (O'Neill 2001)

Canada has an even larger economic tolerance for monopoly than does the United States. "The top ten U.S. chains have less than 50 percent of the grocery market share, while in Canada, only seven chains control 70 percent of the market. Loblaw Companies Ltd. is clearly the dominant power, with over 30 percent of the market" (Barndt 2002: 117). The U.S. figures may have shifted towards even greater consolidation with the rapid entry of

Wal-Mart into the grocery market. The lack of diversity in retail markets is concealed by the multiplication of banners; Loblaw Companies Ltd., the food retailing arm of the Weston food conglomerate in Canada, operates under numerous names in addition to "Loblaws," including Nofrills, Provigo (in Quebec), Maxi, Your Independent Grocer, Atlantic Superstore, Zehrs, President's Choice, and Fortinos.

Not only is the grocery trade controlled by a very few, but food processing (less visible to consumers) is enormously consolidated — and that consolidation has now extended into the organic and natural food market. Thus Philip Morris, which brought us tobacco and its various unfortunate results, owns Kraft, Dairylea, Philadelphia, Vegemite, and various coffee labels: Master Blend, Maxwell House, Mellow Birds, Café Hag, Brim, and Kenco. As Brian Halweil (2000) pointed out, "The merger of Philip Morris and Nabisco will create an empire that collects nearly 10 cents of every dollar a U.S. consumer spends on food, according to a company spokesperson." Philip Morris and Wal-Mart, Monsanto, and others are significant investors in the Hain Celestial Group, which owns much of the natural food industry, including Bearitos, Breadshop, Celestial Seasoning, Imagine Foods, Yves, and Garden of Eatin'. The majority of Hain is now owned by Heinz (see Ruiz-Marrero 2004). Many of these brands will only be familiar to Canadians who have been buying natural food for a long time, from the time before they were purchased by the apparently insatiable Hain corporation. Once under the Hain umbrella, products tend to be withdrawn from the Canadian market, which is judged to be too small to bother with.

Take a step back up the food chain from brands and retail and we find very large, publicly invisible companies that provide the raw materials for the "variety" of goods available. Eric Schlosser (2002: 8) found: "During the 1980's, large multinationals — such as Cargill, Conagra and IBP — were allowed to dominate one commodity market after another. Farmers and cattle ranchers are losing their independence, essentially becoming hired hands for the agribusiness giants or being forced off the land." As Brewster Kneen (1995) pointed out in *Invisible Giant*, the dominance and power of such corporations are largely obscure to the average consumer, because the firms deal in the raw materials of food and have therefore no brand name. Cargill in 1995 was the largest privately owned company in the United States, with interests across the world in grain-processing (largest trader in the world), oilseeds (largest), beef (third), pork (fourth), beef in Canada (largest), flour-milling (third in the United States) and phosphate, a key fertilizer ingredient (second in the world) (Kneen 1995: 10). Since then it has continued to diversify and grow. This kind of profile could be cited for the other giants that together largely control food production and manufacturing in the world. Like the giants of myth and fairy tale, these oversized creatures are not very plentiful but they are unpleasant to meet; just ask all the small dairies and farmers sued by Monsanto.

With Monsanto we reach one end of the food chain as expressed in the rapid consolidation of agriculture. As John Madeley (2002: 121) writes in *Food for All*, "Nowhere is the dominance of TNC's [Transnational Corporations] more pronounced than in agriculture." He adds, "By controlling germplasm from seed to sale, TNC's are moving to monopolistic control of the food chain that allows them to extract maximum profit" (2002: 123). As Monsanto's seed division president reports on their strategy of buying out seed companies, "This is not just a consolidation of seed companies, but really a consolidation of the entire food chain" (quoted in O'Neill 2001). The process is called "vertical integration," a term that lays claim to a level of rationality and efficiency not borne out by the strategy's effects. As numerous activists and scholars have pointed out, the corporate consolidation of food, from agriculture through processing to retail, ensures the application of corporate ethics to the food system. In place of sustenance, we get ballooning profits and a fixation on making money. The average consumer is often a casualty of these goals.

Consolidation of ownership goes hand in hand with the consolidation of ingredients. As Kneen has eloquently shown for Cargill, the multiplication of food products from corn, wheat, or soy — key raw materials for Cargill's processing facilities — guarantees that many of the things you eat every day have Cargill's grubby little paws on them. Kneen (1995: 9) points out that a trade ad for Cargill (targeting the manufacturer customers) demonstrates its ubiquity through the tiny words "wheat flour" on a Campbell's soup can. "The gradually decreasing print size on the [two-page] arrow says, 'It's small, relatively anonymous and absolutely no indication of how big our interest is in your success. Your brand — our flour.'"

Uniformity and Corporate Food

> Monocultures are in fact a source of scarcity and poverty, both because they destroy diversity and alternatives and also because they destroy decentralised control on production and consumption systems. (Shiva 1993: 6)

As many people from different disciplines have pointed out, the diet provided by shopping in conventional grocery stores is surprisingly uniform, given the emphasis on choice and diversity. Even in the produce section, overflowing with a colourful bounty that includes exotics like mangoes and purple potatoes, we have lost a landscape of difference, and at this point seem to have lost even a map to find it again. Thus mangoes are just mangoes to many

Northern consumers, while I can attest from my year spent in Nepal that mangoes actually have many different varieties, shapes, sizes, textures, and flavours. While we may revel in the deep purple of the occasional specialty potato, Andean farmers farm "30 to 40 distinct varieties of potato (along with numerous other native plants), each having slightly different optimal soil, water, light, and temperature regimes, which the farmer — given enough time — can manage" (Halweil 2000). The need for uniformity (tomato slices that fit the round little hamburger buns neatly) has denied us a diversity of diet and flavour, as well as the efficient use of different ecological niches, which most of our ancestors took for granted. Referring to the twentieth century, Barndt (2002: 13) concludes, "Monocultural and cash crop production is a central feature of the global food system today. It has, however, eliminated many types of tomatoes; 80 percent of the varieties have been lost in this century alone." Taste as well as biodiversity are casualties of the growing monotony of our national pantry.

The culture of the food system recites to the populace a fable about a system that can deliver anything anytime. Supermarket aisles and displays create an image of endless choice, of impulse fulfilment. (Papayas in Canada in January? No problem! Especially if we have no idea of how they are supposed to taste.) As if that was not enough, the rapidly expanding world of Internet food sales increases our experience of food as a global market in which everything that is edible is also accessible. The story conceals the grimmer tale of conglomeration and rigid top-down control by a few companies.

Nonetheless, the truth behind the label is not quite the issue because we are addressing cultural constructions of reality. The key is the perception that a serious choice is there — that this is what makes our food system great. In fact, simply to reveal the truth, to enumerate, for instance, all the food companies owned by Philip Morris, seems to me to be a doomed strategy because that knowledge alone is not enough to puncture the rhetorical bubble of the myths that make up our perception of the world. The revelation tactic forgets that food is an emblem of power in which consumers vicariously participate (we are powerful because people marshal food from around the world for our delectation).

This story of food also celebrates our democracy (anyone can "vote with their dollar" for any comestible they want to indulge in). As Patricia Allen and Martin Kovach (2000: 221) state, "Proponents of green consumerism argue that capitalist markets provide opportunities for responsible consumers to 'vote' with their dollars and thereby to solve environmental problems." The entire story is part and parcel of a cultural figuration that leaves no space for hunger, that makes hunger easy to ignore because it doesn't fit the story. Democracy means that everyone can vote; but the dollar democracy of food choices is open only to some people — those, of course, with dollars.

Instead of recognizing financial restrictions, the field opens only to artificial restrictions in the form of dietary issues and health; that is, personal well-being becomes the only standard for what appears on the table, which means more expensive goods, not more equitable distribution. The economics that oppresses and starves the food producers, and leaves so many consumers hungry day after day, is invisible in this handy version of reality.

The straits we find ourselves in, with people starving (perhaps unwilling to pay?) in a world of plenty, with food made of few ingredients, managed and controlled by a few multinationals, reflect not the evilness of human beings but the economic faith that we have allowed to guide our culture and our economic life. The economic gospel preaches that consumers make rational decisions based on self-interest; they buy things according to the simple rule of willingness to pay theory. Significantly, economic orthodoxy says that consumer identity and behaviour, the tenets of WTP theory, are defined by choice rather than, for instance, need. It is not "consumer need theory," or "compulsion to pay theory." It is "consumer preference theory" and "willingness to pay." The doctrine says that each consumer will pay only up to a certain amount for any good. Every good has a price (under this tenet, even air has a price, as well as the life of another person, as in insurance calculations). Every consumer is completely informed, and therefore makes decisions knowing all the variables, the outcomes of not buying. Every consumer is instantly able to know what he or she wants; the market allows people to identify how much they will pay for what they want, to express their desires in the language of money. This allows the economist to generate complex graphs and algorithms that often demonstrate useful things like consumers' unwillingness to pay for clean air, thus obviating the need to worry anymore. This condition translates culturally into strange messages about who we are (we don't "want" clean air?). In much of North America these messages are the key locus of our representation of ourselves, that is, for the construction of identity.

The theory implies that we make consumption choices in a vacuum, weighing them internally and letting our own self-interest guide us exclusively. The theory also implies that consumers have perfect knowledge, and that they are perfectly rational. It doesn't allow for consumers who accidentally buy expensive organic rice and are then embarrassed to take it back once they reach the head of the line, so they buy it anyway. It doesn't account for mothers who buy whole organic milk for recently weaned toddlers because they care about their child's well-being. It doesn't have a place for the young women who shop together and egg each other on to buy that revealing dress (a dialogic process). The precision and narrowness of the economic vision of a market in which prices are bid on and accepted (Leon Walras's famous auction) do not allow for the broader context in which we shop at the co-op every day despite the sales on key items at the supermarket, and we do this because we want the co-op to survive and know that a food system made of Wal-Marts will not work for us. Each of these scenarios may include a negotiation of price, but the multitude of other considerations are so pressing as to be non-incidental. The growing and often crushing debt carried by Northern consumers clearly indicates an irrational attitude towards affordability, aided and abetted by all sorts of enticements, such as credit cards and payment plans.

Although willingness to pay theory, as the centrepiece of conventional economics, has tremendous institutional power, it is still a cultural expression. Thus, if we examine economics as a cultural phenomenon, the construction of identity featured in willingness to pay (the ethics, and who it says we are) reflects a broader culture. The discipline of economics must be recognized in its particular relation to a dominant ideology. Harry Glasbeek (2002: 22) argues, "While no one claims that the idealized market exists in practice, those asking us to adhere to its principles send out powerful economic and political ideological messages."

The Addled Auction: Flat Oceans and Falling Bicycles

> Economists set themselves too easy, too useless a task if in tempestuous seasons they can only tell us that when the storm is long past the ocean is flat again. (John Maynard Keynes, quoted in Keen 2001: 177)

Most non-economists are instantly puzzled by WTP theory — although their doubts may be quelled in the course of Economics 101, in which they trade their intuitive lack of faith for new status and power in society. WTP theory can seem bizarre until one looks at it as a mythology of identity, a culture musing to itself on who we should be and how we should act. Advertisements and TV commercials are just one more manifestation of this story about our identity: rational, self-interested, uninvolved with others, and not answerable to those around us. As Steve Keen (2001: 27) states:

> While economics can provide a coherent analysis of the individual in its own terms, it is unable to extrapolate this to an analysis of society as the simple sum of its members.... Most mainstream economists are aware of this problem, but they pretend that the failure can be managed with a couple of assumptions. Yet the assumptions themselves are so absurd that only someone with a grossly distorted sense of logic could accept them. That grossly distorted sense of logic is acquired in the course of a standard education in economics.

In conventional economics, graphs of consumer preference are usually coupled with supply curves, which vary inversely with consumer choices. Thus supply increases up to a certain point to fill demand, with the two meeting at a magical point ("equilibrium") where the costs of production are perfectly balanced with price (see Keen 2001: 169). Walras's auction imagines the bidding on and accepting of price to reach this magical point. But Keen likens the use of equilibrium to trying to learn to ride a bike by balancing on it while stationary. Even if you miraculously learn to somehow hold your balance while standing still, if you then try to extrapolate your new skills to a moving bicycle the principles are found to be completely different. The first time you try to turn a corner you will fall flat on your face. Keen (2001: 163) frames the ideology of equilibrium as a distorting influence in economic theory: "Economic theory has distorted itself to ensure that a market economy will achieve equilibrium."

Still, as Joseph Schumpeter goes to painstaking lengths to point out, the concept of equilibrium has had a long and distinguished history — from the fourteenth-century scholasticism of St. Thomas through Adam Smith (1723–90) and David Ricardo (1772–1823) to Marie Esprit Léon Walras (1834–1910), Vilfredo Pareto (1848–1923), and John Maynard Keynes (1883–1946). Part of this history entails an ongoing search for sufficient mathematical expertise (a high priest) to model equilibrium effectively. Schumpeter finds the doctrine applied not just to supply and demand but to many other moments of economic modelling. Indeed, the search for equilibrium takes on something of a spiritual quest. As Schumpeter (1954: 971) notes, "The theorist 'prays for' a unique set of variables to solve all simultaneous equations." He acclaims what he calls Walras's "heroic simplifications" (1954: 974) as the conclusive appearance of a mathematician on the field of engagement, and compares Walras's work in economics to the signing of the Magna Carta. Still, he argues that the notion turns up in both physics and the social sciences, not because of a resemblance but "because it is the same human mind that works both" (1954: 970). Schumpeter (1954: 1012) lucidly states the problem with the theory: "We may question the value of a theory that holds only under conditions, the mere statement of which seems to amount to refuting it." He admits that achieving equilibrium variables depends on a "proof" that "has to be purchased at the price of very restrictive assumptions" (969). Speaking of how some economists can be said to have searched for "the dreamland of equilibrium" (618), he concludes: "It is clear from the outset that markets in real life never do attain equilibrium" (1008).

Consumer theory is mirrored by producer theory, in the marginal cost of production, with, however, quite different consequences for the construction of producer identity. On the producer side, supply is determined by a miraculously omniscient company manager or owner who can speculate on the correct amount of goods to make, given the marginal increase of cost with each unit item, to maximize the profit. This is probably laughable in most businesses, but especially so in food businesses. John Harvie, CEO of Co-op Atlantic, an alternative supermarket chain, came to the food business division of the co-op from agriculture. As he told me, "I started in agriculture, then made the leap to food in 1980 and it nearly finished me off." In hindsight he laughed about it: "People thought I was bluffing, they couldn't believe I really knew so little." He could not believe how impenetrable costs are in food: "It's impossible to know what you paid, you can get seven different answers, with volume discount, preferred deal, the date you bought it, depending, depending…." My first and most daunting task in the dawn hours working at GreenStar Co-op was to check and adjust the produce prices based on recent deliveries, losses, inventory, discounts received, seasonal sales, and more.

Brian McCullum, a cattle auctioneer in Sussex, Nova Scotia, described what is really happening in the cattle industry. The plan of production is entirely guesswork, he said, and had recently resulted largely in disaster. "People have to speculate on feeders to survive, that means guessing the price in eight to nine months. No one can do just one or two animals anymore. No one is replacing the farmers who give up." Producer decisions on cost and price are probably more like consulting a ouija board than making a thoughtful, rational economic choice. That is not because producers are stupid or irrational; in fact, the candid comments of Harvie, an extremely skilled and effective businessman credited with tremendous positive change in the Co-op Atlantic empire, show an important variation between consumer and producer identity. Perhaps because the cultural work of economics has less interest in producers than in consumers, these producers may be freer to admit to incomplete information. How often does one hear an "expert" consumer say, "I couldn't tell one product from another, so I guessed"? The act of shopping by definition assumes that consumers know why they buy a product. It might be a breath of fresh air to hear, for instance, a wine expert telling us that one wine seems nice, but then there's price, the label, flavours at first sip, then later sips, front flavour, back flavour, and what you're eating it with, so really, who knows?

In the producer world, farmers know that apple trees do not enter an obedient stasis when they hit the last output that stays within the marginal cost of production. Willy-nilly, they continue to produce fruit, oblivious to the furious sketchings of economists. Nor, as I can attest, do freak hailstorms hold off in July just because the price of lettuce is good for farmers. The extent to which nature intrudes in economics may be especially visible in food production (Goodman and Redclift 1991). However, nature intrudes (or is tangled up with) any and all production to some extent, not least in the particular needs of workers (boredom, carpal tunnel syndrome, love affairs, hunger, light levels).

Although the producer identity figured by economic theory resembles the consumer frame of identity (rational, self-interested, omniscient), the everyday culture does not trumpet the work of the producer identity in the same way. In fact, our relation to production is thoroughly concealed in the popular imagination, as if working were a little shameful, and certainly not in any way constructive of our identity. Beyond a few fantasies about healthy, relaxed farmers standing in their field admiring the sun on their crops, the everyday work of creating food is fairly absent from our cultural icons. Loblaws (always ahead of the pack on the cultural imagination) is now offering up ads that take place in its test kitchens, with scientists taking the place of producers and cooks. As Kneen (1993: 72) writes, referring to farmers who have been reinvented as businessmen, "the farmer is dismissed."

Unlike consumers, the North American producers have been taught that their knowledge is worthless, that only experts (often the same people trying to sell seed or some new technology) are qualified to solve the on-farm problems. Where the consumer absorbs the false identity of the smart shopper, who knows how to sniff out bargains and knows when she or he is being cheated by price differences, the producer is shaped by the community of agricultural scientists as being (falsely) devoid of relevant knowledge. Ads from Monsanto and other corporations encourage a kind of mindless trust, as if you were buying auto insurance ("you're in good hands"). The frequent use of military imagery in the names of agricultural products also invokes our faith in the military as protector of our security.

As in the case of the consumer, the cultural construction of the producer's identity takes place in the key of knowledge, both in the case of the orthodoxy and its resistant alternatives. As Jules Pretty (1995) points out in *Regenerating Agriculture*, recent battles around agricultural modernization centre on the status of different knowledges. Pretty (1995) and Shiva (1998) argue that a traditional agriculture sees multiple solutions to problems, and often addresses a number of problems simultaneously. Traditional solutions embody long-term sustainability, flexibility, and creativity, as well as democratic process. This kind of knowledge is heterodox and perverse. It fails to stay within the neat guidelines of scientific practice, but changes with its landscape and its climate. One thing that kept me committed to working for organic farmers for so many years was the creativity of their solutions to problems. Their strategies were often refreshing and surprising; they often used the same material for many different purposes. Halweil (2000) states:

> Farmers are professional, with extensive knowledge of their local soils, weather, native plants, sources of fertilizer or mulch, native

pollinators, ecology and community. If we are to have a world where the land is no longer managed by such professionals, but is instead managed by distant corporate bureaucracies interested in extracting maximum outputs at minimum cost, what kind of food will we have, and at what price?

Resistance to WTP

In WTP theory, the rational, perfectly informed, and self-interested consumer meets (and opposes) the rational, perfectly informed, and self-interested producer at the point of price, that magical point at which the most preferences of two impossible beings coincide. One writer remarks that WTP theory imagines a kind of zero-sum effect for benefits: additions in one place necessitate losses elsewhere. "We just take it as given," Nystrom (1995: 115) says, "that doing good for others has to diminish the good we can do for ourselves. As Nancy Folbre (1994: 5) notes, there is also an assumption, which anthropologists recognize as particularly characteristic of white Western culture, that identity is singular, not multiple. Feminist economics, among other disciplines, has begun to challenge such a view of ourselves. As Folbre also points out, individuals may "act in ways that seem irrational in the sense that they offer no apparent economic benefit."

In one session of "Imagine Our Economy," a popular economics course run in 2003 by the Catalyst Centre in Toronto, we taped up a giant outline of a generic body, a gingerbread person, on the wall. We asked the participants to write on sticky notes all the different reasons as to why they make a purchase and then stick the notes anywhere on the outline that seemed to relate to the reason to shop. For instance, a participant might place notes on the paper person's belly to indicate the need to satisfy hunger as a reason for shopping or paying, or on the brain if the reason was to learn more (from a new book, perhaps, or from paying for a course). When we were done the huge gingerbread person was plastered with sticky notes — but very few of them named price as a reason for buying something. A great many of the reasons reflected a sense of altruism, either for friends and relatives or for struggling farmers or shopkeepers. Although the participants were mostly politically aware and progressive, many of them were also low-income, and I expected the exercise to produce many motivations, including price, and not that the results would largely skip price. The exercise led me to wonder why price would be the idiom for the economic expression of the relations between buyers and sellers.

WTP is not the only model of consumer identity that occurs in daily practice. Natural food stores, co-ops, and other organizations participate with consumers in reconfiguring their identities. Their ideal consumer is truly knowledgeable, open-minded, and thoughtful. Monbiot (1996b: 2) writes,

"Organic box schemes, farm shops, food co-operatives and fair trade outlets remain all but invisible to most people in Britain, but are growing, in some places, with astonishing speed. They have started treating the consumer as the consumer deserves to be treated — as an intelligent, responsive, social being." Some people in Atlantic Canada, concerned at the lack of education and member knowledge in the co-op movement today, are taking steps to rectify that situation. For them, education in this case means economics education: understanding the economics of food, why it is important to keep money in the local economy (a common theme), and what it means to have a share in the co-op.

Lorri King, the owner of Alternatives, a natural food store, has posted a mission statement on her wall and under that a diagram of something called "The Customer Circle." The circle exemplifies how good customer service can be a complex, long-term process of education. It begins with excellent customer service, which can motivate a customer's healthy choices (focused on the individual). As time passes, customers become more committed to being part of the process (focusing on a community); they start to consider collective issues such as their role in the environment. They then become more loyal and knowledgeable, which allows the staff to provide even better service. This model of education (which details a path from one notion of consumer to another) is quite different from the pabulum that the "Insider's Report" hands out. It requires a long and delicate process, with ties as thin as spider silk being drawn between people over time, infinitesimal connections gradually being made, and a committed relationship eventually unfolding. This complex model of consumer identity recalls our earlier examination of producer or farmer knowledge: intricate, multilayered, and ever-changing.

While consumer theory expresses satisfaction in terms of price, alternative food stores deliberately place price in the context of many other issues. As many of the people I interviewed said, if they have to compete on price alone, they've already lost the battle. In alternative food systems, the WTP model of identity hits a brick wall, and like Humpty Dumpty begins to mourn its broken pieces.

A Story beyond Price

My top goal is to be more than a store. (Sarah Fairley, General Manager, Karma Co-op, 2003)

Sarah Fairley, the general manager of Karma Co-op in Toronto, told me that although the store cannot lose sight of the original co-op goals of providing affordable food, its long-term vision insists on affordability as only one reason that brings members there to shop. If Karma succeeds in its goals, it will be as part of "a strong community," she said. It will be "well-connected to our neighbourhood and the local food initiatives. It'll have a sense of itself as being more than a store. Members will feel that they belong to something rather than just shopping at Karma." Over and over again she emphasized the embeddedness of Karma's goals. She said that members emphasize that other people should not profit "from your need to eat." Her ideal supplier recognizes that "our economic viability is in their best interest… it seems obvious and yet is not obvious so often."

Using very similar language, Linda Tuijtel of Foodsmiths told me, "We're not just a store where you come to shop, we're a store where you come to shop and ask questions and see a friendly face." Molly Forsythe, another long-time manager there, pointed out that emphasizing price is a trap, a quick route to bankruptcy. "We aren't going to price ourselves so we won't be here ten years from now, but… you want to create a business that supports the people who work for you to be able to live and the people who made the products to be able to live." What is Forsythe's hypothetical advice to a new store owner? She would warn them not to "get stuck on pricing."

Lest we mistake this approach as a matter only of the niche market, the Co-op Atlantic CEO also remarked that in the fierce competition of recent years in the Maritimes, you have to "compete as best you can," that is, when it comes to prices "try to compete" on the broader playing field. Still, as John Harvie recognized, this competition "is not something we can expect to win in, they have deeper pockets. If we are trying to compete head to head, we don't have much advantage." Even though Co-op Atlantic is, he said, in most cases "more than competitive," that strategy is not sustainable. "We tend to feel if you live by the sword you die by the sword, and that would be the case if we were just trying to be the cheapest on the block."

These successful businesses replace an obsession with price with com- munity relations — as in Molly Forsythe's comment about supporting workers and producers as well as the store, or Sarah Fairley's emphasis on community — and with service. As Sue Rose of the Herb and Spice store in Ottawa said:

> Quite often I hear that my prices are just as good as theirs in many cases. And here you get service, we'll teach you how to cook it, we'll tell you why organics are worthwhile, we'll tell you why this is not a good thing to have in your food. We can't answer everything but we know an awful lot collectively around here. So I'm not particularly worried about the big stores taking it over.

These strategies are not just a response to being smaller and less powerful than Loblaw or other chains; they speak of a serious and successful alterna- tive economics that challenges the conventional ideas of consumer theory.

Their comments speak about a full-scale alternative system that has evolved from years of careful negotiations with customers' comments and desires. This active listening requires them not only to delve into what customers say they want but also to engage in a continuing learning process in which customers and staff teach each other and develop opinions in concert and in conversation. Together they develop a broader vision of the problems that the customers are trying to solve.[7] Clearly, if these strategies reflect customer desires, and the success of these stores suggests that they do, then customers seem to want much more than to maximize their personal satisfaction and pay the cheapest price for it. They are shopping where they can get knowledge, a friendly face, community, even ownership (in co-ops), and other intangible goods that fit awkwardly into supply and demand curves but keep these businesses thriving. Rose emphasizes the respect that ties the relations in her food economy together. Her advice to a new store owner is to treat everyone, from customer to driver, with respect: "If you give it, you get it back." The only ones that don't get much respect are the drunken shoplifters but, she said, "mostly they get thrown out with courtesy."

The self-interested consumer image disintegrates in the face of this dialogic process of give and take. The customers' construction of identity occurs in the context of exchanging information and thoughts, weighing conflicting knowledge, and even setting strategic direction, officially in co-ops but unofficially in small stores in which customer opinion helps to set new directions for the owners. Rose recognizes that this work may not even immediately result in a sale. She and her husband, she said, "didn't want to be executives managing an empire."

> We like dealing with customers one on one. There's nothing more satisfying than somebody who comes in with a really restrictive diet; they come in and say there's nothing they can eat and I'll spend an hour with them. And they'll say aren't you supposed to be doing something? I'm wasting your time. Well, no, that's what I'm here for. And they'll go away with smiles on their faces, and a few things in their grocery basket, but they're back next week.

The work of learning and changing who you are (a dialogic construction of identity) can supersede money, resulting first in loyalty, but it can also eventually lead to sales. Sue Rose's own satisfaction and goals derive not from the accumulation of financial capital but from the respect that circulates among the participants in this alternative exchange. I asked her what kept her going in tough times. "Mostly," she said, "it's the goodwill of the people I work with and the customers."

Most natural food stores are a kind of hymn to the diversity of reasons to shop. Along with price, the items and their signs or labels may report their origins, their cultivation methods, whether the producers received a fair price, whether the product has been genetically engineered, even the provenance of the seed (as in the old varieties of "heritage tomatoes"). In my own work as a sales representative for Organic Meadow and later the Ontario Natural Food Co-op I gained enormous respect for the careful attention that the owners and staff paid to all the different things that customers ask about.[8] Their displays usually orchestrate a multiplicity of motives, offering up a range of purpose and meaning for the customers' choice. Their displays have to reflect the negotiation of meaning that customers work through as they choose somewhat arbitrarily (perhaps even irrationally sometimes) among factors such as origin, cultivation method, producer support, buying what the kids love, buying what the kids will eat, special sales and deals, and the presence of trans fats or carbohydrates.

These stories teach us a new way of seeing neo-classical willingness to pay theory, which falters before this diversity. The work of the stores and co-ops reflects in their action and successes a growing determination to challenge dominant consumer theories. It would be irrational, following WTP theory, to claim that all of the various motives are expressed in price, because price is both cited as one motive among many and deliberately set aside. The links between the reason to buy and price are not direct or obvious. I am not claiming that natural food stores reflect some "true" desire of customers, because this consumer identity is constructed as well through media dialogue and other texts. But this alternative cultural work of identity, dialogic and multiple, reflects a different process and a very different logic from that manifested in WTP theory. A growing number of people prefer the complex and transformative quality of this identity work to the simplistic calculations of identity offered in a conventional store.

Friendly Monsters

I like watching natural food stores in action, and witnessing the steady rise of so many of them through the shards of an economy that has declined continuously in real wages since about 1973. The story of their success is a story of the existence and healthiness of alternative economic strategies. This focus on willingness to pay theory may seem esoteric, but it is crucial to recognize that the strategies that challenge the primacy of price and consumer single-mindedness are the everyday practice of functional alternatives; they are not just resistance, they are in fact a different way of doing business.

Often theoretical economists, especially when backed into a corner, will somewhat glibly remark that their theories have nothing to do with real business practice, that they are just amusing mathematical theorems that are not meant to inform or model practice. The relation between theory and practice has infected economics for generations; the theorists who model actual practice are often accorded lower status than their more cerebral, abstract theoretical cousins. This distinction, though, is disingenuous. It is a cover for how, as some scholars have pointed out, economics operates not as a science but as a religion, a matter of faith and belief. The mathematical economists may bolt themselves away in monastic splendour, but the doctrines they spin are not neutral or apolitical. As the tenets of a powerful religion that is sweeping across the world, they are deeply ethical. They contain guidelines for right action (self-interest, single-minded rationality, personal satisfaction, individual decision-making independent of a community or others). As John Pottier (1999: 102) states, "One of the strongest manifestations of market 'embeddedness' is that markets are shaped by and in turn help shape, notions of morality and personhood."

Challenges to conventional consumer identity, offered up across the world of alternative food initiatives, thus represent a kind of heterodoxy or alternative faith to the dominant religion and ethics. Besides indicating another path to a more savoury identity and ethics for a consumer, the existence of these alternatives also makes a statement about the dominant ideology: that it is not the only way, that economic systems are multiple and diverse. As Hazel Henderson (1996: 7) says, we should be celebrating the alternatives "rather than fighting over deck space on the old 'Titanic.'" J.K. Gibson-Graham's powerful book *The End of Capitalism (As We Knew It): A Feminist Critique of Political Economy* (1996: 12) argues that we have allowed capitalism and the doctrines of neo-classical economics to rule alone, forgetting that any economy is the "site of multiple forms."[9]

In a sentence that provided an inspiration for my own work, Gibson-Graham (1996: 21) exhort us to challenge the monolithic inevitability of the dominant economics with "an economic imaginary populated with 'friendly monsters' of the non-capitalist sort." I would add to this, echoing their implications, that the face of capitalism is also scored with multiple forms. Like a face about to break into tears, it is just barely holding together. As anthropologists have long taught us, people have invented numerous different methods of exchange and markets, each thick with the expression of the culture's morals, metaphors of identity, and rules for relating to others. Ethnography has shown, as Pottier (1999: 101) writes, that "*marketplaces everywhere and at all times are regulated* through political, cultural and legal conventions."

It is quite common for the ordinary person or student to be told that they cannot talk about economics if they haven't studied it. This kind of exclusiveness is especially dangerous when the issue involves the religious doctrine that defines such a large part of our lives, including our food, how we shape our identities, and often our very survival. Food is an idiom that non-economists can use to meditate on economics and express their opinions and ideas for change. The idiom allows us to recognize that the economy is not some mystical set of theorems but is cultural fodder, owned and operated by all cultural actors. As with any hegemony, cultural actors have complex relations to the dominant ideology of economics. Pottier (1999: 118) stresses this same point: "Empirical research… emphasizes that economic activity is neither autonomous nor natural but *regulated* through cultural norms and practices." In our cultures of food, resistance and challenges to the hegemony of standard economic theory form easily and thrive; they cannot be banished from the contemplation of the economies of food.

Notes

1. This situation has reached crisis proportions, as heterodox economists and graduate students spearhead a movement to allow the teaching of alternative economics. These alternatives include more than classic threats such as Marxist economics; they extend to the application of chaos theory and current evolution theory to the dynamics of economic systems (see Monaghan 2003).

2. To be fair, the limitations of WTP theory are recognized in economic work such as institutional economics and other manifestations. Sophisticated understandings among the elites has not reached basic economics education, however. The spread of an outmoded theory continues as many undergraduates never make it past Economics 101, and popular culture continues to reflect conventional WTP approaches. One might liken the problem to the marriage ritual that I studied in Nepal. The actual meaning of the Sanskritic text (which few people understand) is much less important to cultural practice than the way in which ordinary people understand and act on what they think the words mean.

3. I use advertising here with forethought; advertising occupies a key position in North American culture as a popular art that embodies cultural arguments and narratives. As in any mythological representation, advertising offers us the symbols of our culture in an overdetermined, saturated narrative.

4. Successful shopping is often marked by an almost criminal relation to the store, as exemplified in an ad in which a series of small criminal acts (such as minor theft) are likened to the incredible bargain that you can get from a phone company if you just call. Sellers are often depicted as diehard morons in this landscape — "We're giving it away!" they crow, as if they have drifted beyond any elementary understanding of the market.

5. The Nestlé promotion led to hundreds of deaths as infants and toddlers were separated from the immunity-enhancing properties, as well as the abundance and nutrition, of breast milk, to suck in the unclean and bacteria-ridden waters of the local supply, which had to be added to the Nestlé product. By 1997 Nestlé was continuing to promote bottle-feeding but was buying up bottled water and promoting that as a substitute for the contaminated tap water in the poor countries to which they were marketing (see Campaign for Ethical Marketing).

6. In 2004 Wal-Mart held the position of top food retailer in the world, with revenues almost four times the revenues of the next largest retailer (ETC Group 2005).

7. Many health food stores and co-ops have not, for instance, jumped on the low-

carbohydrate-diet bandwagon because it does not fit a broader mandate of sustainable health (both individual and environmental). Most trends focused on weight loss tend not to drive changes in the natural food industry, although the industry may already cater to the needs of a dieter in various ways (for instance, by offering vegetarian options).

8.   The market economy creates a strange disjuncture between clear demands from natural food store customers and the market's ability to deliver on that demand. Thus, Ontario stores asked for local organic canned tomatoes for years without garnering a response from suppliers. Suppliers were not just being pigheaded; they were running into the perennial logjam created in Canada. The United States has such a large, subsidized manufacturing base that transporting thousands of jars or cans of tomatoes all the way from California to Toronto is less expensive than canning the same product in our own backyard. This calculation applies to conventional food economics as well, and impoverishes the Canadian food supply; various defunct canneries dot the landscape in Canada. The success of alternatives suggests that perhaps suppliers could profit from listening to the demands differently, and trying to respond to them through new principles (de-emphasizing price where feasible). Recently the Ontario Natural Food Co-op (ONFC), a wholesaler based in Toronto, was finally able to offer a highly successful line of local organic canned tomato products.

9.   The book was jointly written by Julie Graham and Katharine Gibson, who combined their names for the authorship.

Chapter 4

Growth and Granola
The Story of the Organic Movement

Volunteers rented a truck once a month, drove to New York to pick up food, and stayed up all night to break the food down into each co-op's orders. ("A Brief History of United Northeast" <www.unfi. com> 2004)

Northeast Co-operatives began with a gleam in the founders' eyes and justice in their hearts. Early on local co-ops around Boston began shopping together for "lower prices for all the co-ops." But in 1973, when they formed an official co-op (New England Food Co-op Organization), their goals were "not only fair food prices and good quality, but also justice in areas of food production and distribution." The rest of the "Brief History" is silent about justice. The history leaps from peak to peak of breathtaking growth (30 percent per year during a time when the natural foods industry was achieving only 20 percent) and mergers. In 1999, after a merger with Ohio River Co-operatives, Northeast became "the fourth largest natural products wholesaler in North America," serving customers "in 22 states." Later, Northeast Co-operatives "merged with" (or was "absorbed by") United Natural, one of the small number of large natural food wholesalers that dominate the natural food supply in the United States.

Tales of early twentieth-century financial success tend to report on the rise of a poor white man who started without anything (except his colour and maleness) and became owner of a successful corporation or franchise (the Horatio Alger story). More recent stories seem to gloat with equal delight on spectacular success and sudden downfalls. The story of the rise of the organic food industry is often told in glowing terms: a story of mountains of gold that grassroots organizations (with justice in their hearts) were lucky and resourceful enough to stumble across. Still, a cautionary subplot may also show its head.

Northeast's narrative of success (where do we invest?) echoes the salivations of conventional business pages as they drool over some dot.com's triumphal progress. Like many of those tales, this one also ends with a downfall. In 2002, "motivated by the company's financial problems, the increasing and rapid consolidation in the natural foods industry, and the desire to preserve service to all its members," the Northeast Co-operatives member-owners approved the merger with United Natural, a conventionally structured private corporation. One critic, C.R. Lawn (2003) asked, "How could Northeast, despite rapid growth, yearly sales exceeding $130 million, a new physical plant, and a strong network of more than 1200 buying clubs, retail co-ops and private stores, nevertheless have lost so much money?"

These intertwined stories are fireside tales of common parlance in the rhetoric of late twentieth-century capitalism. The organic movement, if it had a poet laureate, a Homer of its own, might start with stories of well-deserved and righteous success. Similar rags to riches tales are reported almost every day in the pages of the mainstream business press, and are echoed in the stories of self-made entrepreneurs and the curriculum of universities and colleges. However, the Homer of organic food has other stories up his sleeve, and he will bend your ear if you sit awhile.

About the same time that Northeast was logging one commercial triumph after another in the early 1990s, I exited the world of academics with a newly minted Ph.D. in anthropology clutched in my hand. A few short months later, hoping to broaden my experience of the world, I found myself in New York State managing Finger Lakes Organic (FLO) Growing Cooperative, an extraordinary venture that at that time had a growth rate of about 20 to 25 percent per year. As with many small organic companies, sales rose while margins tightened; this was a challenge that was occurring — and being met in various ways — across North America. Over the 1980s and 1990s the organic movement was experiencing phenomenal financial success while engaging in an uneasy dialogue between its values and businesses founded on moral and philosophical grounds.

When I first joined Finger Lakes Organic I had no business experience, and no credentials beyond my doctorate in anthropology — though at least that achievement implied great listening skills. One of my first rewards from listening came when a key customer called me up and gave me a much-needed lesson in marketing. This co-op manager explained that he had been committed to buying from FLO since the co-op was founded in the 1980s. He believed in buying locally and in maintaining loyalty to a key supplier. In exchange, he explained, the FLO manager (which now meant me) maintained the quality of the produce and the integrity of fair pricing. The FLO manager made sure that the produce intake was done with care, with quality checks and frequent discussions with growers about what customers needed. The FLO manager's responsibility was to price at a level at which the co-op manager could not only sell things on to his customers, with no gouging, but also get as much for the growers as possible. Unaware of this unwritten contract, I had not been fulfilling the proper role. However, I had just written a dissertation about symbolic capital and the creation of trust-based economic exchanges, so I quickly realized that he was describing a homegrown version of what I had studied in Nepal.

The difference between FLO and a conventional business, while superficially small and to some outsiders barely recognizable, set me on a twenty-year course of fascination with alternative approaches to business. FLO, unlike a private business, did not negotiate prices in advance with the growers (member/owners). Instead, to cover its expenses it simply took a percentage off the final price of the product when sold to customers and sent the rest back to the growers. The goal was to get as much as possible for the growers and, as a non-profit, to post only a minimal surplus after expenses. For the managers, this subtle difference resulted in motivations that contrasted strongly with conventional corporate business management. Our trust-based relations with customers meant negotiating prices around numbers that worked for everyone. Sometimes customers were willing or even offered to pay more, knowing that the money was going straight to the growers rather than to profits. Some of the produce I had was well above the quality of regular produce; the FLO growers had high standards. In exchange, customers, especially in New York City, were willing to pay a little extra for the spectacular effect on their produce displays.

The delicate feat of balancing that I and other staff accomplished each growing season included, for instance, explanations to the growers about why the price of carrots dropped in September (everyone has them) and, on the other side, various lessons for the customers, especially about the weather. ("I know you want strawberries but you remember how it rained all night? Your strawberries are now field jam.") I now believe that a degree in anthropology, which focused on communication, listening skills, and even some mediation skills, was better suited to my new line of work than an MBA would have been.

FLO eventually faced the new challenges of an increasingly competitive market and shrinking margins, and the organic movement began to develop in several directions at once. The seeds of that trajectory were all right there in my first lesson at FLO. How do you make money and negotiate moral obligations at the same time? More importantly, the organic movement raises the question of what happens when certain values change or conflict with a different value set. The history of organics tells the story of a negotiation of value systems that still co-exist uneasily in the marketplace and on organic farms everywhere.

Despite these indications of moral complexity, organics is, like the anti-GMO movement, a movement for product replacement, that is, not the pesticide-laden, waxed apple but the chemical-free one — whoever grew it, however the workers were treated, and regardless of where it came from. The story of organics describes a movement to replace the unsafe products of chemical agriculture with food that is free of chemicals and safer for both people and the environment. Indeed, the tendency of the organic movement to split into two trajectories may reside in the emphasis on product replacement. While relations such as I described for FLO were common in the grass-roots period of organics, nothing in the economics of organics guaranteed that these subtleties of dialogics, trust, and symbolic relations would remain an integral part of the movement. On the other hand, the guidelines for the products, if not carved in stone, are at least regulated by and formalized in the various certification rules to which growers must adhere.

Organic food fits into the broader context of the natural food movement, but is a special case in a number of ways. First, unlike natural food, organic is highly regulated. Certification standards (both national and regional) are strict and require organic farmers to keep audit trails of all inputs to their farm. Third-party inspectors, through farm visits and document inspection, declare a farm organic or not, setting an independent seal on the farm or manufacturer. The seal appears on the label of processed foods, and some vegetables. By comparison, the definition of "natural" is loose and open to convenient construction. There is no generally accepted idea of what constitutes "natural" food, although it tends to mean food that does not have chemical additives or hormones. There are only moral pressures, but nothing legal, to stop a "natural" tomato farmer from planting GMO seeds or spraying occasionally with, say, Roundup, if the farmer feels in his or her heart that the chemical will evaporate before the product goes to market (as one natural farmer told me).

The chemical experiment in agriculture began with the end of World War II, when chemical weapons manufacturers were casting around for something else to do with their products. The common use of military metaphors for pesticide and herbicide names is no coincidence. In this war, as in most wars, it is the civilians who have suffered the most. The experiment has left farmers with depleted, chemically dependent soil. Much of the topsoil has simply washed away. The straight pure lines of the monocrop system that characterizes conventional agriculture and facilitates the application of chemical inputs are tantamount to building drainage ditches for your topsoil; the many months that fields lie open to the elements, often without cover crops to hold onto the soil, exacerbate the problem. Topsoil, which nature takes centuries to create, is disappearing in the United States at a rate of two billion tons a year (Sanders 2004). The soil washes into the water systems, causing sedimentation and clogging that alters the ecosystem. This problem is in addition to the toxins and pollutants that are added to the planet's soil, water, and air annually through chemical agriculture.

Organic standards[1] are largely soil and product management regulations. They specify quantity and type of allowable inputs, ban the use of hormones in meat production, and indicate the length of time (usually three years) that any non-organic plot of land has to be farmed organically before it is certifiable. The guidelines are key to creating a stable consumer movement, and to the movement to replace the products of chemical agriculture. Consumers can look for the certification seal and then feel confident that the food is chemical-free.

The existence of a label reduces the need for direct contact with the farmer. It means that someone else (who is rendered more powerful, more objective, by being a neutral third party) has guaranteed the growing methods of the farmer (who can now also be faceless, and send products to the mass market to sell rather than talking to the consumers). As many people have pointed out, organic standards also tend not to address other issues such as ecological sustainability, workers' rights, animal rights, or corporate structure. Allen and Kovach (2000: 224) state, "Organic standards are particularly hard pressed to capture concepts such as holism and ecological sensitivity" (see also Klonsky 2000). An organic farm can raise beef fed organically and free from antibiotics and hormones on a typical feedlot, where hundreds of cows are jammed together suffering short and miserable lives, cared for by undocumented, underpaid, and abused migrant workers and owned by an absent and wealthy landowner. It can sell the beef through mass-market outlets that have a similar lack of concern for quality of life, whether animal or worker. OntarBio, which both produces organic dairy products and supplies the organic meat industry, created its own rules for animal treatment because of this flaw in the standards. The operators' cows must get a certain amount of time to roam around and eat outside in appropriate weather. The co-op also specifies a longer than conventional rest period after birth for the mother cows and does not separate the calves immediately from the mothers, allowing a period before weaning when the milk is going to the calf rather than the customer.

Organic agriculture has tended to devolve to somewhat dry and precise issues of method and input. Standards are set out in incredibly complex and lengthy documents that tend to be incomprehensible to the average layperson. This bureaucratic regulation provides the guarantee needed by consumers who are not in direct contact with producers. As Julie Guthman (1998: 150) writes, "Organic regulation makes organic agriculture safe for capitalism." Such regulation also stamps the movement with the goals of product replacement (scientifically better food for all), while structural changes continue to elude the enterprise. The focus of the movement now raises critical questions. What are the results of the emphasis on replacing unsafe products through conventional marketing techniques? What kind of change does this emphasis achieve? Do we really need organic jellybeans? What other possible kinds of change are jettisoned under the pressures of conventional marketing: growth, profit, and consolidation?

As organic becomes big business, voluntary practices like those of the Organic Meadow dairy producers begin to cut into the primary goals of a farm or organic agribusiness — profits. The United States became the scene of a bloody battle over standards as the corporate players entered the field and then sought to revise the standards to fit their style of agriculture. Before the 1990s, since most companies had no particular interest in the tiny market, the standards were regional and appropriate for growing conditions in different parts of the country. In the 1990s, the U.S. Department of Agriculture (USDA) announced that its new national standards would allow both sewage sludge (full of toxins and heavy metals) and GMO seeds, among other atrocities. Ben Lilliston and Ronnie Cummins (1998) found:

> Among the more controversial proposals were to allow under the mandatory "USDA Organic" label the use of genetic engineering, nuclear irradiation, toxic sewage sludge, intensive confinement of farm animals, and a host of other conventional factory farm agricultural practices. If degraded rules become institutionalized as federal law, the United States will gain the dubious distinction of having the lowest organic standards in the world.

The response from consumers and producers was swift and outraged. Before the USDA closed the door on feedback, it had received 275,603 letters (I couldn't get on the website to deliver mine because of the heavy traffic there). Sheepishly the bureau backed off and eventually finalized standards that are more in the spirit of organic agriculture. Still, key advocates for organic food, such as Ronnie Cummins of the Organic Consumer Association, point out that the standards reflect only the minimum rules for organic production. As Guthman (1998: 135) put it, "In California, conventional agro-food firms are beginning to appropriate the most lucrative aspects of organic food provision and to abandon the agronomic and marketing practices associated with sustainability." The debate continues. Consumers launched a boycott against the gigantic Horizon Organic dairy. In July 2007 a group of small farmers sued Horizon for price-fixing and restraint of trade through monopoly ownership. Organic certification was suspended in June 2007 at a factory farm that supplied Horizon with organic milk (a 10,000-head feedlot in California). Dean Foods, Horizon's parent company, reported profit losses again in the dairy company. Meanwhile Aurora Dairy, another huge organic dairy factory farm, was threatened by the USDA with loss of its organic certification due to impropriety in animal husbandry and organic practices. Guthman (1998: 137) concluded, "The political construction of the meaning of 'organic' and its institutionalization in regulatory agencies has facilitated both the proliferation of agribusiness entrants and their adoption of questionably sustainable practices."

Organic food and its informal cousin, natural food, can boast of spectacular success since the mid-1990s, with growth rates of at least 20 percent a year in the United States and Canada for organic products. In

2005 the USDA reported that retail sales of organic food products in 2003 totalled $10.4 billion, and seemed on track to continue double-digit growth into 2004. A 2007 report from the Nielsen company set the latest retail sales figure in Canada at 28 percent over the previous year; organic farm numbers increased since 2001 and conventional farms decreased by 7 percent (Canadian Organic Growers 2007). These estimates tend to come from tracking cash-register receipts in stores that use bar-code scanning and have agreed to participate, which means that the huge amount of organic food that is moved without the benefit of electronic computation (through farmers' markets, for instance) is probably not registered in the figures. In 1996, when I started working in Canada with organic producers, few organic purveyors had any register tracking systems, and we had no real idea what the growth figures were, except that they seemed anecdotally substantial. Also, most organic produce had to be rung in by the price, not by the bar code, because farmers or their wholesalers had to purchase the bar-codes themselves, and it had not proved necessary to do so until supermarkets picked up the products. Even with the introduction of unit codes (which the register can track), supermarkets suspected the underreporting of sales because the managers believed that the cashiers consistently failed to distinguish between organic and non-organic unit codes. Sometimes figures from the United States would be cited for Canada, even though the market and the movement of new products in Canada are quite different.

Aside from these caveats, 20 percent is usually the accepted growth percentage for the organic food sector. While this might seem unspectacular, the rest of the grocery industry has essentially reached a plateau in sales; any growth now comes from squeezing larger margins from producers and wholesalers.[2] The organic and natural food categories are among the fastest-growing sectors of the food industry. This growth guarantees all kinds of healthy and unhealthy attention from profit-oriented businesses. Since 1999 a disturbing trend in mergers has rapidly consolidated the organic industry, and put ownership of much of it into the hands of familiar players such as Cargill, Heinz, General Mills, and even Coca Cola (which in October 2001 bought out the Odwalla brand) (see Howard 2007).

Big Gets Bigger

> What must be firmly established at the start is that myth is a system of communication, that it is a message. (Barthes 1957)

In the 1990s, huge supermarket-style natural food stores such as Whole Foods Market and Wild Oats spread across the United States and later merged. Whole Foods has expanded into Canada and aggressively absorbed local markets. Driven by shareholder rights (Whole Foods is now publicly traded), they are loudly anti-union. A familiar mythology of origins tends to grow up around these success stories; that is, they are not quite a fiction, but a way of telling customers and staff and the general public about where they came from as a way of saying who they are. Origin stories of the success- ful organic businesses tend to calcify around a kind of "Horatio Alger with long hair" story.

Michael Pollan (2001) writes: "'Organic' on the label conjures a whole story, even if it is the consumer who fills in most of the details, supplying the hero (American Family Farmer), the villain (Agribusinessman) and the literary genre, which I think of as 'supermarket pastoral.'" Pollan explores the "cracks in the pastoral narrative," invoking themes that may be similarly mythical of success and entrepreneurship. In some ways, the history of the organic movement can be seen as a clash of mythologies. Each version of events represents not so much an attempt to paint a realistic portrait as to state a core set of beliefs about how food economics should work.

Cascadian Farm, one of the most successful organic food corporations in the market today (purveyor of frozen foods, including french fries, vegetables, soups, and organic TV dinners) was, Pollan (2001) shows, "started in 1971 by Gene Kahn with the idea of growing food for the collective of environ- mentally minded hippies he had hooked up with in nearby Bellingham" (Washington). The company was eventually bought out by General Mills (after first selling a majority share to Welch's in the aftermath of the Alar sales spike). Kahn himself came "to symbolize the takeover of the move- ment by agribusiness." A vice-president of marketing told Pollan candidly that General Mills had to redirect Cascadian's consumer target away from people who believed in natural food and towards "health-seekers" — "a considerably larger group of even more affluent consumers" who are "more interested in their own health than that of the planet."[3] Unfortunately, the market offers these concerns up as if they represented a choice. Why, after all, are these consumers required to prioritize and simplify their needs? What if they wanted, really, to be able to be healthy, save the planet, and afford it, in no particular order? Such a history repeats itself throughout the organic movement. Pollan explores the value shift that occurred for the hippie farmer to become the millionaire with a Lexus that Kahn is today. Despite Kahn's own judgment, his broad goal of changing the food system (with as many acres as possible converted to organics) represents a choice of values. Pollan (2001) states:

> Organic is nothing if not a set of values (*this* is better than *that*), and to the extent that the future of those values is in the hands of companies that are finally indifferent to them, that future will be precarious. Also, there are values that the new corporate — and

78

government — construction of "organic" leaves out, values that once were part and parcel of the word but have long since been abandoned as impractical or unprofitable. I'm thinking of things like locally grown, like the humane treatment of animals, like the value of a shorter and more legible food chain, the preservation of family farms, even the promise of a countercuisine.

Organics: Long Hair and Bottom Lines

The early beginnings of organic food and agriculture corresponded to the period of various social movements of the 1960s and 1970s (see MacRae 1990; Guthman 1998). The sphere of activity tended towards small-scale operations. Sales were direct or co-operative with highly educated farmers who believed that farming without chemicals, in mixed crop operations, was the right thing to do. A belief in agriculture without chemical inputs in this case was part of a complex whole that included political beliefs and challenges to conventional property assumptions amidst the context of the environmental movement. As Craig Cox (1994) points out, the co-ops were often financial adjuncts to important political movements such as, in the case of the Midwest United States, the antiwar and conscientious objector movements.

At the same time, some early organic farms were multigenerational. They tended to be run by established farmers who had direct experience with the dangers of pesticides or more often simply refused to fall for the blandishments of the chemical salespeople who came around. Generally, farming culture breeds a great deal of caution around new technologies. For one thing, a farmer stands to lose an enormous amount by crop failure, so cautious experimentation makes good sense. The caution may also derive from a general attendance to the logics of nature and agriculture, a slow and unpredictable canvas of change that fits uneasily with the notion of quick fixes (see Shiva 1993; Davis 1998; Gunderson and Holling 2002; Wu 1995).

In Canada organic farmers who are just the latest generation on a multigenerational farm are a common phenomenon, especially in Ontario. Family farms were until recently probably a little more stable in Canada than in the United States, partly because of the strength of co-operative marketing through the various grain and dairy boards (many of which are now gone). Still, we need to look at other factors to explain why, with Canadian agriculture so beleaguered that numerous farmers have committed suicide, a farmer who inherits and stays on the land turns to organic agriculture.

The rise of organics also fits into the broad context of modern environmentalism. History according to textbooks tends to suggest that environmentalism began with Carson's *Silent Spring*, but a concern about the environment among white Europeans can be traced at least as far back as the first smokestacks that heralded the start of the Industrial Revolution, and among indigenous populations probably even further. The broad popular concern began in the 1950s, reached a peak in the 1960s and 1970s, and later dropped off to some extent as economic survival came to the forefront of people's anxieties. The shifting priorities do not belie that the environmental movement created a frame within which new issues around food safety make sense (Hannigan 1995). Consumer anxiety about food may also reflect a growing and individualistic focus on risk assessment and a loss of trust in institutions (regulatory and governmental) (Beck 1994).

The history of organics invites a range in analysis from an agricultural movement to which consumers could express a commitment (through, for instance, Community-Supported Agriculture) to a consumer movement for safe food. As Alan Beardsworth and Theresa Keil (1997) pointed out, food scares laid the groundwork for the rise of the organic and natural food movement. The two authors wonder, "Why do nutritional issues seem prone to this kind of effect?" (1997: 163). After all, the end result of the short-lived Alar pesticide scare was a newly resistant mass market, uninterested for decades in trying organics again. To build an alternative food system on food scares is shaky at best.

Such food scares did gradually alert consumers to the problems of pesticides. Mothers often research proper diets for their children, and they particularly began to do so after various food scares (Alar and Aldicarb in the 1980s for instance; Guthman 1998). Parents began to find and circulate the various studies that pointed out that pesticides were not tested for children, only for adult white males. A growing concern began to form around the omission of children in studies. The bones and organs of children are still forming and growing and their sensitivity to hormones is considerably higher than that of an adult. Studies have confirmed that children are more at risk than adults from pesticides (Consumer Reports 2000). As the decades unwound, consumer concerns became paramount and the budding organic movement and industry were formed accordingly. The industry worked hand in glove with the less stringent natural foods industry and the natural medicine industry. These extensive markets, built on consumer concerns about health and nutrition, are based in high-income populations. They often include movements to reduce obesity, or to reduce weight for culturally based aesthetic reasons, and lifestyle movements that focus on personal improvement and personal health. The issue identification with the concerns of a broader community is muted in these cases.

Although food issues have a resonance with environmental issues, they may find a somewhat uneasy place at the environmental table, like the guest you can't remember inviting. The complex relations of organics to economics, the somewhat unexpected and spectacular financial success of organics, and the tendency for agricultural issues to be buried by the momentum of a consumer-driven movement for clean food have created a movement identity that mobilizes issues that are different from, say, clean air or the preservation of wilderness. Scholars have devoted much ink and many words to the relation between humans and nature. Food and agriculture tend to figure this problem differently, because by definition both eating and food production feature, in Kovel's terms, transformative relations between people and nature, separate but interpenetrating (see Kovel 2002: 103).

If You See a Fork in the Road, Take It

As Guthman (1998: 140) states, "Organic food seems to embody the contradictions that arise when nature is the central idiom and it is also the basis of economic growth." I would argue that there has been a cultural split in the trajectory of the organic movement. Those who focused exclusively on the issue of product (clean food), a common obsession in a consumer-based movement (personal health or safety), mostly traced the route of conventional economics. These businesses discovered and profited from a lucrative niche in the conventional supermarket. Adding a few recognizable products to supermarket shelves changes little in the overall food system, although it may reduce the pesticides in our environment. Even as success broadens (Frito-Lay, owned by Pepsi, brought out an organic tortilla chip; Wal-Mart now stocks organic food), the systemic challenges remain.

Miguel Altieri (1998) argues, "The first wave of environmental problems is deeply rooted in the prevalent socio-economic system that promotes monocultures and the use of high-input technologies and agricultural practices that lead to natural resource degradation." Organic agribusiness depends as much as its conventional cousin on transportation and environmentally destructive irrigation projects. This fossil-fuel dependence and water profligacy belie the movement's environmental success: California, with 1.3 million acres under organic cultivation in 2001 (USDA 2004), is largely an irrigated desert, dependent on cheap (and soon to be depleted) water sources from the Colorado River. Organic carrots from California are cheap because they rely on this subsidized water and are perfectly straight because they are grown in sand. Local carrots in Ontario and elsewhere have a bumpier road of it. In addition, products like the ubiquitous plastic bags of baby carrots, which are actually big carrots whittled down to thumb-size, are the result of unsustainable amounts of fossil-fuel-dependent processing and packaging. These baby carrots have giant ecological footprints.

Organic agribusiness occurs on an impressive scale on California farms, with technology, migrant labour, and marketing methods that replicate the conventional farms in the area. Such huge farms do little to preserve the land. They farm in conventionally long, single crop rows; they weed mechanically, leaving the soil bare. Their input, though certified organic, is expensive and can be imported within the guidelines (that is, they may not bother to compost, but will bring prepared nutrients onto the farm from elsewhere). Their volume ensures that they can afford to ship vegetables 3,000 miles to Toronto, spewing pollution all the way and balancing whatever good the restraint from pesticides might have done. In Toronto, Montreal, or Vancouver, purveyors of California organic produce are able to reduce prices to a point below the level of local smaller organic farms, which they do with regularity during the local growing season. This practice threatens the livelihood of local farms in favour of a few distant (and perhaps absentee) landowners.

Such dumping into the Canadian markets has been practised for decades by the highly subsidized agricultural sector of the United States, to the point that Canadian agriculture everywhere is in danger. Of course, the U.S. system of subsidies is only part of the story; equally disturbing is the lack of attention from the Canadian agricultural and government communities to building local markets for Canadian products. The majority of support for Canadian agriculture in the form of grants and crop insurance is focused on export agriculture and cash crops such as soybeans and, more recently, corn for bio-fuel. The strategies that make Canadian agriculture unfeasible are precisely the same methods applied to Southern countries. As the Canadian Council for Policy Alternatives pointed out, structural adjustment policies that have wiped out indigenous and self-sufficient agriculture in Latin America have been applied with equal success in Canada (Qualman and Wiebe 2002).

When organic agriculture is carried out on the same scale and with the same goals (profit, endless growth) as agribusiness, inevitably the other social effects will follow. In the world of what is significantly called the organic "industry," ongoing discussions question whether organics has lost its soul and become just another big business. Wayne Roberts, a food policy guru in Toronto, discusses the issue and finds: "Most of the world's 850 million hungry people are farmers, and organic and pesticide-laden have the same result for them. Either way, they produce food for a luxury market in the North and don't get to keep much for themselves" (Roberts 2003: 24).

Organics alone may fail to achieve much social change. Specific instances such as Plan B Organic Farm in Ontario and SunRoot Organic Farm in Nova Scotia embed their work in complex solutions to the problems of the food system, and go well beyond organic. The three core farmers at SunRoot (joined at various time through the season by apprentices and members of their Community-Supported Agriculture program) come from backgrounds of social justice and international development work. Their goal is not just to grow food but to "see if we can find ways to grow food for everyone." The determination to grow organically for low-income local people, rather than just the urban market that can afford to pay, led them to create a unique program through the local community services department. The project combines food provision with advocacy training, computer access, self-esteem workshops, and workshops led by the CSA members as well. They let the participants guide them in the workshop focuses, and have extraordinary tales to tell of transformation and growth among the participants, themselves included. One SunRoot farmer, Steve Law, who has an extensive background in human rights and international development work, and works for the Tatamagouche Centre, says that not only is food "an incredible place to start with lots of people with issues around social justice… it is *the* place to start… in some ways this is some of the most important work that I've done." As his co-farmer says, "Food is the vehicle by which people can become politicized" (Evelyn Jones interview 2003).

The SunRoot farm is run by consensus decision-making among the partners (see chapter 9 for more on consensus and food democracy). They let anyone at the farm sit in on the meetings, but the taste for democracy may need to be acquired: "Some people are really excited [at first] and sit through four hours of meeting and they don't want to do it again" (Jones interview). The farmers all have off-farm employment in community and social justice work, which varies from year to year. Their engagement on the farm and the number of people they can accept in the CSA varies accordingly. They have also worked hard to become engaged with the local community: the CSA is supported by the local Family Resource Centre, and they have been on a local board, shopped locally, and established work and material exchanges with the other farmers nearby. This careful attention to process and engagement, which is similar to the Peace Brigades International model in which two of the farmers worked, makes this farm fairly unusual. It may in part explain their persistent success in a difficult sector.

Nothing in the organic food sector forces a focus on repairing inequities in the food system or making the world a better place to be. At the core, organic methods are simply soil management methods, leading to simple product replacement rather than structural or logical change. The organic movement offers no guarantee that an organic farmer or landowner will worry about community health, local hunger, food sovereignty, animal treatment, or workers' rights. Once chemicals were carefully removed from the production arsenal, the farmer was free to pursue whatever other goals he or she desired. This could include, for instance, the tempting rewards of immense profits made by selling clean and safe food to consumers with disposable income. The narrative possibilities (where can the story go easily from here?) steer historical development.

To shift to conventional economic logic and values is to engage in a particular construction of culture and of our (economic) relations to each other. Conventional economics, with its heady celebration of profits and its confidence in growth and progress, necessarily chooses to shape the world in a certain way, and to give us a certain frame within which to live. It imposes a focus on consumers and an obscuration of production; many people don't really know where their food comes from, don't know whether or not it is organic. People manage not to associate their own experience of work (which in this late capitalist world most people dislike and many detest) with the labour issues of food production, as if, as far as food goes, the Garden of Eden was somewhere around the corner, churning out everything we could ever need (as long as we can afford to pay).

This is not because we are stupid but, again, because we are surrounded by the narrative of a consumer-driven economics, a mythology about how consumer choices determine the availability and variety of food. This narrative is close to being a fable (in Barthes's sense of a story that has a creative effect on how we understand the world); consolidation and centralized control of the food system are widespread and increasing. Consumer action alone can blind us and lead us, as Allen and Kovach (2000: 230) express it, to "an assurance that you don't really need to do anything besides alter your buying patterns in order to change the world, hardly the fuel to ignite a transformative social movement. Ultimately, the individual action that is the hallmark of the market cannot resolve collective problems."

Consumer work can change the food system for the better (witness the boycotts of Nestlé when that company was persuading Third World women to stop breast-feeding and start buying Nestlé infant formula instead). But the final results of this important work can also be endangered, as in the progress of organics, if it slips into the tempting unilinear and single-interest focus of economics. Nestlé's solution was to create another product to solve the problem — to offer bottled water to replace the local unclean water, rather than replacing the whole enterprise with a non-market solution (like breast-feeding). The notion of consumer-driven economics obscures the multiplicity of interests and values that finds expression in economic exchange: the producers AND the consumers, the farmers AND the co-op members, the workers at produce warehouses AND the truck-drivers, the owners AND the workers. The simplicity of logic favoured by conventional economics and by popular representations of the economics of food buries the richness of potential coalition. It shortchanges the power of all these different interests to make change through simultaneous negotiation (as if we had held a big dinner party but only provided one chair at the table). It is probably no coincidence that the other tine of our rhetorical fork in organic movement history emphasizes this very logic, of multiplicity, multiple interest, and coalition. In the words of Jules Pretty (1995), "What is needed is pluralistic ways of thinking about the world and acting to change it."

The Row Less Furrowed

The history of organics includes another trajectory, one that is rhetorically and morally different from the forces that led to organic big business and a consumer focus. Small organic farms tend to be complexly integrated with a community of change, and they are key to the success of many local food movements.

Plan B Organics outside Toronto is built on an intricate and thoughtful relationship to the food system. The analysis of the problems in the food system and the creation of innovative solutions are key parts of their work, as they are for many organic farmers. Plan B Organics is run by three young farmers who have managed to solve the outstanding problem of access to land through government support and personal funding. The enormous challenge of getting land and then hanging on to it anywhere that has access to markets (and is therefore ripe for commercial development) has become an insurmountable obstacle for many potential new farmers in Ontario and elsewhere in Canada.[4]

Plan B has also diversified marketing. Its members attend numerous farmers' markets and sell to the Good Food Box program organized by FoodShare, an innovative Toronto food security organization that works on food policy and advocacy as well as food production and distribution projects. Plan B also operates an extensive Community-Supported Agriculture project. CSAs were originally invented in the 1960s with fairly radical roots: they were supposed to be a way in which a community could express its stake in the land and its produce. A CSA member receives a box each week that reflects the seasons (in the Northeast United States and Southern Ontario, spinach and leeks in the spring, no lettuce at the top of the summer, unpredictable explosions of fruit and greens in the fall).

The box received also reflects the fortunes of the farm, including the miseries of heavy rainfall. The working in slippery, muddy fields all day long is reflected in a lack of rain-sensitive crops — such as raspberries — in the box. Members, at least in the original model, pick up food on the farm, and may also help with heavy periods of work. Single-farm CSAs often result in boxes that have mountains of kale or tomatoes; in bad years they might be half-empty. The variability of cuisine and supply is of course the point (the model means that consumers share, to some extent, the farmers' risk) but few postmodern consumers have the patience, understanding. or cooking habits to appreciate this problem. The benefits of belonging to a CSA, as writer Lisa Hamilton (1997) points out, are not strictly quantifiable. "We are conditioned to ask 'How much does it cost? What will it do for me?'"

CSAs now tend to make concessions to consumer expectations of service. For instance, customers don't need to pick up at the farm; Plan B delivers food to various depots in Toronto, from which the boxes are further distributed.

To circumvent the problem of relying on one farm, Plan B draws produce from several surrounding farms; it has created an informal producers' co-op. Its members have struggled to turn the organization into a more formal structure and to co-operate around access to open markets in the surrounding area (sharing trucking or marketing staff, for instance) but have only recently been able to garner seed money for the venture. Alvaro Venturelli of Plan B has also served on the board of FoodShare. Plan B has developed a tree seedling nursery and it was instrumental in founding a new farmers' market at Dufferin Grove Park in Toronto. In addition, the farmers employ youth at risk as part of the work crew at the farm.

Venturelli emphasizes the notion of community health and the interdependence of producers and consumers. Thus he sees the problem of hunger in Toronto as related to the challenges of agriculture in this decade. Plan B's solutions engage other local farmers. To watch an organic (or any small farm) in action pops the bubble of the myth of the lone and determined organic farmer, who fights against the rising tide of chemical farming. The motif of the isolated farmer (like the isolated activist) helps non-farmers to doubt the power to make change and the organizing strengths of farmers. An interknit community, with little real privacy as far as agricultural or marketing methods goes, represents a more powerful and diverse kind of social movement. Like Bove, the activist farmer is always already part of a coalition. In Canada, as an example of agricultural coalition, the National Farmers Union has been instrumental in many important initiatives, including the formation of the marketing boards, but also in coalition with trade unions and co-operative organizations, as part of the rise of the progressive New Democratic Party first on the Prairies and eventually nationally. More recently they have become part of La Viá Campesina.

A farm like Plan B is situated in a community of agriculture. Nearby, non-organic farmers peer over the hedge or rock pile at the luxurious (and valuable) rows of organic vegetables, the floating row-covers, and the mixed plantings. They can easily see how rich the soil is by the colour; they can probably vouch for the considerable yields that come from the labour-intensive organic methods as they watch the carts go by. Farmers are not remotely isolated in this situation; they are engaged in verbal and visual dialogues with the surrounding farmers, for many of whom the chemical revolution in agriculture has been far from satisfactory.

More than the exchange of ideas crosses the hedgerows. In one direction, Plan B farmers trade food for wood to heat their houses, and on the other side encourage a large-scale farm to experiment with compost. Such dialogues and interrelations work along well-worn lines of exchange in a farming community. Tools, ideas, and solutions inevitably circulate; some conventional farmers will scoff at the foolishness of organic methods, while nonetheless taking mental notes. Others may express genuine interest in the ongoing experiment next door, because it is in the very nature of agricultural work to try various things and apply whatever works.

Some of the original problems that organic production was trying to solve have shifted from the organic movement and resurfaced in the issues of land ownership; long-term sustainability of land, water, and air; community survival and the right to food (or to feed oneself); the movements for local food self-sufficiency, and union and co-operative movements for workers' rights (such as fair trade and union-led grape boycotts).

Organic and natural food marketers like to tell themselves that supermarkets are the most important outlet for these novel products. They see supermarkets as the only way that organics will reach the masses, who don't shop at health food stores. This comforting bedtime story ignores actual retail development strategies and the pricing of organic food. Supermarkets all over North America are rapidly withdrawing from unprofitable communities (that is, low-income communities, frequently communities of colour). Like good MBAs anywhere, they reason that since the people there have no money, why offer them goods such as chocolate, clothing, or food? In the language of the market economy, food is just one more commodity, plentiful and available for those who can pay.[5] Presumably low-income people are not really the masses that supermarkets or organics are trying to reach, but with the middle class evaporating into the lower income brackets, the masses who can/are willing to pay for the more expensive organic and natural food may also be evaporating. If the movement really wants to reach all income brackets, people should be (and are) trying to figure out how poor people really get their food (see Koc et al. 1999: 4) and how to become part of that delivery system. (See Chapter 6 on food security and recent initiatives in Brazil, Toronto, and elsewhere.)

Food security and food sovereignty actions around the world seem to have little trouble incorporating organic food into their solutions: FoodShare in Toronto offers an organic option (a Good Food Box available to all but priced to be accessible to low-income communities). In addition, community gardens are generally organic, and other similar cases abound. Organic agriculture, especially in the unsubsidized parts of the world, can be cheaper on an established farm, because the cost of inputs is lower. Once a level playing field exists, organic makes financial sense as well as moral sense. This factor is a strength but also invokes a quandary that the organic movement often finds itself in: what kind of financial success do we really want?

The Values of Narrative Choice

Organic and natural food advocates are caught between the moral grounds of their product (safe food) and the very different morals and goals of a lucrative business sector. Once profits are to be made, and become a primary goal, the cycle of growth and profit is difficult to relinquish. Of course, many natural food wholesalers are not remotely wealthy, but the cycles of debt, new product development, and growth required to maintain the traditional financial success drives them farther from the nebulous goals of changing the whole world. The historical unfolding of the movement tells us that the story is more complex than a movement for social change that has become big business and sold its soul. Organic food has spread by means of multiple social tentacles, some more self-serving than others, some more driven by conventional goals of profit and growth, some with other ambitions. The debate clearly remains undecided. The struggle itself may be in the nature of organics.

Each pass of a bar code on the register, each new profit percentage racked up, cannot quite shake off the history of a particular moral stance that has infected the symbolics of profits, growth, and wealth. A mass market is not free of moral positions but represents an elaborated and strictly enforced value system. The problem is not the loss of morals but the choice of one set of values over another; the analytical question is why this choice proceeded as it did, and how the various value systems interact.

As spectacular financial success accrues in some parts of the organic and natural foods movements, and fortunes are being made, social justice issues adhere to other historical developments. As Roberts (2003: 25) points out, the buzzword outside that bastion of supermarket economics, North America, is "agro-ecology." He reports that agro-ecology focuses on food, fibre, and fuel, and that it uses mixed agricultural materials to enhance soil productivity, to provide on-farm nutrients, and to preserve soil for the future from erosion and nutrient loss: "Productivity comes from having a wide range of plants and animals, which mimics the diversity strategy of nature in the raw."

Sometimes referred to simply as "sustainable agriculture," the mostly Southern agro-ecology initiatives tend to be locally based agriculture solutions with some principles in common. Miguel Altieri (1998: 70–71), an important scholar of this philosophy, writes, "The goals are usually the same: to secure food self-sufficiency, to preserve the natural resource base, and to ensure social equity and economic viability." The initiatives tend to be much more than environmentally friendly agricultural methods; they include the farmer to farmer popular education movements, land reform movements, and the restoration of indigenous agriculture varieties and methods.

As Pretty (1995) points out, the alternatives to environmentally and humanly unfriendly agriculture, conventional or organic, are plentiful outside North America. A powerful sustainable agriculture movement, which Pretty calls "regenerative agriculture," is sweeping through the rest of the world. It draws on centuries-old subsistence agriculture techniques to pose a challenge and resistance to Green Revolution methods and the incursions of agribusiness. Agro-ecology has seeped into North America as well. Lisa Hamilton (1997: 1) writes, "The mistakes of the last decade which lost organics to corporatization spawned a new movement and, in turn, a market immune to co-opting. The more specific sustainable agriculture movement not only nurtures the soil and its plants, but grows ecosystems and communities." Michael Sligh and C. Christmas (2003: 30) write, "It is time to strengthen the natural links between the organic food label and other production process identifiers, such as fair trade, energy use, and local food claims."

Pretty (1995: 12) reports from an extensive database set up at the University of Essex on the array of different approaches to sustainability across the world. He argues that sustainable agriculture is not just a product (an organic papaya) but a process, and a way of thinking: "As situations and conditions change, so must our constructions of sustainability also change. Sustainable agriculture is, therefore, not a simple model or package to be imposed. It is more a process for learning."

The sustainable agriculture movement marks an important attempt to redress global food problems. Some interest in sustainable agriculture has also developed in North America.[6] This interest recognizes the power of indigenous models for change; the producer cultures of the world may be the greatest sources for the yeast that begets social change in agriculture. In the North, both academically and culturally, there is a tendency to posit a radical and culturally constructed separation between food and agriculture, producer and consumer. The impenetrable depth of the producer-consumer split damages the ability of people to make intelligent change. This split is presently one of the key economic logics challenged by sustainable agriculture initiatives.

The progress of the separation between the organic industry and sustainable food movements is uneven and complex. Supermarkets try to engage the discourse of community as a marketing device, designing their produce sections to look like farmers' markets; natural food supermarkets may make attempts to structure their supply to be more than just whatever organic food is cheapest. A rapprochement might be effected, but the grounds of compromise may fail to solve the deeper problems (even if they wanted to). The corporate lack of face to face experience with customers (the mass-market "farmers' markets" are strangely empty of farmers) introduces a challenge of trust, which in turn makes innovative community-based solutions harder. For instance, extensive regulation (required by the emphasis on an arm's-length mass market that cannot afford the lawsuits that such formalized relations inspire) makes it very hard for local producers to start in small-scale production, to market locally and face to face, and thereby to establish trust relations as the basis of a market.

Finding an Economics We Can Believe

The discourse of product replacement (organic cola instead of Coca Cola) opens the door to a consumer-driven movement. For consumers, then, the issue is how to make good choices, keep healthy, and not to pollute one's body, as if the environment that mattered most was the internal one. The poisoning of nature in this scenario is a problem only insofar as we want to avoid poisoning ourselves when we consume. The notion of the environment as a context becomes obscured by the focus on correct food products; the aims of organic get split into sustainable (producer, external issues) and clean safe food (consumer, internal issues). The market economy is in no way excluded from this framework. Economic motives of profit and growth face little resistance. Organics is whittled down to food for those who can afford it, and adheres closely to the economic theory of consumers' willingness to pay. The project to simply replace the products of an inadequate food system with better consumer products has distinct limits when taken alone. As many researchers have asked, do we really need organic Twinkies? It is as if you saw one child being mean to another child, but when you tell the child to stop it they shrug and say ok, and start bullying someone else instead. The problem isn't the choice of victim (or food); the problem is the behaviour.

The history of organics brings to light a key struggle not just between cultural constructions of reality but between a more disturbing clash of value systems. Dissatisfaction with the progress of organics represents not so much a mealy-mouthed distrust of success but a genuine concern with a moral system that relinquishes justice in favour of growth and profits. As Robert Nelson (2001) points out in *Economics as Religion*, despite protestations from mainstream economists to the contrary, economics is a system of beliefs and constraints for living, just like any other cultural system. It has its own trajectories, which it must argue out with alternative systems such as grass-roots food movements; it has its priests (business columnists, for instance), its soothsayers (Milton Friedman), its acolytes (Bill Gates), its heretics (Joseph Stiglitz). Once we recognize economics as a cultural system, we must also recognize that every orthodoxy has its heterodoxy (see Bourdieu 1977; De Certeau 1988), and that the dialogical exchanges between the two accomplish the practice of culture (see Bakhtin 1981). The struggle between two dogmas tends to reinforce the resistant power of a third alternative, neither the orthodoxy nor its opposite, but a sort of perpendicular cousin. It is this third alternative, at odds with a battle between capitalism and not-capitalism, that we are in search of here.

Even though the attractions of financial success can take a food movement in various unconstructive directions, it is nonetheless extremely important to replace the products of the food system, as well as to take action on other fronts. The sales growth and lucrative products of the organic and natural food industry should go hand in hand with the fight for land and sustainable agriculture. The stories invoke each other, like an epic told over a series of cold winter nights; the storyteller weaves around the listeners a tapestry of information and moments to ponder and to act upon.

Notes

1. As with most highly regulated sectors, there are various standards in different countries and even within the same country. The debates over which standard is "better" can be heated and sometimes arcane, although at other times public input and understanding are crucial, as in the 1990s when the U.S. Department of Agriculture tried to get sewage sludge included in the new national standards.

2. In the case of the strategy of large supermarket empires like Weston (Loblaw), the goals are to bypass or purchase the lower links in the food chain (vertical integration). Thus for risky aspects of the food system such as primary production (farming) and processing (especially in new markets such as organics), large food corporations contract with existing companies to produce products under the corporation's brand name. If the product doesn't sell, most of the loss will be located with the processor or farmer, who probably invested to meet the new market's demands. If it sells, the corporation may take over the manufacturing, hacking off another chunk of the pie for itself.

3. General Mills' clear choice of affluent consumers contradicts the breezy argument that many, including Kahn, offer to defend the industrialization of organic: that this is the only way in which the price will become affordable for everyone. General Mills clearly moved the company away from a concern with the poorer consumers, not towards any charitable goals. While the Pollyannas of organics may believe that it will all trickle down, the food system continues to fail those who are imagined to wait for the drops from above.

4. An important innovation in Ontario called CRAFT (Collaborative Regional Apprentice Farmer Training) brings farm apprentices from organic farms together for training by seasoned farmers and extensive information exchange. The apprentices are usually part of the WWOOFERS (World Wide Opportunities on Organic Farms) program, which matches workers with organic farms all over the United States and Canada. See Fairholm 2002.

5. The dastardly economic formulation of "willingness to pay" (which obscures all signs of social injustice) implies that all those poor people, agonizing over paying the rent or eating, are just unwilling to pay for food, choosing to spend their non-existent money on something else. WTP enshrines an egregious example of blaming the victim; the poor who are "not willing" to pay are by this logic like bad children who are "not willing" to eat their spinach.

6. See the work of Food First in Rosset's documentation with others of the bricolage of sustainable practices in Cuba. A range of novel sustainable agriculture practices were initiated to respond to the ongoing U.S. boycott and the collapse of Cuba's key trading partners in the Soviet Union. Food First was launched in San Francisco by Frances Moore Lappé and Joseph Collins following the publication of Lappé's groundbreaking book *Diet for a Small Planet*, which alerted people to problems in the food system in the 1970s.

Chapter 5

"Rich With Others"

Co-operatives and Capital in Atlantic Canada

A cross Atlantic Canada, the growing pressure from hungry and ruthless supermarket giants (Weston/Loblaw, Sobeys, and now Wal-Mart) has wreaked havoc on the economic landscape of food. People are dumbfounded by the logic that results in enormous sprawling box stores, with all their bells and whistles, in a lightly populated town such as Antigonish. Since the mid-nineteenth century the grocery trade has squirmed and whined about the low-volume markets in Atlantic Canada, the great distances to travel, the remoteness of the communities, and the general lack of financial gain to be had from operating in the region. Now the companies cannot get enough of being there. Meanwhile, the co-operative movement, established initially in the nineteenth century to supply the deficit, thrives in a diversity of sectors. Somewhat bemused, the co-operators have risen to the new challenge from corporate stores, with instructive results.

Co-ops exemplify Gibson-Graham's "friendly monsters" of capitalism. They are firmly business enterprises, highly successful in the market economy, with a mandated democratic structure (one member/one vote). Their mission is to meet the member-owners' needs — not to profit, or to grow, just to meet their needs. Co-ops worldwide abide by the same seven principles: 1) voluntary and open membership; 2) democratic member control; 3) member economic participation; 4) autonomy and independence; 5) education, training, and information; 6) co-operation among co-operatives; and 7) concern for community (International Co-operative Alliance 2008).

Like mint in a garden, they are ubiquitous in their distribution. In 2005 almost half a million people were members of Canada's 1,260 agricultural co-operatives (Canadian Co-operative Association 2005). Consumer co-ops logged $9.2 billion in revenues in Canada in 2002. In the United States, the National Co-operative Business Association (2008) reports that the top 100 co-ops have combined revenues of $117 billion. Their numbers include the Land O' Lakes and ACE Hardware co-operatives. There are 270 telephone co-operatives, 250 purchasing co-operatives, 10,000 credit unions (co-op banks), and over 3,000 agricultural co-operatives. Almost half of the electricity distribution lines are owned by rural electric co-operatives. Four in ten Americans are members of co-operatives. The co-operative movement has spread around the world. The Canadian Co-operative Association (2005) estimates that 800 million people are members of co-ops globally.

Co-ops continue to thrive in Atlantic Canada, despite vigorous attacks by private corporations with their enormous purchasing power. On a trip a few years ago to Atlantic Canada, I was delighted to find myself in small towns where most of the businesses seemed to be co-ops or credit unions. In fact, as big business gains in power and abandons more communities, co-operatives may even experience a resurgence. Co-operatives continue to exist Canada in almost every imaginable sector, from health care, food, agriculture, and renewable energy to housing, filmmaking, ambulance services, home-care services, banking, forestry, outdoor recreation gear, and funeral services. Their survival rate (estimated in a Quebec study) is 64 percent over five years vs. 36 percent for the private sector (Canadian Co-operative Association 2005). Canada's largest non-financial co-operative is the giant Co-operatives Retailing System (CRS) in Western Canada, which combines the Federated Co-operatives Limited with hundreds of retail co-ops across the region. The FCL provides distribution, marketing, and administration services to its 275-member retail co-operatives, reaching 1.2 million individual members through the co-ops. The mission of this behemoth "is to improve the economic position of its member-owners within a responsible democratic structure" (see Federated Co-operatives Limited).

How do co-operators realize such a mission in their everyday practice? A few years ago in Atlantic Canada, in the midst of the thumping and shouting from the supermarket giants just down the street, the Fredericton Direct Charge Co-op had a membership meeting. One topic was: What should we do with the members' surplus this year? The goal of a direct charge co-op is to set its prices just high enough above cost to cover its operations. The co-op finds ways of returning any surplus or savings to the membership. Since a co-op is democratic (one member/one vote), the question of what to do with the surplus must be brought to the owners of the co-op — that is, the membership. In this case the members voted not to receive the extra as dividends, but to renovate the store. Their participation did not end there, however; the co-op solicited its members' opinions on how the store should be renovated. This process occurred over many meetings and necessarily paid more than lip service to the idea of a member voice. The results are spectacular. The store is huge and busy, and displays innovative, member-driven marketing strategies. For instance, member input led to wide aisles (something that in conventional business terms cuts into the retail space — and theoretically less shelving means less inventory displayed means fewer sales). The members wanted the wide aisles so they could stand in them and socialize, which would be considered a hindrance to sales in other businesses but makes perfect sense to a co-op. Strong relations among co-op members means stronger decision-making and more democracy; in other words, a stronger co-op. Member requests also led to a complete redesign of the shopping cart so that, for instance, soft goods such as bread would not get squashed at the bottom of the cart.

Co-ops 101

Consumer co-operatives in Canada hearken back to 1844 and the Rochdale Pioneers of England for their inspiration — a movement that began in response to the loss of control over economic relationships through indus-trialization and the loss of access to land for subsistence. Co-ops often cor-respond to the rise of immiseration of the masses from unequal control of the economy; such misery can be counted first and foremost in the increase in hunger and starvation.

In the mid-nineteenth century mining communities in Canada began to set up co-ops, often founded by immigrants who brought not only baggage and songs, but also ideas, from their home countries. In the early twentieth century co-operatives were founded not just in the Maritime provinces but in the mining communities of Northern Ontario and Alberta and British Columbia. Across the border in the 1880s the consumer co-op movement blossomed from the powerful trade unionist movement and the Knights of Labor, while in urban Ontario trade unions led to the formation of (mostly short-lived) co-ops. Meanwhile dramatic developments in many producer sectors saw the formation of producer co-ops. In the Western provinces this activity eventually led agrarian, farmer-owned co-operatives to form consumer co-operatives on the side. They were sometimes overshadowed by the producer sector but were staunchly defended. Originally the farmers co-operated to buy farm supplies such as binder twine or to purchase a car-load of apples or flour in volume. These associations were loosely organized, undercapitalized, and frequently in danger of dissolution.

Between 1926 and 1958 the consumer co-op movement consolidated under wholesale co-operatives (MacPherson 1996). The co-op movement expanded and gained in support as the Depression of the 1930s unfolded and people struggled to make ends meet. In each province scattered retail outlets, usually after much fuss and negotiation, eventually started up co-operative wholesale operations to supply goods. Some of these ventures, such as the Federated Co-operatives Limited, which eventually merged with Alberta wholesale operations, survived. Calgary is the only major Canadian city that successfully fought off the encroachment of big private stores, largely because of the strength of its existing co-op store. In Ontario the consumer co-operatives failed notably. As a result the province today has a much weaker co-operative presence than any other jurisdiction (see MacPherson 1999: 336).

In the 1960s, as prosperity unrolled across the country, co-operatives became less essential and the rise of consumer society put a great dent in co-op aspirations. Many faded away. At the same time a new wave of co-operatives began, featuring a turn to niche marketing such as natural foods. Strong co-operatives have persisted both in major cities and in isolated communities where box stores have not been interested in setting up shop and suppliers were hard to come by. In the Maritimes stores experimented with the practice of direct charge — in which the goal is to end the year with zero profit — and service fees, with members paying fees that, when accumulated, covered the costs of running the store. After paying the fees, members could buy their groceries at a price close to cost.

The goal of many food co-operatives initially, even before the trends of the 1960s, was to broaden access to good food by buying in bulk, reduce expensive packaging, and sometimes teach people to use whole foods and raw materials. By combining the buying power of many relatively powerless people, they sought to create an organization that could fight off corporate control of the food system. In Atlantic Canada, the co-ops (which now reach over 200,000 people) began because the leaders, mostly Catholic priests, believed that people should control their own economic destiny.

The Maritime movement echoed co-op movements around the world; there was even some exchange between the Atlantic co-ops and Mondragon in the Basque area of Spain (MacLeod 1997), which now boasts about ninety co-op enterprises with annual sales of over 13 billion Euros in 2006 (Mondragon 204). Co-op Atlantic spans the Maritimes with a diversity of co-ops. Not all Atlantic co-ops are members of Co-op Atlantic, the second-tier wholesaler for the retailers, but the majority of them join. Where else, said my informants, apparently a little puzzled by the question, would they get their supplies? The structures are elaborate and complex. The Fredericton Direct Charge Co-op has seats for staff on the board as well as for consumer members. The Co-op Atlantic board is made up of people who either sit or used to sit on boards for their local co-ops. Many of them come from producer families who sold to the co-op (like the huge Scotian Gold apple co-op in the Annapolis Valley) and also bought their food and supplies at the local retail co-ops. Many of them bank at a local credit union, and get their insurance from the Co-operators, an insurance co-operative. Communities frequently boast both a farm supply co-op, which is a sort of hardware store-cum garden centre, as well as a local grocery co-op. In addition the town may house other co-ops, including a forestry co-op and perhaps a funeral co-op. Board members across the Maritime provinces were instrumental in founding the Co-op Management Program at St. Mary's University in Halifax to train co-op managers in co-operative business management. This program, of course, is also a co-op. Co-op Atlantic has over 135 member co-ops (who send representatives to the AGM who vote on the direction of the co-op). Through the local co-ops and the AGM structure, the 200,000 co-operative members/owners can have a say in what their local co-ops and Co-op Atlantic do next.

The response to the growing inequities around food in the 1980s in Canada and in the 1960s in the United States led not to co-op formation but to the creation of food banks that distributed food to the hungry. These two solutions have significant differences in values. Still, both of them tend to recognize a right to food for everyone and a need for more equal access to the food. A co-op tends to be a long-term solution that does not provide much support in emergency situations, but builds in principle a food system that everyone owns, and that therefore abandons no one. One goal in Karma Co-operative's mission statement, echoing the goals of many food co-ops, is to "exercise political and economic control over our food."

The history of co-ops does not always demonstrate a successful ability to fulfil that goal. The moments of triumph give hope to many co-operators who work in neo-liberal economies of food that seem to require hunger in order to function. In the minds of many economic theorists, scarcity is key to making a market work. That might be all well and good in the case of, say, peacock feathers, but it is not so great in the case of bread and milk. Oddly enough, the occasional failure of co-ops (which occurs on average half as often as the failure of private businesses; even less often in the case of worker co-ops) is often used to prove the failure of the idea. Conversely, the collapse of a private business is usually blamed on the owner's failure to follow economic principles properly, rather than given as proof of the errors in the principles. Clearly in the battle over economic theory, the playing field is surreptitiously uneven.

When I asked him what I should be focusing on in my interviews, long-time co-operator and co-op educator George Labelle said thoughtfully:

> As co-ops grow, there'd be less need of government, less need of social services, less scope for other businesses, because the co-ops would grow and they'd take over the social aspects and they'll eat into the whole economic pie. Nobody talks about that anymore, they've forgotten about it…. A vision like that would be helpful.

The co-operative solutions to financial challenges speak of another way of doing economics, of an alternate set of principles that is deep-rooted and diverse, multigenerational, and capable of intelligent change in the face of new challenges. The extent of Co-op Atlantic's endeavours is marked by the response of people in that region to my question: Is a full-scale co-operative economy a long-term plan? Instead of scoffing or even laughing outright at what seem an over-ambitious vision, the people I talked to tended to say that they weren't there yet and had a way to go. What astonished me about

Atlantic Canada in particular was that the economic terrain is so interwoven with co-operatives that to the people there my question not only seemed reasonable, but also required a thoughtful response. Many co-ops elsewhere are so unique in their community, and often so isolated in the region, that the idea of a co-operative economy is unthinkable.

This thinkable possibility in the Maritimes places the co-ops in Atlantic Canada on a par with Co-op Italia in northern Italy, the Mondragon co-ops in the Basque region of Spain, and the Federated Co-op system in Western Canada. The depth and breadth of their work often occupy them to the extent that they are so busy figuring out how to be better co-ops that they cease to muse on conventional economics. In this way, they fulfil Gibson-Graham's behest that we study the real workings of alternatives instead of imagining capitalism as a monstrous beast that the alternatives nibble away at like parasites (Gibson-Graham 1996).

The Co-operative Difference: Capital in a New Light

The relationship of the co-op movement to conventional economics and the business management practices taught in the average business school is a subtle one. It exceeds the simplistic concept of a dominant system that has an alternative, resistant system nipping at its heels. The co-op system does not hesitate to cogitate upon and to confront other systems. At the same time it operates on its own terms, spells out its own strategies, practices, and goals, and borrows and reframes economic practices from other venues. What are the principles driving this alternative economics? How do essential terms operate in the co-operative system and relate to conventional economics?

Alternative economics has a solid history, replete with tried and true theories and practices. The only question is why conventional economics so relentlessly ignores these proven practices. Mark Lutz (1999: 7) writes, in reference to the neoclassical theory of the self-interested individual: "It is a question of false methodology, which prevents complete understanding of how the economy really functions and diagnosis of its malfunctioning. In other words, the neglect of a social perspective seriously impedes the vision of conventional economics, leading to a whole set of questionable assertions and findings."

The co-operative difference inheres particularly in a reframing and enrichment of the key notion of capital. What does each economic system mean by capital? What is capital in the co-operative system? How do co-operators talk about it? What are they trying to figure out about it? What makes it increase? Accumulate? Circulate? What are the key principles of capital in the co-operative system? What in an alternative system functions and is invested as capital or accumulated value? Co-ops benefit particularly from a rich and creative flexibility with regard to what has been called symbolic or social capital.

Social and symbolic capital is the intangible wealth generated by relations based on trust or faith in each other, which instils a commitment to shared interests and causes and to the complex interdependence that characterizes strong community relations. In his analysis of social or symbolic capital, Bourdieu (1977) describes an intangible fund that can be reputation, trust, honour, or a similar symbolic good that accrues through social relations and also defines the movement of financial capital. It is the glue that links participants in economic exchanges. It is not, as some might argue, unique to alternative economic forms, but innovative and alternative economics in all its forms uses it deliberately and consciously rather than denying it and concealing it as in conventional systems. A number of terms have particular relevance to the place of capital in the alternative system: 1) members' voices/words; 2) knowledge; 3) faith/belief in others, or trust.

Members' Voices and Muddy Interests

Sheldon Palk, the general manager for thirty years of the highly successful Fredericton Direct Charge Co-op, says the secret to his success is people. He views his responsibility towards people/members as complex and dialogic, as an ongoing prescription for his behaviour. This goes beyond the poverty of "we care about our members," because active listening must be added to concern. He explains that he believes that "if you listen to your members, then it's hard to go wrong," and then immediately shifts to lauding the staff as well. Any member is likely to be integrating and juggling multiple interests in relation to the co-op. A fair amount of integration as well as tension occurs among different interests in a co-op. Workers are usually members as well, so they have a voice in the strategic direction of the co-op. In some co-ops (like the Fredericton Co-op or the few worker co-ops) workers have seats on the board. A co-operator in Atlantic Canada might be on several co-op boards, and often is on various boards in the course of his (or less often her) lifetime. Leonce Losier, a long-time co-operator, until recently on the board of Co-op Atlantic, has been on the board of his local credit union, worked with a regional francophone co-operative (Coopérative Regionale de la Baie), and is also involved with a funeral co-op. In a region with a limited population, this work means that he is probably working with other people who are also wearing multiple co-operative hats.

The muddiness of interests is a strength. Co-operatives that are not embedded in co-operative networks tend to have a much more simplistic, unilinear approach to members' voices, which often become somewhat symbolic and even discounted in the general operations unless there is a crisis. It is much harder to ignore voices that keep popping up from different perspectives — working for you, on your board, sharing a membership with you, all at once. The experience led me to question a simplistic approach to conflict of interest, which is the subject of much regulatory concern. I realized that the notion of a singular point of view in a tight community with no overlap to other interests may be a fiction that can seriously impede community functioning. The strange idea of this single-mindedness is echoed in willingness to pay theory. After all, wouldn't a multiplicity of knowledge and experience, if transparent, help rather than hinder a co-op? However, this is not to say that the same middle-aged white men should be running everything (as in corporations, where the same people show up on boards and in positions of power with surprising frequency). A co-op and its members can benefit from multiple and overlapping interests only when the diversity of interests in a community is represented in it.

As an outsider, in my initial interviews with people involved in the co-op movement I clearly struggled to understand the structure, while for local people it was obvious and unproblematic. The tolerance of complex and overlapping interests comes partly from a genuine commitment to the power of varied opinions, deriving from long-term experience and multiple interests. Such a commitment is more than a matter of curiosity or a public relations attempt to make members feel good. Rather, it derives from a belief that negotiating these interests — that, is, democratic process — lies at the heart of making a co-op work. It astonished me that over and over the first step a manager would take to solve some financial crisis would be to ask the membership what to do.

These opinions, and the process of weighing and sorting and eventually investing in them, represent a complex capital fund that accrues value and produces genuine business strategies and change for the co-operatives. Yet this is a capital with a difference — as long as the members are engaged and participating in the co-op, this social capital fund cannot run out: they will always have informed opinions, which the managers need only mine (and the managers clearly spend a certain amount of time figuring out how to get at those opinions).

Co-operative Knowledge and Education

Co-op Atlantic devotes considerable attention to the issue of knowledge and its circulation: how to get it from the members, how to pass new knowledge back to them. In the case of the Fredericton Direct Charge Co-op's renovation process, once the members had voted to use the surplus for a renovation, the question was how to find out from them what they wanted in a new store design. Not only did the staff show the members the blueprints — they taught them how to read them. Then they listened to their opinions.

This reminded me (by invidious comparison) of the recent travesty of democratic process at the Royal Ontario Museum in Ontario. The multi-million-dollar renovation, supported by the government (unlike most co-op renovations) began with a worldwide competition among top architects for the best new design. The museum chose one design that looks as if a spaceship had landed badly on a Roman temple. Once they had ripped out one side of the museum to make room for the spaceship, they dedicated a whole room to the people's opinion. The blueprints were posted on the wall, and little slips of paper were provided so visitors could write down their thoughts and post them on the wall too. Then we, the populace, would see what everyone else thinks in a nice safe atmosphere in which, since the decisions were already made, our opinions were utterly meaningless (a point reflected in the flippant tone of many of the notes on the wall). Governments and corporations alike often use this sort of theatre of participation (a parody of democracy) to conceal extremely limited processes of decision-making.

The co-op movement in Atlantic Canada was energized from 1920 to 1950 by the popular economics education work of Moses Coady, Livain Chiasson, and Jimmy Tompkins and many others connected with the Catholic church — work that has a resonance with the wave of liberation theology emanating from Latin America. They believed that people should control their own economic destinies, and to do that the economic system had to be transparent enough to allow people to make intelligent choices. The study clubs that gathered people across Atlantic Canada to address these issues together had the practical goal of establishing co-ops, both producer and consumer (see Race 1999). The Coady Institute still thrives in Antigonish, although its mandate has shifted to international development.

Many co-operators see a renewed need for education. Francis Porelle, a Co-op Atlantic board member and also long-time board member of Shediac Co-op, a strong organization in the Acadian area of New Brunswick, argued that the co-ops will grow with more education, not with more competitive prices. Another Co-op Atlantic board member commented that although most people in the region are aware of the movement, they lack a real philo-sophical understanding of it. There is a rift between older co-operators, who may have been around when the study clubs were operating, and new co-op members who may even be unaware that they are owners.

The co-operators I talked to argued that a lack of knowledge of broader economic functions was preventing people from seeing beyond one-off price comparisons. The co-operators analyzed the long-term pricing strategy of the corporate grocery giants. The co-ops, they maintain, have kept the big guys from sending prices through the roof, as they would do if the other competitors left the field. Because people don't understand the broader picture, they don't understand that the community will be worse off if the co-op fails. As Lutz (1999: 7) points out:

Consider, for instance, the sum effect of *individually* rational choices on an independently owned, local bookstore: when discount books are purchased at the supermarket rather than the local bookstore, people are choosing the same for less. But such prices eventually drive the specialty store out of business, thereby narrowing future shopping possibilities. The English economist Alfred Kahn referred to this type of problem as the "tyranny of small choices" adding up to an undesirable aggregate outcome.

Simple conventional economics dictates that if the co-ops and other rivals disappear, the victor left on the charred battlefield of food will necessarily raise prices because customers will no longer have any other options for their groceries.

This predictable and recurring process contrasts with a co-op's commitment to fair prices and transparency. It is not uncommon for new co-ops to devote considerable meeting time to arguing over whether they should express their prices in the conventional way, as a penny or two short of a dollar ($.99 or $2.98) or end the pretence and post the price as $1.00 or $3.00. They see pricing goods a few pennies short as a blatant attempt to obfuscate the truth, in effect lying to your member-owners. Still, this particular dishonesty seems difficult to avoid. Customers have the vague impression that the rounded-up numbers are higher, and they simply don't buy as much. Some cases of cultural mystification are just too big for one store to take on.

The co-operative culture of knowledge evinces a healthy attitude towards mistakes. If you can imagine that your store of knowledge capital is always growing, that you are always learning more, then mistakes are a necessary part of the process. More than once someone explained to me that the co-ops don't crucify people for mistakes. Losier said to me, "You don't hire people not to make mistakes." This extraordinary comment only makes sense in a culture in which growing knowledge matters to the health of the economy. A genuine, lasting education inevitably involves mistakes from which the member, manager, or worker arise better equipped to deal with the next challenge.

Economic knowledge must grow and circulate for co-operatives to survive; it is an essential source of member commitment. If the understanding of the broader local and community economics wanes, then the base of commitment (the members' non-financial investment in the co-op) rapidly fades as well. I asked a "member-relations representative" at the Metro Credit Union in Toronto (now swallowed up in a merger) why they were using doughnuts from a U.S. company to do a fundraiser in Canada (where people are proud of their own doughnuts). The member-relations representative just laughed. A co-op that cannot even respond to a member questioning their abandonment of community commitment is a co-op that has lost its economic knowledge and the ability to pass it on intelligibly to its members.

One co-operator described his commitment to co-ops in terms of knowledge. Alistair Marshall, a long-time member of the Scotian Gold Apple Growers Co-op and a member of the board of Co-op Atlantic, said he originally joined Scotian Gold because he was selling his product to the Co-op and wanted to know what was going on in the business. That is, he took ownership as a member-owner. He asked, how do you instil in people a knowledge that it's their co-op? With Loblaw, he added, the money leaves the community; with the co-op it stays — an important point mentioned by numerous co-operators I talked to, but one that is rarely heard outside of alternative currency groups. As the local food and local economy movements grow, the local circulation of capital may become a more familiar idea. There is a key interchange here between symbolic capital like knowledge and financial capital; without the symbolic capital of knowledge, money will leave the community, providing profit for strangers and impoverishing ourselves, our friends, and our families.

Trust as an Economic Practice

The workings of knowledge in strong co-ops leads us to the important factors of faith and trust. An almost miraculous leap of faith underlies the assumption that 200,000 widely scattered people, if they have sufficient knowledge to understand the workings of a business and local economies, will collectively continue to make the right decisions for the welfare of the co-operative and its members.

One manager who had been managing co-ops for his entire working life said he had faith in the co-op system and in the CEO John Harvie. Another manager cited the local members as the key to his success (he received credit for turning a failing co-op around). He mixed their knowledge and their trust in the system together:

> We have 8,000 members, only 4,000 from Shediac; 2,000 of them are active, they support the co-op day in and day out, they do their whole grocery order there and really understand the system, they want to help, they know they can depend on the store, they know it was founded by the people of Shediac.

Part of the concatenation of trust and faith is that loyal members believe they are treated fairly, that prices are fair or honest. Several co-operators emphasized the need for fair and honest prices rather than cheap prices. Their emphasis recapitulates the argument about knowledge and the sense that if the deception involved in conventional economics is laid bare, people will put their loyalty in the co-ops.

Managers also talked about the importance of promises, the verbal contracts between members and the co-op that are sealed with trust. A manager who has for some reason depleted his symbolic capital will not be able to muster trust from the members or the workers and will be crippled in operating the co-operative. The power and efficacy of the member's voice or opinion depend on the foundation of trust, the honesty and belief that they can offer to one another. Belief in a system and belief in the other people in that system cannot be disturbed by a few errors or failures; it persists as a much deeper asset.

In practice trust represents a broad attitude of faith in your fellows. How do co-operators talk about faith? Research is still needed on the important relation between the church and the co-operative movement in Atlantic Canada. Losier told me that the early credit union in his area of rural New Brunswick (Tracadie) took deposits in the church on Sunday, after service, making a clear identification between the symbolic capital of faith and the accumulation of economic capital. People do not refer to the church in relation to present-day co-operatives, but they do use the term "faith" quite often to explain co-operative success. Faith and trust tend to run together in this context.

The Gift That Grows

The circulation of trust and other social capital has extraordinary power to knit an economic system together and even to direct the more prominent circulation of economic capital. Such capital is not depleted by circulation; one can give one's trust to someone else and still have plenty to give. The more bonds of trust that are established, the stronger one's fund becomes. The fund of trust is thus (as in a gift economy) increased by being passed around, and it operates in distinct counterpoint to the movement of financial capital (which increases if loaned but not when given).

In such a context economic insecurity takes on a whole new meaning, shedding new light on someone's remark that Maritimers are so used to being on the edge financially that a crisis has to be extremely serious before they even notice it. They may live on the edge financially and yet remain rich in other forms of capital, imparting a non-economic security that adds to their stoicism in the face of financial hardship. When someone tells Losier that co-ops should behave more like conventional businesses, he says absolutely not: in a co-operative he is "rich with others." Co-operatives are successful because they rely on wealth shared with others.

The difference between profit and savings or surplus is as thin as the difference between an original and its mirror image. The terms may replicate each other and yet retain a crucial reversal of meaning. Profit, the ultimate goal for a conventional business, implies hoarding; something is "kept back." Surplus, the co-op term, suggests an unintended overflow or extra amount that must be used or distributed. A surplus at the end of the financial year means that co-operators must gather and decide what to do with the extra. Managers sometimes correct each other's use of the word "profit," sometimes with humour but with a clear recognition of the importance of the difference.

Talkative Food: Homegrown Beef and Symbolic Capital

Co-op Atlantic is especially proud of its highly successful agri-food strategy. This strategic direction, a joint approach developed between the food and agriculture divisions, expands on the concept of "reciprocal business," which means that manufacturers or producers buy the raw ingredients for their processing or animal husbandry through the co-op, and then produce a product for the co-op stores. The initiatives, which include products such as hay, blueberries, chicken, turkey, potatoes, or peanut butter, represent a unique coalition of local production and local consumption. The work has mobilized member/owners of co-ops and producers of various products across the Maritimes, and engaged government and media support. The strategy led to the production of Atlantic Tender Beef, recipient of the Canadian Grand Prix Award from the Canadian Council of Grocery Distributors.

Co-op Atlantic began to offer Atlantic Tender Beef in the co-op stores in the late 1990s. Atlantic Tender Beef is local food on a grand scale: that is, the beef is born and raised in the Maritimes, fed on grain and potatoes grown by local farmers, with minerals purchased from Co-op Atlantic. The processed beef is then sold back through more than a hundred local co-op stores under the Atlantic Tender Beef label.

Ed Hanscomb, meat manager and later the food category manager at the Fredericton Direct Charge Co-op, was enthusiastic about the Atlantic Tender Beef: "It's not just about beef, there's a lot more to it — it talks about farmers, it talks about community, it talks about retailers, it talks about co-ops." These products are not silent commodities but they enter the field trailing a host of social relations, inflicting the commodity market with a transparency of the non-economic that is precisely what ensures its successful operation. That is, they make the social relations explicit and thereby capitalize on them. The success is marked both economically and symbolically: stronger communities, stronger coalitions among producers and consumers, more money marked as local, giving it a history, a place: a symbolic value.

The very notion of social capital is worth exploring. The literature about it focuses mostly on Robert Putnam's (1995) definition of social capital as "networks, norms and social trust that facilitate coordination and cooperation for mutual benefit." For the most part, this literature seems to de-emphasize the "capital" aspect of Bourdieu's original reading of the term and focuses on analyzing the glue that holds a society together.

Bourdieu's "symbolic capital" carries interesting additional implications in that it must be shared and circulated (and thus obeys the imperatives of gift exchange systems). It also bears a complex and non-obvious relationship to financial capital in any form of economic relation, whether capitalist, socialist, or "heterodox." The additional and challenging implications of symbolic capital occasionally arise in the general literature on social capital. For instance, Patricia Wilson (1997: 756) points out that social capital:

> Flies right in the face of two central tenets of mainstream econom-
> ics. First is the assumption of scarcity. Social capital is free.... The
> concept of social capital also mocks the other leading tenet of main-
> stream economics — the idea of "economic man," the individual
> separate self rationally calculating the costs and benefits of his every
> action on the basis of self-interest.

Strategies and Multiple Practices Revisited

There is a danger of descending (or rising) into idealism here. As sometimes occurs in the scholarly literature, the temptation to see a vision of a new economy (of food or anything else) risks the fanaticism of a new convert; it brooks no deviations or complexities. Thus the literature tends to polarize points of an analysis, leaving food co-ops in the unsavoury position of end-lessly failing to achieve a brilliant ideal. The realities of practice are much more interesting. As in any cultural system, people engage in an intricate dialogue between different systems and their various rules. The tightrope of culture balances hectically between many conflicting points. Co-operative democracy is a balancing act that occurs somewhere between disappoint-ment and hope. The power of the co-op example is that it is constantly chal-lenged to reconcile an alternative economics with conventional problems of economic capital and financial viability.

John Harvie quoted the saying, "Understand the rules of the game you are playing so you can break them intelligently." He advocated a philosophy of business mindfulness: that the practitioners have to be mindful of co-op principles, that is, piercingly aware and deeply cognizant of them, in order to be able to bend them responsibly. Co-op practice in the Maritimes recalls a traditional story about strategies: an old monk and a young monk are travelling together and come to a young woman hesitating on the bank of a river; she is worried about getting her clothes wet when she crosses. The old monk picks her up and carries her across the river, despite the taboo against touching females. The young monk is astonished. After pondering this event for many miles he finally challenges the old monk about it. The old monk laughs: "I put her down hours ago, but it sounds like you are still carrying her!" Equally, an analysis is probably most useful if it avoids undue agitation over apparent breaches of co-op values.

Throughout the interviews, in addition to discussions of trust and member voice, the people I spoke to mused on the relations among multiple economic positionings. One manager saw these relations as a constant shuttling between goals and strategies; in a financial crunch period, the social may take a back seat to the economic and co-op focuses on short-term goals while keeping the long-term social vision in mind. The directors see their board as marking a spectrum from social to economic goals. One director might say that co-ops are not there to compete, while another might say (with a sidelong glance to the first director) that the co-op must first and foremost make the financial side work. The interplay between these goals is significant. While each individual may see the relation between goals as a spectrum or even a contradiction, the net result of the dialogue will be a complex negotiation of multiple ends and means. Economic terms such as capital, value, and interest are like puns that work across multiple languages. Practice deliberately avoids choosing one meaning over another but instead manages to operate, in fact to thrive, on the double entendres of meaning, as in the definitions of capital.

This analysis of symbolic capital leads away from the question "why do some systems clearly negotiate symbolic capital?" (implying that others don't) and towards the question "what non-economic goods are valued in this system?" Every system negotiates social or symbolic capital; it inheres in the ethics of how we relate economically to each other, and in whatever is accumulated and circulated as non-financial wealth. If the co-op capital requisites such as members' voice and trust do not figure heavily in the conventional system, then what interacts with economic capital as its symbolic counterpart? The symbolic capital in a corporation is substantially different from the corporate public relations output about social relations, corporate concern about community, and other crocodile tears. As one instance of the mobilization of symbolic capital, many women, and men too, speak with frustration of the corporate glass ceiling that prevents women from rising to senior management (a phenomenon to which co-ops are not immune). Women cite the importance of the old boy's network from which they are excluded, often ostensibly because of domestic responsibilities that often require them to be at home rather than in the workplace. The old boy's network is not some special financial market or other "inside knowledge," but the network of acquaintance and shared experiences — golf and barbecuing, for instance — as well as similarities of race, class, age, and gender that smooth the exchange of corporate symbolic capital. This network fosters the information exchange, promotions, favours, and access to powerful others and to important opportunities that allow the insider (by definition mostly white and male) to rise.

As many social economists have pointed out, economic exchange in any form cannot be extricated from the social. The question is how the social is configured. As Lutz (1999: 88) says (quoting the economist John Hobson), "Ethics do not 'intrude' into economic facts; the same facts are ethical and economic." Any system of economic relations is a value system. The position of values within each system indicates the interplay of symbolic capital with economic goods.

Symbolic Capital and the Necessity to Circulate

It is not sufficient, as I have done so far, simply to identify the place and appearance of symbolic capital in Atlantic co-operative economies (member voice, trust/faith, and knowledge). We must ask the important questions of capital: how does it circulate, and how does it accumulate?

Just as capital stored under your mattress for thirty years will fail to have an impact, however small, on the economy, symbolic capital must get out into the culture and be passed around. Losier commented, after a tour stop at a store, that the problem with some co-ops is that the members don't understand the need for circulation — they want to take everything out but not put anything back in. He was deliberately vague on the object of the circulation, clearly implying that he meant more than money; he meant participation, or "sweat equity."

Later Bryan Inglis (vice-president of agriculture), speaking of the success of the agri-food strategy, emphasized that the system has to be structured in circles, with the strategies passing all kinds of capital back and forth among the different sectors. This means that goods have to circulate within the system, not just anywhere, but specifically (symbolically) within the community of Co-op Atlantic. Failure to do this breaks down the accumulation of trust. "If you don't do it right," he explained, "the producer thinks you are taking advantage of them."

If the producer viewed this circulation as purely financial, then the question of trusting each other would not need to arise. Several people reported to me that, during a recent restructuring, the trust between members and other stakeholders had been shaken, but was gradually being rebuilt. This necessity is reflected in a kind of patience that people have about adjusting for errors that might have been made. Rebuilding trust cannot be done with a sweep of a pen over a chequebook; it requires time, patience, and energy, and a different approach to your economic partners.

In the Co-op Atlantic case, an anemic system of knowledge circulation has presented a challenge for symbolic capital in recent years. Most co-operators recognize the importance of knowledge, of having it and passing it on through education. Obviously, no matter how much one gives away, like trust one's own store of knowledge remains or even increases (as people say they learn by teaching). This symbolic capital system must be strengthened, say many co-operators, in order to strengthen the stores.

Most strong co-ops have some member education, with kits on the co-op principles and benefits to hand out to new members, and newsletters. A Regional Co-operative Development Centre (RCDC) did extraordinary work, especially in educating youth about co-operative leadership and practice. The program echoed the popular education techniques of the study clubs in earlier decades of the twentieth century, although the focus for the RCDC was on co-operative relations (teamwork, trust) rather than popular economics. Other local innovations include the work at the Braemore co-op on outreach to lower income people. The co-op brought people in for five sessions over five weeks, educated them in its operations, and gave them a courtesy card to shop and compare the co-op to conventional stores (Chiasson 1989). The co-operative education mandate is a driving force behind the new international Co-op Management Program based at Saint Mary's University in Halifax.

This type of education is not disinterested. It is driven by the knowledge that learners have a stake (an interest) in store operations. Moses Coady was careful to emphasize that study clubs would only succeed in teaching people basic economics if the group had the goal of starting a (co-operative) business together and therefore had a stake in the circulation of economic knowledge. Thus the increase of local knowledge will be an increase in all kinds of capital: economic as well as symbolic.

Co-ops may benefit from their willingness to nurture and to expand on the circulation of symbolic capital, using it as a strength rather than a secret source of power. In this way they can have an advantage over conventional businesses, where the place of symbolic capital is obscure and may circulate stiffly in a narrow circle, excluding many and falling short of its full promise. Lutz (1999: 161) writes that a conventional system without any consideration of social relations actually suffers from a dangerous poverty: "In a world of selfish economic traders, opportunistically dodging any kind of social values that would counsel moderation and restraint, a world devoid of moral character and conduct and respect for others, a world in accord with the postulate of economic rationality, it is questionable that commerce would prosper."

The Religious Practices of Homo Economicus

A number of scholars, applying various levels of rigour, have explored the values of the conventional economic system and point the way towards the place of symbolic capital. A key problem in this investigation is that the conventional economics system has become like the air we breathe; the system is a given, and reigns with an extraordinary kind of indubitability. As John

McMurty (1998: 67) points out, "No traditional religion has declared more absolutely the universality and necessity of its laws and commandments than the proponents of the global market doctrine." Lutz (1999: 262) also compares conventional economics to a religion: "In a way, economics has been filling the vacuum left by the Medieval church."

Nowhere is this argument more carefully elaborated than in Robert Nelson's brilliant *Economics as Religion* (1999). Economist and theologian, Nelson presents an intricate historical argument tracing the development of the values of economics and various Christian precepts, recognizing not only that each school of economics may be enthroned as a faith but also that the resemblance in each case may be to a different facet or version of Christianity (which, of course, is not a singular belief system). His analysis points us towards symbolic capital in conventional economics. As he points out, the religion espoused in economic practice exhorts the believer to work hard now to receive the fruits of labour in the future (retirement). The promise of retirement enforces in our society a dedication to bone- and mind-breaking labour, to investment in banks ("savings"), and various retirement schemes. Without a clear doctrine, such dedication and abnegation would probably be much harder to maintain. Capital in this cultural context accumulates for the average person only as a (speculative) future fund. The things that people are shown truly to derive profit or benefit from — time with family, time to do the things they want to do, freedom from stress and domination in the workplace — are all offered only in the future, by retirement. The vernacular religion of retirement is preached by advertising, radio business commentators, investment brokers, and family. Sometimes TV advertising will even portray retirement in the same way that heaven used to appear in movies — peaceful and happy, with a warm golden glow over everything. The sun is always shining.

As Nelson points out, the promise of heaven on earth constrains our behaviour to the greed and profit accumulation necessary to lubricate the neo-liberal market system. This is a cruel symbolic capital; you must wait decades to reap the profit. Workers can be kept nose to the grindstone by the promise of long-term profit in a system that is largely confined to short-term gain. Only a powerful mythology could inflict such a state of affairs.

The tremendous effort that has gone into re-creating economics as an objective and value-free science has failed miserably in eradicating values from economics. Lutz (1991: 51) suggests that the long list of progressive or non-classical economists who have tried with mixed success to make the morals of the economic system transparent "may take comfort in Sismondi's teaching that 'facts are more obstinate and more rebellious,' that 'they do not manifest themselves less from its being supposed that they can be refuted without being heard.'"

Symbolic Capital and the Roots of the Co-op Difference

Given the conscious emphasis that co-operators put on symbolic capital, what are the results of this emphasis in co-operative economics? The co-operative difference changes 1) the definition of business success; 2) the rift between producers and consumers, which is rapidly becoming cancerous in the conventional system; 3) the attitude towards conflict; and 4) the distribution of power and how it can be used.

How does a co-operator define success? As one manager explained, a successful business is different from a successful co-operative — if you focus on the business side, chances are it is not a co-operative at all; you have lost your identity. George LaBelle, co-operator in the Maritimes since 1948, said, "It's a social thing; most co-ops are business enterprises to meet a social need. They were never intended to just make money for shareholders or people on the Board." One manager remarked that he wasn't marketing the product but rather the agri-food strategy itself (that is, the symbolic meaning). The advertising will tell people that "the co-op is here to grow the economy and the community it is in." He added that if it was just a brand it would fail. The Fredericton co-op identifies success with how much money it returns to the community members in "savings." The manager of the Shediac co-op, Jean-Claude Bertin, emphasizes that the co-op is a community-owned store. It's not there to make money; it's there for the convenience of the community and to create jobs in the community. The Fredericton general manager says entrepreneurs can't believe the zero-base budget, that the co-op operates with no profit to show at the end. There are no geographically scattered shareholders getting dividends. The extra all goes into the local economy.

In the general economic system, an artificial rift between producers and consumers is partly responsible for our inability to see beyond conventional economic patterns. Unfortunately, co-operatives have a history of aiding and abetting the problem for many reasons, not least because movement leaders Beatrice and Sidney Webb in England were loud proponents of consumer co-operation and believed that letting farmers work together was dangerous. Their legacy plagues the movement today. However, co-operatives can also focus on mutual interest; that is part of their mandate. Thus it is a natural development that an initiative like the agri-food strategy, which genuinely unites the economic and symbolic interests of producers and consumers, should come from a powerful co-operative network rather than a corporation.[1]

No Democracy without Conflict

Co-operative process also repositions debate and conflict. A private corporation has little place for disagreement. A co-operative relying on the accumulation of symbolic capital must promote, and cannot survive without, a well-informed membership with access to plenty of forums to have a say. In practice, this means lots of disagreement, even shouting matches. When many opinionated people with plenty of juicy information who have had the power of decision over millions of dollars collectively for decades get together to make a decision, it seems unlikely that there will be meek and passive assent to any suggestion.

I asked people why they thought outsiders saw the Atlantic Canada co-op relations as so conflictual. Alistair Marshall said that it was because people are very independent and have differing opinions. Co-operation leads them to work together to find democracy through their difference. Once they do manage to come to agreement, they will stand behind what they have created. His comments suggest that starting a co-op is not to be taken lightly, which speaks to the weight of true democratic functioning: democracy, like a co-operative, in actual practice is disputatious and even occasionally unpleasant.

On the subject of conflict in democracy, writer Hilary Wainwright (2003: 142) quotes an African-American orator who fought against slavery, Frederick Douglass: "Those who profess to favour community and yet deprecate conflict and risk are men who want crops without ploughing the ground. They want rain without thunder and lightning. They want the ocean without the awful roar of its waters." I have over the years listened to numerous people explain that they have abandoned the co-op movement because co-ops have too many meetings and the meetings are too acrimonious; they had to discuss things with people they didn't like or disagreed with. Such comments seem tantamount to saying that rather than working things out with someone you don't like, you would rather have someone with no interest in your welfare make all your decisions for you, including what you eat, how safe it is, how much of your paycheque goes to pay for it, and often the quality of your work life as well. Sheldon Palk said sometimes he wonders why they have to have so many meetings, but then he realizes that the meetings are how they make decisions: "It all happens right here." The power derives from the workings of the collectivity, not from his position as general manager.

The process that allows disagreement to wend its way towards a committed decision is certified again by symbolic capital: trust and faith in each other. Francis Porelle said the board of directors believed in the general manager (Harvie) and had an excellent relation with the management team (vice-presidents). They had faith in each other, they did not mistrust each other. He said they might have some hot discussions, but they were sincere and open; that is the only way to work. Harvie has an in-depth knowledge of his directors' philosophical positions because of this democratic process. He named at one point the spectrum of opinion (from idealists to "capitalists") and could indicate where the various directors tended to fall on the spectrum. He startled me at one point when I mentioned a question I was asking in the interviews (what is the most important thing going on right now at Co-op Atlantic?) by knowing intuitively and with a fine precision what the individual directors would say in response to the question.

Several people likened conflict in the co-operative context to a family process. One remarked, "I don't think it's very deep. It's sport. We are from Atlantic Canada. We are Maritimers. When it comes to face the outside world we are not divided. Blood is thicker than water. It's like, I can make fun of my own family, but you can't. We can fight amongst ourselves, it's our business." In this context, calling it "our business" is enlightening — in a co-operative business, fighting in order to reach consensus is part of the business. Without it you can't make decisions.

A sad breakdown of democratic decision-making in the broader culture prevents people from seeing the value of democratic conflict. Split-second, impulsive, and wholly self-interested decisions are promoted through advertising and even in business management training. (See the popularity of the book *The One-Minute Manager*. Do we really want our food system to rest in the hands of managers who think they can get anything worthwhile done in a minute?) In advertising we are told (in a whiny overdub), "You know you want it," as if that alone was enough to make a complex decision like buying a car, or getting the right food. The subtext is, "Don't think about it, just do it," which is counter to the co-operative process of knowledge exchange and democratic decision-making.

I am aware (because many co-operators wanted to talk about it in interviews), that some serious shakeups had occurred in the past decade with Maritime co-op mergers, management changes, and some store closings. The loss of financial equity in these events may pale next to the loss of social capital (trust), particularly in towns that lost their co-op. It is not surprising that co-op history often focuses on conflict (to the exclusion of other issues). For outsiders to the co-op, conflict is often read as an ongoing failure of the co-op model. But conflict also reflects an aspect of democratic functioning with which (white, upper-class) North American culture is especially uneasy. To achieve democratic practice in a diverse culture and in a challenging economic climate, people will inevitably disagree, and there will probably be hard times. The real question is how well and how constructively a democratic organization can negotiate conflict and come out on the other side with a continuing faith shared by participants.

One mark of the direction that Co-op Atlantic will probably take is that after some lean years, food sales began to climb again. The question of conflict and its final resolution seems to me to be internal to Co-op Atlantic and its over 200,000 co-operators; it is a matter of an unfolding process rather than analysis by outsiders (Co-op Atlantic has plenty of insider analysis at its fingertips already). As people told me when I asked about why outsiders think they fight all the time, it is acceptable for them to fight amongst each other (like family) but it was their business to sort it out on their own. For this reason as well, it seemed quite problematic to me to make any current conflict part of the historical record (beyond this note).

New Definitions of Success

Part of the tremendous success of the agri-food strategy, as perceived from within by managers and directors, is the coalition built through the initiatives. Ed Hanscomb emphasized that the co-op was about community, and that in the case of the agri-food strategy everyone got involved, even the government; "producers, retailers, consumers, everybody working together." This emphasis infects the movement of power as well; if the most powerful co-operative is the one that supports a coalition, power derives from social ties and the tensile strength of the bonds. While position in a management hierarchy or as a director also brings access to power, power must be shared across sectors of supply, membership democracy, and reciprocal business. Co-ops can falter when people forget that principle. Norma Tomiczek, a Co-op Atlantic director, remarked that people get hooked on the whole corporate, commercial store ethos because they think they have no options, no way of getting control. The perception of powerlessness prevents people from joining co-ops; there must be a recognition of the access to power (shared with thousands of others) that comes from co-operation.

The most interesting and challenging aspects of alternative economics are in the places in which a dialogue (even a shouting match) occurs between different definitions and uses of economic terms. These words illuminate each other: the uses and circulation of "capital" in the co-operative system contrast with a different application of "capital" in non–co-operative systems. The Co-op Atlantic example also represents a large-scale working model of an economics that incorporates the justice issues that arise in the uneven distribution and access to food that characterize the global food system. It provokes us to think ahead. How might we organize society once we do incorporate social equity into our everyday exchanges?

When we allow competing discourses or alternative economics to arise, especially in the territories already claimed by the orthodox economic doctrines (such as supermarkets), the patterns of the orthodoxy cease to be concealed. They rise like invisible ink from the blank page. The recognition of alternatives inaugurates a dialogue that, once begun, cannot be undone; the revealed can never quite be re-covered. Likewise, the inequity, mistrust, delayed satisfaction, and symbolic desolation of conventional economics may never quite recover from our participation, whether intellectual or practical, in co-operative economics.

Note

1. I make a distinction here between the delicate and difficult work behind this coalition-building and the use of such a coalition as a mythology to attract customers, as in the case of Loblaw store designs that imitate open-air farmers' markets while its product comes from wherever it is cheapest, and when it buys local only when the farmer can "compete" successfully with the underpaid producers in the South or subsidized farmers in the North.

Chapter 6

Hunger and Sovereignty

Strategies of Justice
in the Food Security Movement

On packing day each week, the warehouse space at Field to Table in
Toronto fills with volunteers who work a long line of fresh vegetables to
complete hundreds of Good Food Boxes that go out to people, low-income
and otherwise, across the city. The volunteers get to take their own box
home and also share in a communal lunch with the staff and director. This
organization, part of FoodShare, houses rooftop gardens, beehives, an educational composting project, a community kitchen, and an incubator space
for start-up food businesses, and it organizes workshops and food groups and
networks around food issues.

FoodShare is an organization built around the issues of food security
and food sovereignty.[1] Food security, according to the United Nation's Food
and Agriculture Organization (2008), "exists when all people, at all times,
have access to sufficient, safe and nutritious food to meet their dietary needs
and food preferences for an active and healthy life." It means that everyone
has access to food regardless of ability to pay. In some ways the work of co-
operatives echoes concerns of food security initiatives and also raises questions
of capital as well as equity — while movements that focus on new products
such as organics, natural food, or GMO-free food tend, as we've seen, to work
to answer questions of safety and challenge the dominant consumer theory.
For its part, food sovereignty refers to the struggle to acquire control over food
production and consumption. La Vía Campesina, the radical organization
that has united a coalition of peasants and small farmers across the globe,
believes in a people's right to food sovereignty: "the right of each nation to
maintain and develop its own capacity to produce its basic foods, respecting
cultural and productive diversity." The organization later included in its goals
the "right of peoples to define their agricultural and food policy" (quoted in
Desmarais 2007: 34).

These rights — and the initiatives following from them — are necessary because the world, both North and South, is in a hunger and nutrition
crisis. Worldwide more than one in eight people were going hungry in the
1990s (FAO 2003). The Bread for the World Institute (2008) reported that in
the United States, "35.5 million people, including 12.6 million children...
live in households that experience hunger or the risk of hunger." According

to the Canadian Association of Food Banks (Pegg 2007), 14.7 percent of Canadians live in food insecure households. Contrary to general opinion, people seeking help from food banks often have at least one family member employed. Studies in Toronto in the 1990s indicated that people would pay their rents before buying food; the housing crisis in Toronto increased the level of hunger in the city (Husbands 1999).

In March 2007 the Canadian Association of Food Banks reported that 720,231 people used food banks that month. A disproportionate percentage of people who benefit from food banks are children (almost 40 percent), for whom food shortages during growth and development can lead to serious problems. The percentage of employed seeking assistance is especially high in Alberta, even with its so-called booming economy.

One is reminded of Ebeneezer Scrooge and his journey from "are there no workhouses?" to a moral awakening. Dickens's tale speaks of the limits of the charity solution to a broader problem. After he recovers from his miserly ways, and gives Bob Cratchit a huge turkey, Scrooge also raises his employee's salary. As Raj Patel (2007) and others point out, famine is not a scarcity of food; it is a scarcity of justness, expressed in the uneven distribution of wealth. As in India, where people starved when the granaries were full, "merely having the food around doesn't guarantee that the poor will eat" (Patel 2007: 130).

Food banks address the emergency aspects of hunger and food insecurity. As Marlene Webber (1992: 84) writes, "Within the food bank movement, charity and justice clash." Many people within the movement themselves recognize that as the food bank model overlaps with charity models, it tends to re-create the problems it is trying to solve. Food security organizations such as FoodShare (as well as some food banks) work beyond the bounds of emergency food distribution. They address the issues of access and distribution and engage in legal and policy debate. Their initiatives run the gamut from the distribution of food to the hungry to advocacy for governmental changes to the way in which people get access to food. This work overlaps with and extends the work of food provision to the hungry. Susan George (1990: 226) emphasizes this point when she writes in *Ill Fares the Land* that the right to feed oneself should be more important than the right to food.

The Two-Headed Monster of Scarcity and Surplus

Debbie Field, executive director of FoodShare, points out in *Food 2002*, a report on a broad consultation on hunger and food security in Ontario: "Hunger in North America is an incredible paradox given the substantial overproduction that the conventional agriculture system continues to support" (Field and Mendiratta 1999: 44). The food system, inasmuch as it is embedded in the market economy, necessarily depends on the principle of scarcity to operate. "If poverty were not a money-maker, in a world glutted with food," writes Webber (1992: 13), "there would be no reason to starve people."

As numerous food access workers recognize, the food bank solution is a symptom, not a solution. Food banks may ease immediate and devastating hunger in the short-term (although they never have as much as people need; often food banks have to limit clients to one visit per month). They cannot address the structural problem of a market that requires scarcity to function. If the commodity system depends on consumer willingness to pay, it must necessarily include prices that are too high for some. Prices are supposed to achieve a state of equilibrium at the point of maximum yield for the producer; that is, as high as possible without driving away too many customers. In that balancing game, which is supposed to represent a rational give and take between producer and consumer, some consumers will necessarily drop out early, like players in a poker game with a poor hand. This can be amusing when the stakes are poker chips or extra money, but becomes much less entertaining when the stakes are the next meal or two.

Frances Moore Lappé echoes the approach of co-operative economics when she argues in her speeches and books that we focus our attention not on the scarcity of food but on the scarcity of democracy. Patel (2007: 130) writes (referring to the Nobel-prize winning economist Amartya Sen): "The only way that famine can be overcome is to guarantee rights to hungry people that trump those of grain-hoarders.... And the only way that Sen sees this as possible is through, at a bare minimum, a functioning democracy." As many scholars point out, our world has plenty of food — in fact it has had a surplus of food for many decades — but the culture of a rigid market-driven system denies access to that surplus for growing numbers of people. The shift to a non-profit solution (food banks) represents only the leanest of changes.

The production of surplus is integral to the functioning of the food system and its big retailers. The creation of food charity is an inevitable result of that functioning. Political economists such as Harriet Friedmann (1993) explore the history of food charity that starts with the creation of cheap exports and "food regimes" that the U.S. system depends upon. They ask who really benefits from food aid. Global food charity — food aid — is a lynchpin in the structure of the global food system. Surpluses generated by U.S. agriculture are typically dumped in other countries (including Canada), with the result of wiping out indigenous agricultures (which can't compete with the cheap, subsidized U.S. food). Surpluses are essential to price control. They drive out small producers at home and abroad and feed off expensive subsidy programs (expensive to those who pay taxes).

The logic of food aid replays the logic of this competitive dumping, and largely fails to solve the problem of hunger. As John Pottier (1999: 144) points out, "Time and again external aid imposes a structured response... the rigidity of which thwarts local initiative." He argues that famine relief tends to be distributed along local lines of established power. It is organized in such a way that it fails to reach most of the people who really need it, and equally fails to establish any program that would solve the hunger: "Relief and prevention work, like development aid generally, can only be truly effective if potential recipients have the power to determine what is used and how.... Such a dialogue must never be considered a luxury" (1999: 167).

The Recipe for Hunger

Hunger can be traced to the breakdown of local agriculture. Food aid tends to exacerbate the problem, weakening moves to restore local farming. The crisis of indigenous agriculture is not politically innocent but tends to be the inevitable result of national shifts towards cash crops (such as coffee or cocoa) and large-scale agribusiness. National governments choose or are forced down this path under the pressures and attractions of free trade and offers of generous loans (to be paid back by the tax-paying populace). Farmers who take the loans offered to them are driven to focus on cash and export crops to gain the means of paying off their debts. This situation often means that they must forgo agriculture for subsistence. The foreign currency is gathered in, taxes are applied to maintain debt payments, and local land is consolidated for cash and profit-driven agribusinesses. Subsidies tend to target export-oriented production, further crippling subsistence agriculture. In other words, the rising need for cash leaves little room for subsistence agriculture. Arundhati Roy (1999: 22) writes: "Indians are too poor to buy the food their country produces. Indians are being forced to grow the kinds of food they can't afford to eat themselves." The food aid solution, either nationally or internationally, fails to stop the cycle of export, debt, and local hunger. Food donations are necessary to prevent starvation in the immediate moment, but additional measures are required to keep the emergency from recurring.

Food banks and food aid may be simply stopgap measures. They maintain the formulas of scarcity and uneven surplus that lead to the problem in the first place. Though they are admittedly inadequate to address the structural problems that created the unequal distribution, they are important expressions of the principle that would remove food from the market system. One solution advocated by food change organizations is to separate basic food from the market economy, while allowing luxury food to flourish in the world of competitive pricing and scarcity. Debbie Field imagines a new way of organizing food: "Basic foods such as fruits, vegetables, grains or beans could be available to all at cost or free, removing the stigma from those who have been forced to rely on food banks" (Barnes 1999). This approach would remove food from the roller-coaster of the market economy and put it in the sphere of human rights. Indeed, many key food initiatives begin by declaring food a human right, a position supported in theory by the United Nations.

During the lengthy process of *Food 2002* in Toronto, FoodShare and others sent invitations to over two thousand people and fifty organizations to a series of meetings to answer the question: "What would it take for everyone in Ontario to have access to affordable, nutritious food by the year 2002?" The *Food 2002* report cited numerous projects around the world that have reduced the dependence of food on the market economy. Izmir, Turkey, has staple stores. Kerala state in India subsidizes grain for everyone. New Zealand and other Southern countries subsidize local staples. Field points out that the Canadian marketing boards, by removing the prices of some grains, dairy, and eggs from the ups and downs of the market, keep the price steady and avoid debilitating dips that could destroy the farmers.

Mary Douglas (1982: 17), an anthropologist, pointed out that hunger and physical subsistence issues are functional aspects of food that should be examined separately from cultural and symbolic analysis: "It is unlikely that a physiological and material concept which is implicitly static can be used for a comparison of social relations which are essentially dynamic." She gently separated subsistence and material food issues from "design" issues and "luxuries" (1982: 106), which are the garden in which social dynamics flourish. Yet, like many theorists who try to establish analytical categories, having separated her factors she has to keep wrestling them apart. "No serious writer on the problem of poverty would defend a grossly materialistic view — either of the condition or the remedy," she argues. "To treat subsistence as a means of obtaining other objectives makes some basic layman's good sense" (1982: 16, 21). She restores subsistence to social dynamics but uses it to challenge conventional economics, arguing that subsistence should be registered as a cost, not an objective, of consumption. Economically, material needs represent a baseline from which an economic anthropology, exploring the social dynamics around food, can spring.

Food security organizations, by arguing that basic food is not a commodity, often breed novel ways of approaching the system and innovative solutions that sprout in and around the basic food bank function. The Stop Community Food Centre in Toronto boasts a community garden (from which they report the harvest of 2,400 pounds of organic produce) and a drop-in café in addition to supplying food baskets to those in need. They offer a community kitchen, a perinatal program, and one-on-one family support for people with newborns. In 2007, they announced a move to the Green Barn, an innovative project to be housed on an abandoned industrial site, which will provide additional growing space. They plan to extend their harvest in a new year-round greenhouse. They will provide food systems education there in addition to their other programs. The space is shared with artist studios, environmental groups, and a public park (Stop Community Food Centre 2007).

In the United States and Canada, the organization Food Not Bombs hands out food to the homeless and hungry wherever they are. They set up tables and field kitchens in the areas where the homeless live and provide free food visibly and in public to anyone who gets in line. They combine this food bank work with political work. Food Not Bombs will show up at political protests and feed the protesters and participate in political theatre (bread AND circuses). Their work's radical difference lies in their unwillingness to hide that they are handing out food and their belief that hungry people should be allowed to eat without shame. This simple formula has led to reports of police harassment, violence, and arrests of various Food Not Bombs members. These incidents indicate that the difference between an enclosed food bank outlet and a visible public space shifts the initiative from something well within the acceptable and necessary aspects of a market economy to something that is apparently much more dangerous, that alerts local security forces to imprison these makers of soup and bread (Butler and McHenry 1992). One wonders, for instance, whether the supermarkets that gain so much mileage from their prominent food donation barrels would be quite so enthusiastic about distributing surplus directly from within the store, or about operating a soup kitchen from their own deli during store hours.

National and International Fights against Hunger

The local work of food security organizations also reflects national and international work. A pair of World Food Summits (the first in 1996, then a follow-up in 2002) announced the laudable goal of reducing world hunger at a rate that then rapidly eluded participating countries. The first summit pledged "to cut the number of hungry people to about 400 million by 2015," although "progress" towards the goal "remained disappointingly slow" (FAO 2004).

The recognition that food aid is insufficient is reflected in the aims of the Food and Agriculture Organization's interest in sustainable practices. The FAO (2004) stated:

> The Special Programme for Food Security aims to help those living in developing countries, in particular low-income food deficit countries (LIFDCs) to improve their food security through rapid increases in food production and productivity, by reducing year-to-year variability in food production on an economically and environmentally sustainable basis and by improving people's access to food, in line with the 1996 World Food Summit Plan of Action.

In addition to consultants and "technology transfer," the FAO lists people's participation as a key feature of this strategy — which still needs to be assessed through field research.

The Non-Market Possibilities for Food

Pottier (1999: 11) remarks on the change in the attitudes of international organizations to food problems, but questions the efficacy of the strategies. "In its initial conception, food security was a global supply problem; what the world needed was more secure flows of basic foodstuffs at stable prices." He cites the Rome declaration at the 1996 World Food Summit as an indication of an important shift, but points out that genuine commitment to these goals means an attention to both the local and the various: "If the Rome declaration is a serious commitment to understanding the problem of hunger as poor people experience it, then policy-makers will need to develop not an appreciation of easy-to-sample 'food preferences,' but an understanding of local perceptions as socially constructed, contested and negotiated" (1999: 16).

Pottier's brilliant study *Anthropology of Food* describes the social construction of famine, and ties the issues of social relations to the satisfaction of material needs. He quotes Susan George to emphasize that transfers of power, not food, solve food security problems. His strong ethnographic data (based on years of research as an anthropologist and as a consultant for famine relief organizations in Africa) demonstrates the manner in which food aid does not simply go to the most hungry but proceeds along existing social lines of power.

Equally, well-meaning (or not so well-meaning) development initiatives assume from the existence of hunger that local agriculture is a problem needing an external solution. This approach smoothly continues the institutions of colonialism under the guise of aid. It transfers power from the food producers to foreign agencies, shattering the reliance on indigenous knowledge and distribution networks. According to Pottier (1999: 169):

> As a self-fulfilling prophecy, the discourse of stagnation and breakdown ensured that guardianship in farming would move from the farms to the research stations, where a different world-view prevailed. A further assumption was to believe that higher crop yields would "trickle down" to those who worked the land. This assumption turned into one of the most powerful myths of the twentieth century.

Anthropologists have been exercised for years about whether anything can escape the work of social construction. That is, is there anything outside the work of culture? The most intriguing arguments may occur in studies of health and medical practice that explore the relation of mind and body and cultural constructions of illness. Perhaps the most interesting outcome of this debate is the indeterminacy of the relation between material needs fulfilment (biology) and culture. The arguments of Pottier and others suggest that food banks and food aid are not culturally neutral but thoroughly embedded in the culture and values of the conventional economics of food. Food security initiatives are arguably not exactly non-economic; in some ways they operate inside dominant economic relations, which would suggest that a simplistic view of market relations misses the richness of the successful alternatives within the mainstream culture.

FoodShare presents concrete challenges to conventional food distribution. For example, community gardens, often initiated by food security organizations, are frequently on public or municipal land, which means that they can alter notions of private property and land use. They are often managed collectively, and gardeners often share tools and materials (for instance, buying seeds, composting together). Many community gardens reclaim vacant lots. In the 1990s in New York City, a group of vacant lots was beautified through local residents' volunteer labour. When the lots, now green and growing, were suddenly discovered to have market value, the city recalled them so that they could be sold to developers. Some of the lots were saved when Bette Midler and the Trust for Public Land purchased more than half of them to protect them from development (Halpern 1999).

In 2007 FoodShare reported that it distributed between 2,500 and 3,000 boxes of food each month; the work continued through their move to a new centre that year. They offer the standard Good Food Box, an organic box, and a Wellness Box featuring smaller portions of chopped food that goes to seniors and others with food preparation barriers such as arthritis. They also have a box and a program on healthy eating and cooking for survivors of breast cancer. Out in the field they run urban agriculture and community gardening programs, with a sprouting operation, greenhouse, beekeeping (run by a co-op of volunteers), and mid-scale composting that processes one tonne of organic waste each month. They have programs going in the schools, as well as internships for young people with barriers to employment. They partner with local community organizations to provide local produce through Good Food markets. Meanwhile they do "Baby Food Basics" workshops to teach new parents how to make baby food, ensuring that they know exactly what the baby is eating. FoodShare also does extensive policy and advocacy work with the city and the Toronto Food Policy Council, national work through Food Secure Canada and informal networks, and international work with the sister city of Belo Horizonte, Brazil. From crib to cronehood, from Field to Table, as they say, FoodShare strategizes to change the food system (FoodShare 2007).

The range of strategies of an organization like FoodShare is breathtaking. It can be tempting merely to list its programs, to gape in wonder at its commitment, energy, creativity, and dedication (or even better, to get involved). A celebration of diverse strategies is, however, not enough, just as a pile of computer components is not enough to run a computer program. We need instead to pay careful attention to the articulation (following Roland Barthes) of the parts. We must also ask a hard question of inspirational lists like this. What is the point of having so many strategies when each one is not just extraordinary but also represents a compromise with the exigencies of the moment? That is, each strategy may well draw criticism — for instance, outsiders complaining that subsidized food boxes unfairly compete with other home-delivery companies. Certainly we must remain alert and be able to provide critical analysis, as the practitioners themselves do. We must ask where the most useful critical feedback might come from. That is, do the thoughts of those not engaged with these programs have a useful part to play in the development of FoodShare's project of social change?

A more interesting question from the outside perspective might be to ask how FoodShare arrived at this diversity of strategies, and to observe this diversity as a strategy in itself. FoodShare's work recalls Gramsci's "war of manoeuvre," which "subsists so long as it is a question of winning positions that are not decisive, so that all the resources of the state's hegemony cannot be mobilized" (Gramsci, in Forgacs 2000: 230). In its work FoodShare has managed to create a structure that is organized loosely enough to allow people's power and creativity to bubble to the surface. Many of its projects are driven by people who come to the organization because they want to initiate something — they have an idea or a dream, which the organization's atmosphere can incubate through the fertile soil of democracy. These projects may move on from the organization's embrace or remain an integral part of its operations. Beyond all the diverse strategies, in FoodShare's work it is this manifestation of democratic functioning that is most extraordinary and inspirational.

Field emphasizes the importance of integrating agriculture, health, and social justice issues (interview 2004). She sees food security as three overlapping circles: individual food security, community food security, and the social food policy agenda. These come together in the programs and initiatives that FoodShare pursues. Field explains that their model is encapsulated in the words "Eat it! Grow it! Share it!" FoodShare, in partnering with Belo Horizonte in Brazil, finds that despite their different cultures they are "part of the same movement."

The Right to Food: The Case of Belo Horizonte

The municipality of Belo Horizonte made a spectacular series of experiments in redefining food and market relations. In the early 1990s the Brazilian town declared food a human right, elevating the municipality to the only place in the world to enshrine this approach in official policy and rhetoric. The department responsible for food security there defines it as the principle "that all citizens have the right to adequate quantity and quality of food throughout their lives, and that it is the duty of governments to guarantee this right" (Rocha 2000). Brazil as a whole later followed suit.

The web of redefined relations that spreads outwards is inspiring. On a daily basis the government publishes the prices of basic food, scotching any attempts by food-mongerers to inflict higher prices on an uninformed public. Thus all neighbourhoods, even low-income areas in which residents might have fewer food options, have uniform pricing on basic items. The government program also provides school meals (one meal a day to all students). A Popular Food Basket is sold to low-income families and brought to their neighbourhoods (Rocha 2000: 7, 11). The municipal government also regulates farmers' markets; farmers can have prime marketing locations in exchange for an appearance once a week in low-income areas. Like FoodShare and various food policy councils in Canada, the Brazilian project emphasizes food that comes directly from producers. It has developed a complex system to fit the needs of a diverse populace. Like FoodShare, the Belo Horizonte model extends far beyond food banks into a multitude of strategies that all work on the problems slightly differently.

The government-run Popular Restaurant, for instance, offers meals for all, rich and poor, at low prices; the meals are nutritious, plentiful, and consist of several different dishes, including dessert. The program serves 12,000 meals each day. Businessmen eat elbow to elbow with street dwellers, artists, and other ordinary people. The government also provides a cheap flour enriched with calcium and other key vitamins. Some initiatives target the hungry (Popular Food Basket); others offer cheap food that anyone with a little cash can have (Popular Restaurant). As many people have observed, initiatives that cut across class, making food available to all, lift social change out of the charity model and into a place where the existing structures of society are reconsidered. The administration of the various strategies is a government responsibility, but, as Cecilia Rocha (2000: 18) puts it, the programs "are 'owned' by many different groups and institutions. It is this widespread 'ownership' that may guarantee their sustainability in the long-run."

For years FoodShare has maintained a healthy dialogue and exchange with Belo Horizonte. Field told me about the spectacular instance of participatory democracy that she witnessed at the Second National Conference on Food and Nutritional Security held in Olinda, Brazil, in 2004. Brazil took the extraordinary step, after electing the popular leader Lula da Silva as president, of inscribing Belo Horizonte's food policy as national policy. It remained to be seen if a policy designed and maintained as a municipal policy linking neighbourhoods and regions could possibly work on such a grand scale. In 2006 Lula da Silva's campaign highlighted the success of his Zero Hunger Program, and he was indeed re-elected with over 60 percent of the vote (Raffensperger 2007). His program was not entirely unheard of, however; many of the initiatives simply restored programs that were part of the Citizens' Action against Hunger and Indigence and for Life that had been eliminated during a previous administration. Field pointed out that in Brazil this work fits into the concept of social responsibility that comes out of liberation theology; the approach teaches that we should not wait for a future heaven but change ourselves as we struggle now.

Food security in Brazil encompasses principles that move well beyond access to food. The programs include health as well as pleasure, equity as well as cultures of food. The guiding principles include comprehensiveness, intersectorality, equity, and social participation and control. The programs and strategies range from emergency food measures to policies to build the family-farm sector, and includes a complex definition of "local." According to a statement from Brazil's Food and Nutritional Security conference, "Mere physical proximity is not enough to generate systematic and synergic [sic] relations between the agents involved" (Ayala 2004).

In keeping with a history of liberation theology, food security in Brazil also includes a radical notion of education:

> It is not a mere transmission of knowledge from one group to an-other — from health and nutrition professionals to the population at large, for example. Rather, it is an exchange of personal experience and the joint construction of strategies that aim at implementing healthier eating practices in the various spaces of society. (Ayala 2004; see chapter 9 for more on education for democracy)

The proceedings from the national conference record an extraordinary canvas of strategies to change and democratize the food system. We must ask of this inventory, as we did with FoodShare, how they got to this place. Field emphasized the process of the conference itself as extraordinary; there were over 1,000 people, with 900 delegates from each of the states as well as Brasilia. In addition there were several hundred government and outside observers. The entire group broke into smaller groups that focused on specific issues and strategies, developed detailed recommendations, and brought them back to the plenary to share with the other delegates. The plenary reviewed the recommendations, overturned one of them, and published the whole thing in the conference proceedings, which according to Field is probably the most complex book available on food security.

The food security work in Brazil is embedded in structural changes that do more than breed an explosion of diverse and spectacular strategies, though they do that as well. They have attended carefully to the articulation of the strategies, a focus on structure that is echoed in the process of the conference itself. Across Brazil, from municipal agencies to school food boards to food and nutrition security councils, complex democratic relations are negotiated and formulated among various structures that address ways of changing the food system.

Complex democratic decision-making bodies are not new to Brazil, nor are they unique to the work to change the food system there. Brazil is also famous for its successful development of the participatory budget process, which allows for the active involvement of local citizens. Like the conference itself, participatory budgeting involves the division and articulation of society into issue-focused decision-making groups. The citizen groups work through democratic dialogue and decision-making, delegation, reporting, and careful processes. The decision-making groups are nested and interact in a hierarchy that ensures broad participation in the process as well as clarity of democratic responsibility (that is, people are aware of the sphere of their opinions and the spectrum of influence of their voices). The results are actions and innovations that inspire others. Porto Alegre, the municipality that gave rise to the participatory budget process, was appropriately chosen as the site of the first World Social Forum, where people from around the world met to discuss and strategize for a different, more democratic world.

The continuing dialogue between FoodShare and Belo Horizonte is useful precisely because the participants all recognize the difficulty of transferring a model from one cultural context to another. For instance, farmers' markets (and recently street food vendors) face a number of obstacles in Toronto that are particular to the cultural context. One can foresee various objections in the Canadian context to the strategy of separating food from the market economy. Broadly, one might wonder if a rapacious capitalist economy would willingly leave a broad and profitable field like basic food out of its inexorable expansion and growth (see Daly and Cobb 1989; Douthwaite 1992; Kovel 2002 on the necessity of growth in the conventional economy). On the other hand, some visions of the market economy overestimate its cohesiveness and rationality. Many of these strategies draw on the existing cracks and resistance in the market economy; like Canada's marketing boards, ensuring fair prices for farmers, many strategies already exist interstitially, gnawing away at the core of conventional economics. For instance, in Canada the publication of basic food prices was also tried at one point but, unsurprisingly, did not survive as a strategy.

As many scholars have pointed out, the notion of an unobstructed market economy is a myth. For instance, the U.S. food industry survives through the support of government sponsorship (for new corporate development), tax cuts for corporations, subsidies to depress prices, redefinitions of the corporate identity to give corporations the attributes of a human person in the eyes of the law (subject to, for instance, free speech and privacy protection), and extensive transportation subsidies, including highway construction. Without such measures, the edifice of a healthy food economy would probably collapse. These factors suggest that "separating" food from an unfettered market economy is a strategic, fictional image. Food security organizations are really only redefining and changing the emphasis of exchange relations, drawing on existing possibilities in economic relations.

Strategic Work and Multiple Practices

Community food security in general seeks complex solutions to the problem of food security. As Patricia Allen (1999: 117) puts it, it "seeks to re-link production and consumption with the goal of ensuring both an adequate and accessible food supply in both the present and the future." Foodshed analysis, for instance, is used to place people within the local system of resources and access. Allen (1999: 120) states, "Community food assessments of the food and agriculture system provide an opportunity for people to understand the forces that constrain or enable their access to resources in the food and agriculture system."

FoodShare and similar food security organizations work strategically and therefore insert pressure at multiple points of the system. Thus they advocate both government subsidies for basic food (like Belo Horizonte) and a guaranteed income. In the interests of practicality (with over 8 percent of Canadians experiencing hunger on a daily basis), these projects support a space of food distribution that gets food to people regardless of the ability to pay (people, for instance, can receive food based on labour alone). At the same time they seek to change economic policy, clearly recognizing the larger problems of the food economy itself.

In a strategic, functioning organization like FoodShare, social change is achieved through a series of compromises and strategies that as a whole serve to shift the society towards fairness, justice, and food sovereignty. Taken as a package, the work of FoodShare invites us to rethink the structures of economics and to applaud the resilience of food initiatives in the face of a web of economic relations that uneasily tangles with the need for food.

Note

1. Various fruitful debates exist over the proper term to use to describe a world in which everyone has access to adequate food: food security and food sovereignty are just two examples. Here I am using "food security" or "food access" because they are terms that recur in the literature and serve an obvious purpose.

Chapter 7

Fair Food

Restoring Equity to the Food System

Shifting to diversity as a mode of thought, a context of action, allows multiple choices to emerge. (Shiva 1993)

All gardeners are subject to moments of surprise. What is the mint plant doing way over here? We tug and find a powerful root system that is merrily spreading through the garden, deftly snaking through the weaker species. The mint has a persistence and rowdiness that somehow match the plethora of food-based social change initiatives that provide alternatives on the food economics terrain. It seems almost better than the metaphor of the choking mat that is the "grassroots."

Such discursive niceties aside, our inquisitive plant has poked its head through the food system in a number of places, making its home through various innovative positionings. I have explored initiatives to change the products of a dangerous food system and questions of safety and faith in science and technology. Alternative enterprise structures (co-ops) led us to issues of capital and democracy. Evidence moved us quickly to initiatives that raise questions of distribution and access. We have explored innovations that challenge the process or logic of the food system and question, reframe and reinvent the logical postulates of food economics.

Jules Pretty, in his comprehensive review of global sustainable agriculture initiatives, argues that sustainability is not just a matter of getting the technologies right. He says it requires a new way of approaching problem-solving, in particular "pluralistic ways of thinking about the world and acting to change it" (1995: 15). Likewise, Vandana Shiva makes the delicate point that the enforcement of monocultural agriculture (single crops, large-scale plantings, technological solutions to irrigation and pests) is not just an agricultural imperialism but an intellectual imperialism, an attempt to replace indigenous logics with a foreign, politically dominant logic. Shiva (1993: 6) states, "Monocultures are in fact a source of scarcity and poverty, both because they destroy diversity and alternatives and also because they destroy decentralised control on production and consumption systems." The failure of a simplistic, imposed agricultural logic was particularly evident in the widespread disappointments of the Green Revolution.

Economics as an Ideology

The principle of consumer self-interest assumes that a person's identity is bounded by the self, and that the social is an amalgamation of the workings of self-interest. The precepts (such as willingness to pay) drawn from this principle, and baldly stated, can seem absurd. Even embedded in North American culture people can see that they construct their identities dialogically, bouncing them off others, adjusting and fitting and generally behaving with various social interests and values in mind. It requires various amusing contortions (on display in economic texts about willingness to pay theory) to imagine that a mother who decides to buy organic whole milk for her newly weaned baby is acting solely on self-interest. The contortions tend to launch us down the path of evolutionary arguments: that a mother protects her gene pool by nurturing her baby. An ethnographer would argue that the mother could provide many reasons for her behaviour, and that few of them function only to protect her gene legacy.

The WTP work of identity construction is odd but absolutely indispensable to the self imagined by economic theory. Much of economics, both of the everyday newspaper variety and in university teachings, devolves from this very Western mythology of self: as something contained by clear boundaries that are preternaturally impenetrable; rational; self-interested; and capable of being fully informed.

One result of the fantasy of an island-like self, full of individual and self-contained preferences, is that the consumer is imagined to be an isolated factor in the economy, a phenomenon that thus easily splits consumption off from issues of production. This separation allows for a food system that depends on an irrational separation of and distance between sectors of production and consumption. The absence of the producer, except in the addiction of marketing folks to hazy scenes of happy pastured cows and hayseed farmers gazing over sun-swept lands, creates a food system that is much more exercised about consumer issues than about producer issues. Our food mythologies skew towards consumer demands, needs, and desires in a hopelessly irrational fashion. Meanwhile production has become dangerously consolidated and invisible, with power in the hands of a few transnational middlemen. How many frequent bacon-eaters have ever been to a large-scale hog operation with its numerous sewage lagoons and raw stench filling the air? Our plates of food typically feature products of uncertain origin; the only reliable characteristic in North America, and increasingly in the South as well, is that the food probably travelled a long way through a long chain of hands to get to our mouths.

When I moved to the neighbourhood that I now live in, I immediately tore up the lawn and invited in a riot of flowers, vegetables, and herbs, some of which, like the mullein candles with their soft ears of leaves, were "volunteers." The kids in the neighbourhood were fascinated (especially by my failure to make the proper distinctions between weeds and plants), and they delighted in the various tastes I gave them from the small patch's bounty — sour cherries, basil, tiny cherry tomatoes. The four-year-old living next door, with a poet's fine regard for rhyme, ran up to me one day and exclaimed, "Before we knew you, we didn't know things grew!"

La Siembra Co-operative in Ottawa, and other fair trade organizations in Europe and North America, seek to redress the problem of our alienation from production by reducing the number of links in the food chain for a few key commodities, including coffee (the second-largest commodity market in the world after oil) and chocolate. When Kevin Thomson of La Siembra presented the food chain for chocolate at an Ontario Natural Food Co-op annual general meeting, he asked one person to stand up for each link in the chain as he enumerated them. About twenty-eight people were standing when he completed the chain. Some fifteen or more sat down again when he took us back through the chain, this time for fair trade chocolate.

The Fair Trade Solution

Fair trade initially focused on the ills of the trade in coffee and chocolate, both of them extremely lucrative commodities subject to trade and speculation on the global market. Within this system, prices are subject to speculation and futures trading in which huge sums can be lost and gained (Ransom 2001). Coffee, a cash crop originally encouraged by colonialist administrations, tends to replace subsistence crops in local agriculture. The theory is that access to money enables people to eat better and to gain access to a larger food market. Governments also generally need more money brought in by cash crops to pay off debts forced on them by the global strategies — such as structural adjustment schemes and the privatization of public resources — of the International Monetary Fund and World Bank.

In the fields of the farmers in the mountains of Peru and elsewhere, coffee production faces fluctuating prices on the world commodity market. The access to markets usually comes only through middlemen or "coyotes," who control the price at the farmer's expense. For a farmer who has to plan months ahead, and harvests only when the climate dictates and the beans are ready, the situation can mean destitution at worst, and tremendous un-certainty at best. In small-scale village economies, the same middlemen who declare prices for the latest harvest are often the money-lenders to whom the impoverished farmer must go in times of need, or even just to get the materials to plant another crop. The farmers themselves gain no benefit from the speculation because they cannot afford to wait for the price to rise. Furthermore, during the three-year period that it takes for coffee bushes to grow, the market they were planted for can evaporate.

One country, Vietnam, encouraged by the IMF and World Bank schemes and attractive loans, decided to enter the coffee market on a large scale. Their entry created a glut of products, and prices fell to unsustainably low levels. Within five years coffee prices on the world market fell by two-thirds, to below what it cost to grow the beans in Mexico, for example. Despite this, your cup of coffee at the local Starbucks or Second Cup held its price steady. The system guarantees that it is not the producers who are pocketing the difference. In the early 1990s countries such as Mexico were getting about a third of every dollar they spent on coffee. Ten years later they were getting less than 10 cents. In Central America about 600,000 coffee workers lost their jobs (Roosevelt 2004).

Fair trade attempts to address these problems. The movement began over thirty years ago, focusing on importing handicrafts from developing countries to sell to Northern consumers. When it is applied to coffee, fair trade reduces the number of people and corporations who have their hands out as the lucrative bean passes from the bush to your cup. Laura Waridel (1997: 35) outlines the process:

> Fair trade coffee is sold directly from producer cooperatives to fair trade organizations (FTO). Fair trade also guarantees a price, and protects the farmer from speculative fluctuations on the commodity market. The cooperatives and FTOs sign contracts in advance to ensure a decent price and a guaranteed market for producers, no matter what speculation or changes may occur on world markets.

A fair trade producer co-op receives either a minimum price for a pound of beans or the market price, whichever is higher, and a 20 cent premium for organic. In addition, 10 cents a pound goes back to farmer groups for community development. The fair trade price is guaranteed not to fall below a certain level, regardless of what the market is doing. The price will be raised to meet the market price in the unlikely event that it is higher than the fair trade price. The rules against middlemen in the fair trade world are so strict that producers are allowed to sell only their own coffee — even relatives have to join the co-op before they can sell their beans for the fair trade premium.

Fair trade extends well beyond the reduction of middlemen and a fair price guarantee. The principles of fair trade, according to Ransom (2001), include: 1) democratic organization; 2) recognized trade unions; 3) no child labour; 4) decent working conditions; 5) environmental sustainability; 6) a price that covers the cost of production; 7) social premiums to improve [local] conditions; 8) long-term relationships. In general fair trade coffee is shade-grown without chemicals; these characteristics not only deliver a flavour as good or better than regular coffee, but also ensure that producers can buy food and other essentials for their families. An important side effect is the flocks of birds that once again have access to favourite habitats. The very details of a fair trade program — which are sometimes muted in marketing materials — are what establishes it as a new economic logic emphasizing alternative economic goals and processes.

If it were only a pricing mechanism, fair trade would inevitably fail. Many farmers would not be able to resist the urge to go back to conventional brokers if the market price suddenly spiked. Even though fair trade organizations would meet price spikes, suddenly flush middlemen might tempt producers with immediate cash. But the strength of fair trade is that it also depends on long-term relations and democratic processes such as co-operatives, or producer control through co-ops or unions. These initiatives are less likely to disintegrate under an occasional bullish market.

Fair trade has encouraged a shift towards sustainable practices through farmer to farmer exchanges and support through the fair trade organizations themselves. The initiatives embed new ways of doing economics in agricultural methods, ensuring long-term stability. Farmers report transitions from heavy and dangerous pesticide use, including DDT, lindane, and paraquat (banned in the United States, but not in Mexico, where it is cheaper than the existing alternative chemicals). Farmers bring in goats to do the weeding, and chickens to produce good fertilizer (Oxfam-Québec and Argus Films n.d.). The living sources of nutrients and other sustainable practices on their farms free them from some of the debt cycle that recurs in chemical agriculture as soils deteriorate and the system becomes ever more dependent on expensive chemicals.

At the consumer end of the shortened trade chain, fair trade is spreading like wildfire. Growth numbers have averaged 75 percent per year since 1998, when TransFair, the certifying association in North America, first established the label. Early growth figures surpassed numbers for organic growth (TransFair 2004a, 2004b). Campuses and institutions everywhere are introducing fair trade coffee in cafeterias. The Faculty of Environmental Studies at York University in Toronto helped to spearhead the Las Nubes fair trade coffee offered by Timothy's and developed through the Las Nubes Centre for Neotropical Conservation and Research, Costa Rica.

Fair trade restores the producers' work to our knowledge and awareness. It ensures that consumers take the responsibility to find a food chain that is sustainable for consumers and producers. Jeff de Jong at La Siembra Co-operative emphasized the importance of knowledge and trust among the participants in a trade chain (echoing the concept of social capital unearthed in the Co-op Atlantic case). He described a well-functioning fair trade system as one in which "good information is being passed from traders and manufacturers and producers and good relations are being formed." He stressed the importance of sharing and trust among fair trade organizations, contrasting that with conventional businesses. "Because we share values, there's a trust level there and we're more open with each other in sharing information and developing partnerships."

At the same time de Jong said he saw this work as a collective effort that goes beyond selling, in their case, more chocolate. The values shared among fair trade suppliers, producers, and certifiers may propel them towards working with the biggest markets they can find. De Jong sees fair trade as a movement that they are trying to grow; they are not just selling product. In this way it resembles an environmental movement more than other food initiatives; that is, a movement where the goal is to transform society's values.

Starbucks Enters the Arena (Kicking and Screaming)

Starbucks showed remarkable resistance to the fair trade ethos in the face of consumer demand. Journalist Margot Roosevelt (2004) noted, "Starbucks only grudgingly entered the Fair Trade market four years ago after protesters scheduled rallies against its 'sweatshop coffee.'" This consumer movement included rallies and a fairly successful boycott strategy (see Organic Consumers Association 2003b). The eventual result was that, after much hemming and hawing, Starbucks brought in fair trade beans — despite an initial belief that the fair trade coffee was not up to its standards. The case represented a familiar example of corporate foot-dragging. Supermarkets used this ploy for years to keep organic produce out of their stores, until the profits to be made finally brought them to change their minds. Before that, they would cite an unsubstantiated failure of organic produce to live up to their "specs" — gassed, poisoned, coloured, and waxed conventional product. Preternaturally shiny apples say nothing about their flavour or nutritional value, but they have become so familiar that their unwaxed organic counterparts seem dull by comparison.

When Starbucks did finally put fair trade coffee into its lineup, despite a plentiful supply the coffee-purveying giant refused to make it a daily coffee, citing lack of volume as the excuse (Organic Consumers Association 2003a). It eventually discovered that there was enough volume after all. Now, once a month, it offers fair trade coffee as the daily coffee. The huge company rakes in the kudos for social responsibility, while this tiny measure represents a drop in its enormous bucket, representing only 1 percent of total sales.

Starbucks' choices carry a sobering message. Once each month, its choices tell us, it is worth supporting farmers. The other thirty-odd days the farmer is out of luck. Of course, the corporate messages claim that this practice is due to consumer demand (which is said to be insufficient — we don't "want" it) rather than corporate strategy. We just aren't "willing to pay" for a better deal for farmers. If the company instead posed the real question

— are we willing to trade Starbucks' obscene profits for a better deal for the farmers? — most of us would probably say "yes."

The Starbucks case raises cautionary thoughts about the danger of the dissolution of fair trade principles into another gourmet brand or niche product. Is it possible for fair trade to achieve the kind of change needed when each day it becomes more neatly absorbed into existing economic structures? Does the brand success of fair trade improve its ability to achieve the goals of producer survival and fair pricing? Perhaps the recent financial success of fair trade is a dangerous turn of events — in the same way that organics risked losing its ideals through commercial success. As a *Time* magazine article revealed, mainstream analysts judge fair trade products from the perspective of the socially less interesting world of branded products: "The big guns are stepping in not merely because they pity poor farmers but because they sense a competitive edge." Here a certain shift has occurred. *Time*, determined to use a conventional economic standard, treats fair trade as just another novel product, like bagels or kiwis. To be fair, writer Margot Roosevelt (2004) shifts to a recognition of this problem at the end, although she places it in the wider culture rather than in her journalistic milieu: "Increasingly, politically correct labels are becoming a brand attribute no different from price, performance or advertising." The rhetorical emphasis throughout the article drains fair trade of most of its meaning; thus it is either charity (pity for poor farmers) or a viable and smart financial move. The report ultimately reduces the complexity of the issues to, "Does it sell?" The complex principles of democracy and co-operation, sustainable community development, and accessible health care have been stripped away. What we are left with is a novel product with a handy official label that allows retailers to charge more.

Starbucks, though, is only one moment in a widespread movement of change. Fair trade has swept through Europe and the United Kingdom. The BBC News reported in March 2004 that the supermarket giant Tesco "launched... its own fair trade brand while the rival Co-op chain is doubling its line" (Jones 2004). The report indicated that the supermarket chain Co-op was predicting fair trade sales of 21 million pounds of coffee in the next year. The United Kingdom is the second-largest fair trade market following Switzerland. Fair trade does not confine itself to coffee and chocolate anymore. Its lineup of products now includes fruit, juices, vegetables, snacks, wine, tea, sugar, honey and nuts. In 2004, responding to pressure from Wild Oats (a natural food supermarket) to expand the fair trade produce possibilities, TransFair announced the certification of bananas, grapes, pineapples, and mangoes.

In 2003 the *Natural Foods Merchandiser*, the main natural foods grocery magazine in the United States, asked whether fair trade would become a growth sector in the next wave of major profit-taking (Nachman-Hunt 2003).

The area has indeed expanded. Canada produces fair trade hemp ice cream. Kenya produces fair trade roses (conventional cut flowers are especially heavily sprayed by workers who are unaware of the ingredients and are not given protection from their toxicity). Pakistan has weighed in with fair trade soccer balls (a fair price to producers along with supportive regulation frees up families who in financial desperation otherwise send their children to work). As an innovation in logic, fair trade principles solve different problems in different places: how to make a living growing coffee in South America, how to make toys without using child labour in South Asia.

As the fair trade market explodes, we must inquire into the effects of its goals and principles. For instance, the market experiences growth partly because of the nature of twenty-first-century economics, as well as the nature of the products. Coffee is a drug.[1] The importance of coffee and chocolate in our culture, and the symbolic and physical loads they carry, make the choice not to eat them at all inconceivable to many of us. Entire holidays have been created largely as a means of delivering chocolate to consumers. Coffee's main effect is to keep people alert and functional so that they work inhumanly long hours and juggle child care, education, multiple jobs, and shrinking salaries. Chocolate, we are told, replaces natural serotonin and treats the sadness that seems to pursue so many of us through our privileged lives. In addition, although fair trade establishes sustainable livelihoods for numerous farmers, the fair trade coffee and chocolate industries are built on products that are not food and not locally grown. Historically, these crops represent the dislocation of subsistence food agricultures by export commodities (including not only coffee, chocolate, and sugar, but also bananas and other tropical fruits).

TransFair and other fair trade organizations are worried now that a corporation (whose sole goals are profit and growth) has entered the fair trade arena. Starbucks offers only a miniscule percentage of its coffee as fair trade, but because the fair trade label is relatively new and small-scale, Starbucks immediately became TransFair's largest customer (Wheeler 2002). By the methods of conventional economics, the needs of the largest customer (volume, efficiency, uniformity) supersede the needs of small farmers and suppliers. Thus TransFair executive director Caroline Whitby reported that the organization, pressured by corporate sellers, was forced to consider the certification of plantations, as long as that step would not "take away from what the small farmers have." That question has turned into a full-scale battle; some fair trade producers left TransFair over the issue.

In time, then, as predicted, fair trade became a significant market force. Starbucks was one of the largest customers, accounting for about 10 percent of all fair trade certified coffee. Certification was extended to other products, including almonds, pecans (grown in the United States), cranberries (Massachusetts), and fruit of various kinds. The question of the place of corporations sits uneasily in the sector. As one Canadian fair trader told me, "Each country has its own debate and its own personality around that debate." Each product also raises its own issues. TransFair has had, for instance, to deal with tea. Given that almost no small-scale farmers grow tea, can fair trade rules be extended to plantations that treat their workers decently if the fair trade organization can provide a premium directly to a group or union of the workers? The answer for now is "yes."

The market growth has meant increasing production volumes. Can we really object to a movement that has persuaded McDonald's and Dunkin' Donuts to carry ethically produced coffee? Yet to see ethical coffee in such a venue may give us qualms. Even Wal-Mart is testing the product in some Texas stores. Dean's Beans founder removed the fair trade label from his coffee, frustrated that TransFair USA seemed to be most concerned with the large companies for whom fair trade was a tiny part of sales and a minor commitment from which they could reap disproportionate public relations points. Dean's Beans lives fair trade principles in its products and business. One newspaper reported: "The company shares profits with farmers and funds reforestation initiatives, health programs, and women's loan projects from Nicaragua to Ethiopia. Its ten employees enjoy profit sharing and full retirement plans and the company contributes to programs for the disabled and the homeless across the state" (Dicum 2006).

The co-director of Equal Exchange, a wholesale purveyor of fair trade products, told the newspaper that his co-op would drop the TransFair label if the certification organization gave its stamp of approval to plantations. Indeed, it seems indispensable to the transformative power of the fair trade concept that fair trade producers are in a position of power that derives from democratic and co-operative structures. They are not just receiving a higher price but must be able to demand that higher price through collective power despite their small size as individual producers and small farmers.

Ransom (2001: 25) bemoans the situation and sees a danger that fair trade might become a consumer movement. "For the time being, far too much still depends on the strange and manipulated tastes of the consumer." The shift from innovative trade process to novel consumer product changes the economics of fair trade. Consumer-driven movements risk diverting attention from producer concerns. The radical disjunction between producer and consumer created in our everyday ways of talking about economics makes it difficult for us to keep the two in mind at once; it goes against the cultural grain. Thus fair trade represents an important feat of rethinking; but as with most discursive changes, once rethought it always risks retranslation into a more digestible, familiar form. While fair trade engages the issues of logic and process in the food system, it uses the strategies of product replacement to do it, thus inviting the structures of consumerism to take over. Although at its ideological heart it is an attack on an economy driven by consumer self-interest, it reframes an interdependent economy (thinking of the farmers while buying coffee or cocoa) within the guidelines of personal choice and shopping. It does not ask us to consider coffee in general, only to consider a better coffee. It teeters on this important brink, a breathless tightrope act that seems to speak with many tongues, inviting multiple interpretations.

Time magazine and the *Natural Food Merchandiser* are largely blind to the more radical implications of fair trade, embedded as they are in the conventional understanding of economics. Their analysis sets a discursive trap, leaving only an impoverished debate between two colourless positions. The plaintive question "has fair trade lost its soul?" scowls across the table at "will it sell?" and one doubts that a fruitful dialogue will be forthcoming. Their approach cannot really answer the question of what challenges fair trade offers to conventional economics, because they are not open to any threat to the established economic faith.

Mainstream economics assumes that products must be submitted to competition to sell (which is prevented if the price is protected through fair trade guarantees). Thus in a BBC interview on fair trade, an eminent London School of Economics professor, Andrei Sarychev, asserts, despite widespread impoverishment, widening gaps between rich and poor, and the accumulation of global wealth in the hands of a few, that fairness results only from competition (Jones 2004). Such a bizarre set of beliefs no doubt makes room for the tooth fairy as well. As many economists and social theorists recognize, the free competition can easily result in the very opposite of fairness. Fair trade does not question the need for trade, as some calls for returns to the small and local might, but wants to restore its human purpose. As David Ransom (2001: 26) puts it, "Either it enhances human well-being as a whole or it is a worthless enterprise that enriches some, impoverishes many more and gets us precisely nowhere."

The concept of fair trade agribusiness might appear to represent an insurmountable contradiction. Since the rules and ethics are different for these different economic systems, the reconfiguration of fair trade as large-scale agriculture might have to be consigned to the world of fantasy. This problem arises, however, because conventional economics is assumed to be monolithic and uniform; if one follows Gibson-Graham in imagining an economics whose face is actually crazed with alternatives, then a new field opens up to consider the progress of fair trade and perhaps organics as well. After all, Mondragon and Co-op Atlantic teach us that co-operative and democratic principles can be applied on a large scale. Is there a way of certifying large-scale farms (which could be formed as co-ops) to maintain democratic principles? If the answer is "no," then how do we expect democracy to work at the scale of, say, a nation-state?

It is easy to decry financial success, to worry that it will spoil the high ideals that a food initiative grew upon. But if we argue that financial success is not in itself a problem, each case must be examined carefully for its relations to the market economy. We must examine each initiative for its tendencies and the understandings that average people have of the movement as they conduct the work of the cultural construction of reality. Just as economics fails to be a uniform discipline, so too do the solutions insert themselves at different points and triumph in different ways. The most interesting questions focus on the details of this insertion and this triumph.

The Economic Is Always Social

Economic relations, seen from the point of view of cultural analysis, are simply another set of rules for shaping social relations. The world imagined by economists who voice a fanatical belief in free trade is simply a world that most people don't want to live in. It tends towards removing the necessities of life such as health care and accessible nutritious food from a portion of the populace who can no longer afford these things; it tends towards wealth transfers towards the richest in society; it tends towards gutting social protections such as environmental regulations. The free trade society, however, like any society, has a complete and functioning set of social values embedded in and necessary to the rules of economic relations — precepts that begin with the false notion that at our core each human being operates solely on self-interest.

Fair trade practice reveals the social that is often denied in mainstream economic theory. Fair trade picks at various threads in the old sweater of economic theory. For instance, trade is already highly regulated; fair trade is not reinventing that wheel. The United States and Mexico are bogged down in an impenetrable wrangle over "dolphin-safe" tuna; Mexico objects to the U.S. desire for dolphin-safe tuna as — what else? — restraint of trade. The United States continues to have a heavily subsidized agricultural base, tilting the playing field towards their farmers and ensuring that in a one-legged race, they get to use all three.

Fair trade simply offers new kinds of regulation, changing the embedded social values from self-interest (consumers) and profit-accumulation (corporations) to mutually accountable producers and consumers, and co-operatively structured firms. It is significant that the largest purveyor of fair trade in the United Kingdom is the Co-op supermarkets. The reconfiguration of the social values promoted by fair trade fits the mandate and declared attitudes about socio-economic relations that are the foundations of the co-op movement. Above all, the alternative economic relations offered by fair trade initiatives challenge the ingrained metaphors in standard economics that pit producer against consumer.

The Crosses of Economics: On Economic Symbols

> Those with common sense are becoming aware of the fragility of a food system that creates so much distance, both socially and geographically, between an unprecedentedly urban world of consumers and a global farm, linked by the perpetual motion of an oil-fueled transportation network and a shaky international monetary framework. (Friedmann 1993: 213–14)

Open any basic economics textbook and you will quickly be treated to a graph of breathtaking simplicity, the supply and demand curves, often flattened (abstracted) into a neat "X." This "X" is the cross of economics before which many resounding pronouncements and prescriptions for behaviour are handed down. Easy to grasp, a breeze to memorize: price comes to rest at the intersection of the two halves of the "X." As producer and consumer numbers vary in response to each other, the elegance of the graph can obscure the symbolic character of the image, while opening the intellectual field to glistening horizons of mathematical calculation. An ethnographer of economic culture finds a rich mine of meaning in such persistent and recurring images. Why figure the relation of producer and consumer as uncompromisingly opposed? Why does the graph only intersect at price? How does that image of opposition influence our culture's relations of exchange?

A metaphor or image as fundamental as the supply and demand "X" functions as a kind of doctrine. It shapes behaviour and how we see the world; it is also unlikely to be challenged from within, because it forms part of the tissue of belief. This way of seeing things — the deep split between producer and consumer — is central to the construction of our food system as a global industrial system. It cannot be denied that it shows up as well in the work of many alternatives. Although it might be difficult to imagine a food system that does not make a strong distinction between producers and consumers, there have been notable attempts to do so.

In the initial chapter of *Debunking Economics*, Steven Keen challenges the smooth relation between supply and demand, carefully shattering the reassuring curves of consumer preference and marginal costs. When he is done with it the cross is a mess of squiggles; his injection of humour alone is enough to start readers thinking about new ways of seeing the producer-consumer relation, just as the ritual clown pulls down the comfortable everyday strictures of cultural behaviour and tradition and allows us to think anew.

The image of the supply and demand "X" builds on the notion of conflicting (radically opposed) interests. Producer and consumer interests are simplified and assumed to be predictable. To achieve this effect, the theorist must make what economist Joseph Schumpeter calls "heroic simplifications." Hold time constant; imagine all consumers are the same; imagine there is one commodity. From the ethnographic outsider's point of view, how different is this mythology from the stories that imagine the sun pulled over the horizon each day by a team of galloping horses, or stories that animate the world with different energetic spirits? As with most mythologies, this one takes on powerful and creative power in the culture. It shapes how we view each other, how we view the people we buy products from, how we place ourselves in the economy. This mythology, like all mythologies, engenders a distinctive blindness. How is it that we can all participate in production of various kinds, including household work, office work, or work in an auto-plant, and yet at the same time be able to disconnect our consumption strategies from our knowledge of production?

The Search for Other Mythologies

Shiva (1993: 85) deviates from standard analysis in questioning "this ideologically constructed divide between consumption, production and conservation." The clarity with which she perceives the artificiality of the producer-consumer division derives, perhaps, largely from her awareness of the perspective of the Third World, in which "in the self-provisioning economies of the Third World, producers are simultaneously consumers and conservers."

In a conversation between two farmers working to change the food system), one of them, Signe Waller, emphasizes that the food system systematically distances producers from consumers: "The distribution system is geared to introducing as many middlepeople as possible" (Waller and Rose 1995: 3). For Waller, as food distribution stretches thinly over the global landscape, the numbers are disheartening:

> Consumers paid $55.5 billion for fruits and vegetables in 1980. Farmers received $11.7 billion, or 21.1 percent of that. The rest, $43.8 billion, went for marketing. Then, in 1991, $108.5 billion was spent on fruits and vegetables (about twice what was spent 10 years earlier). But farmers in 1991 received only 14.6 percent of the total consumer expenditure for those items.

Brewster Kneen (1993: 17) also describes the process that creates the space between producers and consumers, "separating people from the sources of their food and nutrition with as many interventions as possible."

George Monbiot (2001: 1) points to an interesting resonance between the construction of economic relations, whether state or corporate, and the development of the food system: "The global war against the peasantry has been prosecuted with equal vigour by state communists and corporate capitalists. Both have sought to stamp out economically dependent people. Both have claimed that, by centralising supply and distribution of food, they can guarantee the world against famine. And both have engineered starvation." Harriet Friedmann (1993: 213) explores the rift historically within the context of food: "A specialization of agricultural production opened vast spaces between where people lived and where their foods originated, between the work they did and the objects they used."

According to Monbiot (1997: 2), the consolidation of power in a few megacorporations in the food industry inhibits "the two remaining means of public restraint of their activities: government regulation and genuine consumer choice." His perspective, though, emphasizes and decries the loss of consumer power to centralized, monopolized production. Other texts do the opposite, bemoaning the rise of consumer sovereignty, and of the power that has passed into the hands of the rapacious, self-interested consumer, to the detriment of the food system. One natural food store owner talks about "the destructive consumers," people who wreak havoc on the way to the dinner-table (for instance, by rapidly switching loyalties from small businesses to supermarkets and back). Such analysts agree that there is a power imbalance, but as we skid up and down the cross of supply and demand we seem to be between a rock and a hard place.

The Agri-Food Solution

The Co-op Atlantic agri-food strategy is a brilliant solution to the split between producer and consumer. It embodies in action the principles for a popular food education. Dean Baglole, head of the beef producers co-op, explained to me that the strategy works especially well in Prince Edward Island because it gives farmers a place to send the grain and extra potatoes that grow so well there, and then to spread the manure back over their fields for the next harvest. Both the CEO John Harvie and Bryan Inglis (vice-president of Agriculture) reiterated to me that the beef is not a brand; it is a story. According to Inglis, the story is that "your neighbour is growing your food, all the money we produce or make goes back to the community, so it's full circle." When the Atlantic co-operators first got the ball rolling on this project, the only beef-processing plant in the Maritimes had been bought out by Maple Leaf (based in Ontario) and promptly closed. The producers were left with nowhere to ship their cattle but off to Ontario and sometimes Pennsylvania.

What did they do? Like all good co-operators when beleaguered, they formed a co-op and took control of their economic destiny. Co-op Atlantic formed a partnership with a beef producers co-op (which now boasts 186 farmer/owners, most of them in Prince Edward Island but some of them in other Atlantic provinces as well). The partnership built a beef-processing plant, which is now open and operating, on Prince Edward Island. When I spoke to people the project was just a gleam in everyone's eye — they were excited but not sure how to convince all the farmers to sign on and commit.

True to the legacy of Coady educators, the co-op hired someone who set out across the Maritimes to meet farmers, call face-to-face meetings, and answer the same questions over and over, putting a face on the multimillion-dollar venture. When it came time to sell shares, they sold out in two weeks, with a waiting list for more. The sceptics who hung back cannot sell to the plant but will have to continue to ship to Ontario. As one manager from Co-op Atlantic remarked, "If this model works it scares the hell out of the big boys." He expected the next hurdle to be when the big boys in Ontario raise the price they offer to the Maritime farmers in an attempt to entice them away from the new plant.

Reciprocal Business: A Natural Strategy

Inglis pointed out to me that the agri-food strategy was not really new to Co-op Atlantic, although trying to get the story out to consumers is new. Co-op Atlantic integrates agricultural production with consumer operations. For them this is considerably more than the vertical integration practised by conglomerates such as Cargill. They have, for instance, a complex arrangement, which they call reciprocal business, with grain producers and co-ops. Before the season begins the co-operators buy their farm input from the co-op store. Co-op feed stores (co-op farm supply stores and garden centres) then receive, grade, and sort the harvested grain. When the farmers bring in the grain the stores just settle up. Co-op Atlantic even adds a premium if the farmers bring in the grain themselves. Other co-ops package their seed for them in the slow winter season, and one co-op makes up the birdseed that Co-op Atlantic sells. Tom Trueman, a dairy producer, farm-equipment store owner, and member of the Co-op Atlantic board, commented that the goal was to integrate the different parts of the food economy: "all sectors... from gate to plate." The initiative is unique, he said, because it is a coalition of producers and consumers.

Written Contracts Are for Suing

In my first research trip I was groping to figure out how Co-op Atlantic managed to bridge that chasm between producers and consumers. How did they actually manage to get these two facets of the business working together? I figured that there must be contracts with the beef farmers, and that they must have taken a long time to hammer out. But when I asked Inglis about that process, he was definite, there were no written contracts. He said that written contracts are only for suing, and why would you sue your best customer? The farmers may be selling you beef one day, but they will be back buying grain from you the next.

The Co-op Atlantic model is unique in seeing it this way. It reflects a regional history of producers and consumers overlapping messily in different coalitions in the co-operative movement. People are often simultaneously members of producer and consumer co-ops; many consumer co-ops were originally offshoots of producer coalitions, in which the co-operation to sell a product was easily incorporated into the co-operation to buy a product. Still, Trueman took pains to tell me that a "disconnect" does exist between producers and consumers, although there is no antagonism between them — which is a significant reflection of the Atlantic difference. Most other approaches, even when they promote the idea of a coalition of producers and consumers, still configure them as radically separate, viewing each other across a gaping chasm with few grounds on which to begin a conversation.

A much more complex view of economic relations comes from starting with the question of interests rather than supply vs. demand. As Nancy Folbre (1994) points out, people move through fields of shifting interests, negotiating and co-ordinating multiple needs. Such a complex identity challenges the simplicity of a purely self-interested consumer or producer, and economic decisions become multifaceted and fraught. The work of Atlantic Canadian co-operators speaks of an elaborate field of shifting interests, in which producers sit on the boards of consumer co-ops, workers share boards with consumers, and different interests compel complex negotiation. One of my first naive questions in my research in the region was why this multiple positioning did not result in a conflict of interest. Wide-eyed stares in answer to this question made me realize that for them identity is always complex. Each actor's position is multiplicitous and dialogic. They consider multiple interests a strength rather than a threat.

Note

1. Many would argue that chocolate and sugar are drugs as well. Recently the nuclear industry in Toronto had the bright idea of using chocolate to seduce women who opposed nuclear power (research, they said, had shown that women were more resistant to nuclear energy because they are "uninformed," possibly even stupid). They enticed them to a huge "information" session with the promise of gross amounts of chocolate, thinking apparently that the drug would put them in a pleasant state of acquiescence and that, like addicts everywhere, they would do anything for chocolate.

Chapter 8

Living by Our Food
Farmers' Markets, Community Gardens, and Relocalization

The dangerous inequities of a corporatized food system have generated an astonishing level of ingenuity and resourcefulness in responses around the world. The initiatives are often small-scale and personal, community, or regional solutions to global problems. Many of them fit the philosophy of relocalization. Vandana Shiva (2000: 37) says that relocalization: "implies, very simply, that what can be grown and produced locally should be used locally, so that resources and livelihoods can be protected." From think-tanks to farmers to respected scholars, the cry has gone out to relocalize (Friedmann 1993; Gorelick 2000; Rosset 2000).

Farm Folk/City Folk (2003), an extraordinary organization in Vancouver, supports numerous initiatives to relocalize, including farmers' markets, community gardens, and good food boxes. One section of its website asks the question, "Why relocalize our food system?" It also provides the answers: local food is "fresher and tastier, improves local economy, conservation of local farmland, builds community, food safety, etc."

Steven Gorelick (2000: 35) explores the policy changes necessary to relocalize. In his vision, "Farmers' markets, roadside stalls and farmgate shops could be set up to bring local food straight to consumers, cutting out the middlemen and bringing all the proceeds of food production straight back into the local economy." Peter Rosset (2000: 36), former executive director of Food First, advocates for "a personal connection to food: farmers' markets, community-supported agriculture and other such schemes bring home to consumers where their food comes from, and what effect its production has on landscape and environment."

What does relocalization look like? When people get right down to doing it, what have they invented? While the philosophy of relocalization catalyzes action, what decisions do people make when they get down to the business of trying to put their vision into practice? A movement's vision functions a little like the mythology of ritual practice; it is ambiguous enough to inspire all manner of different actions. The practice squeezed from the vision is a matter of the negotiation and construction of a shared reality, which in the end might reflect on the vision as a shiny spoon might reflect a face, a bit distorted, even a bit weird. Depending on the emphasis of the initiatives, there can be a continual slippage into various structures that continue to set producers in opposition to consumers.

The producer-driven or producer-focused initiatives are at one end of the spectrum. In Canada some of the best examples are co-operatives, in which the producers build a coalition in order to pool their strength against corporate economics. The Peace and Environment Resource Centre (2004) describes one such venture: "In Harriston, Ontario, 40 producers have formed the Farm Fresh Poultry Cooperative. Believing they could obtain a better price for their product by processing it themselves than by selling to the large corporations that dominate the sector, the co-op has experienced remarkable growth in its first two years." Cases like this keep some of the power in the food economy local, and more of the money remains in the local economy.

Relocalization in a global economy is not always easy and requires wise marketing and commitment. Sally Fallon (2000: 44) talks about how a small farmer can survive by championing the local: "One way this can be done is for small farmers to specialise in local food and drink, and to produce individual products based on local environments and traditions, which large producers cannot hope to match." Regions even have begun to brand themselves. The Charlevoix region of Quebec rejuvenated its local economy when people there created an integrated line of locally produced products, marketed and sold under one general local banner.

This emphasis on local production reaches a zenith in the slow food movement, which began in Italy and now has chapters all over the globe. Believers in slow food search out local, artisanal foods, organic if possible, and cook from scratch, sitting down together for extended meals that allow eaters (with time and money) to savour and appreciate the flavours (see Stille 2002). The movement introduces a note of conscious ritual into the localization of food, serving to remind us that in most cultures food is heavily freighted with ritual, albeit perhaps not always so conscious. The founder of the movement, Carlo Petrini, emphasizes that the movement is about restoring a sensuous quality to food. Slow food brings an important complexity to the local food movement's vision of land. Petrini (2001: 8) emphasizes the French term "*terroir*" in our knowledge of food. "*Terroir*" translates loosely as "territory," but includes "the combination of natural factors (soil, water, slope, height above sea level, vegetation, micro-climate) and human ones (tradition and the practice of cultivation) that gives a unique character to each small agricultural locality and the food grown, raised, made, and cooked there."

Connie Berry (2003: 27) suggests that we consider applying fair trade principles to dealings with local farmers.

A pioneering initiative just launched in the U.K. will use a certification label to market products from small-scale organic British farmers. This means that consumers, for the first time, can know not only that their product is organic (certified separately) and domestic (promoted through local marketing programs), but also that the purchase supports small-scale producers and ensures they were fairly compensated for that product.

Fair trade principles in the United States have recently been extended to a few American products, in a natural progression of the movement.

Another common initiative is the farmers' market, although there are many versions in Canada, only some of which actually focus on local production. Many farmers have import licences and offer imported fruits and vegetables at their stalls without necessarily differentiating the imports from their own products. Consumers may be sufficiently uninformed to think that those lemons come from somewhere nearby (perhaps an Ontario greenhouse?). Generally if food is available locally, farmers will not import it, even if their farm doesn't have the item. At the Ithaca Farmers' Market in New York State, people can only sell products that they grow or make themselves (the percentage of craftspeople to farmers is also controlled). Farmers' markets can have numerous effects beyond simply getting immediate cash into the hands of small farmers (by definition a cash-starved sector, especially at the beginning of the season). Consumers and producers meet and learn from each other, the producers find out what the customers want (as one farmer told me, it is much easier to plan when you talk directly to the customers and can just raise what they want). The consumers get a much better idea of what it takes to raise their food. The principals can also address issues of pricing, leading, one hopes, to a better understanding on the part of the consumers about subsidies and the challenges of the unsubsidized small organic farmer.

Many "buy local" initiatives work in tandem with the drive to build local production capacity and to return some control to small producers. These marketing programs reflect and support the producer initiatives, and build consumer support for newly empowered producer groups. In Belo Horizonte, the "Direct from the Producer" and "Straight from the Country" programs identify produce as locally produced and marketed by farmers (usually from small neighbourhood stalls or trucks). The people I met in Atlantic Canada frequently emphasized the importance of buying local. The great success of the Atlantic Tender Beef program derives from people's desire to buy home-grown food. Even without much marketing at the beginning, the program did remarkably well.

In Toronto, Local Flavour Plus, now called "Local Food Plus" (LFP), has created a label program that identifies a broad package of important food factors. The label certifies a sustainable food based on agricultural methods, treatment of workers and animals, and distance travelled. Toronto's largest independent grocery store, Fiesta Farms. managed to survive in 1995 when the giant Loblaw opened down the block in a clear bid for its customer base. In response Fiesta Farms began to provide its customers with product from the fifty certified farms and processors of Local Food Plus. "It's ethical food," *The Toronto Star* (Parker 2007) reported. The localization movement has been criticized for ignoring the marginalized (see, for instance, Allen 1999) and for providing delicious, expensive artisanal food only for those who can afford it. Through Fiesta Farms, LFP is able to reach mass-market customers. The store's grocery manager is not starry-eyed about the ideals of localization; he says that it was the bottom-line that convinced him to take up the LFP products. The impact of social capital and ethical purchases on his store, then, is not better karma but better business; once again, we see that the two are not incompatible.

The research of numerous community economic development organizations makes the case for the economic impact of local businesses on a region. One study (Civic Economics 2004) showed that 50 percent more of every dollar spent with local firms as opposed to chain stores stays in the local economy, while local firms have 70 percent more impact per square foot than do chain firms. Renewable energy studies show the economic impact of community-owned energy generation to be five times greater than the impact of commercial installations with non-local ownership (Welsh 2005). Economies of scale, even in the case of the energy production, do not seem to apply. Aronowitz (1996: 99) concludes: "Economies of scale have more to do with centralization of power than saving resources. When placed in the context of both political participation and ecological criteria, bigness turns out to be an obstacle, a negativity." Despite clear and professional research to the contrary, economic development efforts by cities and states continue to focus on enticing multinational corporations to set up shop (offering tax breaks, subsidies, and, where necessary, grovelling). Old mythologies die hard, particularly when those with power and wealth are heavily invested in them.

The fate of the South Central Farm of Los Angeles stands as an example. The farm, established in 1992 and located at 41st and Alameda streets, with 14 acres of land and 360 plots, had become one of the largest urban gardens in the country. Hundreds of low-income families had grown food on the farm; it represented a powerful symbol of urban renewal and hope. But in 2006 the farm was ploughed under after years of wrangling with the city and a prospective buyer. Backed by high-profile defenders, including Daryl Hannah, Joan Baez, and Martin Sheen, the farmers hung on to try to save their farm until the bitter end, occupying trees and trying to stop the bulldozers. Eventually many of the farmers moved on to "put down roots in other community gardens around the city." Some of them found a new piece of land north of the city (South Central Farmers 2008).

The proliferation of community gardens changes food relations in numerous ways. Life Cycles, a project in Victoria, B.C., runs a "Home Grown Gardening" program that, according to the Peace and Environment Resource Centre (2004), "helps social assistance recipients to develop organic gardens in backyards and balconies. This initiative allows participants to stretch their incomes while increasing their control over the food system." Backyard Bonanza in Ottawa, providing free seed, workshops, and seminars, involved 440 families in a project to start new backyard and container vegetable gardens. To some extent such projects challenge private property because they are often on public or reclaimed land and involve communal gardening (either together or in adjacent small plots) with tool-sharing or pooled seed purchases.

In the United Kingdom the Federation of City Farms and Community Gardens supports the development of community gardens. Related initiatives include the Women's Environmental Network, which works to enable minority women to grow their own food (*The Ecologist* 2001: 55). FoodShare has had numerous community garden projects, including a beautiful plot at the Centre for Addiction and Mental Health, a garden planted and maintained by clients of the Centre. FoodShare also inaugurated a creative initiative called Seeds of Our City, which brought new immigrants together to share seeds and knowledge from their countries of origin (Baker 2003) and conducted research on diverse forms of agriculture. This remarkable program begins with the new immigrants who often bring with them into the country a few seeds from beloved plants. The program emphasizes and celebrates this tradition, which both enriches our plant diversity and multiplies our agricultural knowledge through exchange.

The initiatives to encourage people to grow their own food clearly link producers and consumers. Still, such movements also raise class issues. In today's economy, many low-income people are forced to work long hours for low pay as well as maintain a household and raise a family (without, except in rare places like Quebec, much help from the state). To tell them to grow their own food in addition seems like an unsustainable solution. Likewise, as Canadian agriculture collapses and farmers leave the land in droves, how can we expect immigrants to take up the slack (as a recent Canadian initiative does)? How is that different from encouraging immigration so that there will be a pool of people to do the dirty and thankless work that established citizens don't want to do? One rancher in Nebraska told a reporter that passing the farm on to his son would be nothing less than "child abuse" (Halweil 2000).

Only broader systemic changes can solve these problems. Many community garden initiatives are part of larger urban agriculture movements. In the United Kingdom an extended battle for access to common lands finally resulted, Michael Wale (2001: 54) writes, in the "1908 Small Holdings and Allotments Act which came about as a result of years of pressure from ordinary people for a share in the land again. The Act required local councils to provide land for the creation of allotments." Since then citizens have continued to struggle for access to those patches of land, threatened by developers and indifferent local government. In Havana, Cuba, an extraordinary 90 percent of the produce consumed is grown in the city. As a team of Cuban writers states: "This urban production is based on three principles: organic methods, which do not contaminate the environment; the rational use of local resources; and the direct marketing of produce to consumers" (Campanioni et al. in Funes et al. 2003: 220).

Another point of community intersection with the food system occurs in community manufacturing initiatives such as FoodShare's kitchen incubator. In these community kitchens an entrepreneur can try out new recipes and begin production in a certified commercial kitchen without the enormous capital outlay needed to start up alone. These businesses may build on an initial success to start a full-fledged business on their own. Does the initial community-supported start-up change the kind of business they become? That is, is there a debt of social capital and interdependence that circulates through the community from such a venture? Does the addition of new small businesses localize production or just contribute to the proliferation of middlemen as they begin to sell to distributors and other links to reach larger markets? Is there anything in a business that began as community-based that keeps it from entering the conventional grind of profit and growth?

Further research might provide some detail on the effects of success on community-based businesses. The research may well show that a commitment to community values has to be constantly renewed and reshaped. For instance, WOWFoods delivered organic produce and groceries to people's homes. It began as a collective that grew out of an alternative currency system. As it grew it was reconstituted as a small private business, expanding its organic lineup to include other groceries. A few years later, as supermarkets everywhere began to carry a basic selection of organic items, the company cut back on the grocery inventory and opened an organic bakery at the Ignatius Centre in Guelph, where various non-profit programs and social justice initiatives also find a home base. In the course of succeeding while remaining dedicated to community, most community-focused businesses must similarly invent and reinvent their strategies. They have to reaffirm their values on a continuing basis.

Although relocalization strategies are frequent, initially they had a limited impact on the wider society. The idea of relocalization seemed unusually slow to bring about change. Whereas questions of food safety (such as pesticides in milk) easily captured popular imagination, localization seemed esoteric, with marvelous instances of success without a corresponding shift in cultural rhetoric or practice. In my own experience as a sales representative I found that although owners and staff at natural food stores and co-ops were staunch supporters of local food, that commitment did not always translate into actual sales for the products. We all devoted a certain amount of energy to trying to figure out why people would ask for local but not buy it. It is as if the store was a museum — a place that curated a display of ethics ("buy local!"). The customers were not always ready to put that ethics into action but felt good just seeing the products on the shelves — an unsustainable situation for a small store.[1]

Organizations like Farm Folk/City Folk and FoodShare in Toronto recognize the importance of getting government support for urban agriculture, rooftop gardens, and community gardens (see also Hines 2001). Local action alone is not enough to bring about substantial change. Both organizations lobby and advocate in addition to initiating and maintaining projects. One of the greatest obstacles to making lasting change is that the playing field is not at all level: organic farmers and small-scale producers get little help from government; agricultural supports in Canada are geared almost exclusively to agribusiness and to building an export market, not to feeding Canadians; and the continued dumping of highly subsidized U.S. produce (some of it grown on U.S.-owned Latin American farms) in the Canadian market makes life difficult for Canadian farmers, both large and small. A successfully relocalized food economy requires political will as well as a shift in social values.

Escaping the Producer-Consumer Split: Other Countries and the Dilemma of Distance

Cuba provides a stunning example of how to do things differently in the economies of food. Cut off from international trade by the continuing U.S. boycott and the collapse of the Soviet Union (its key trading partner), Cuba turned inwards to solve its food crisis. One collection of articles, *Sustainable Agriculture and Resistance* (Funes et al. 2003), makes the difference between vision and real practice spectacularly clear. The rules for creating food security for all in Cuba are under messy negotiation, trial, and error. Success has come from a multiplicity of strategies. The small island country has created a complex web of different kinds of ownership, farm structure, worker relations, and state and farm relations. Contributor Richard Levins (in Funes et al. 2003: 276, 277) asks, "What if development is seen as a branching pathway, with choices all along the way?" The goals may define all the difference between progress in the classic sense and Cuban development. "What if," Levins continues, "economic development is not a goal in itself but a means to enriching life and preserving nature, with emphasis on equity, health, education, culture, recreation and mutual caring within an environment which is sustainable, diverse, and people-friendly?"

In the wake of the failure of the state farm system, Cuba moved towards various forms of worker collectives (though one scholar worries that this might represent a return to private property (Álvarez in Funes et al. 2003: 72). The priorities are to feed everyone and to preserve an economic solvency that includes full employment, healthy environmental goods, and the protection of people's health (Levins in Funes et al. 2003: 278). The strategies the Cubans applied include both centralized and market economic mechanisms, different forms of property and management, modification of agronomic practices and technological change to achieve sustainable agriculture, and the development of a participatory economy (Martín in Funes et al. 2003: 58).

Many different factors have contributed to the success of this new direction, which almost incidentally brings producers and consumers closer together simply by linking their interests. This level of commitment and involvement by the state often eludes progressive food programs and policy initiatives in Canada. The system in Cuba is flexible, allowing for the interaction of many different solutions, management structures, and property rights. It is clearly always under construction and open to change as necessary. The system is facilitated by the collective membership of the farms, which provides easy access to decision-making processes through the co-op commitment to democratic process. Although Cuba, in being cut off from its major trading partners, may provide a unique example, does this mean that a country like Canada has to wait to be severed from its trading networks before it begins to solve the ills of our food system?

Also in the South, the programs in Brazil's Belo Horizonte combine and conflate the interests of producers and consumers, low-income, food-insecure people with the middle class, and government with farmers, in a complex series of food security issues that interlock but approach the problem from different angles. One initiative connects to another, making a reasonable logic out of many different approaches to food. In Atlantic Canada, a vast co-op network turned a natural tendency to coalition-building into a solution to this old quandary: how do we link producers and consumers? How do they come to work together and not just tolerate each other?

Such innovative solutions to the producer/consumer split occur around the world and across cultures. Originally formed by women to get better prices on milk, the gigantic seikatsu-buying clubs in Japan are now so large that they wield considerable consumer power. Their vision takes the economy in a new direction, not just to put the screw to the producers but to start "free schools and worker collectives so that people can begin to free themselves from the grip of the centralized economy" (Pretty 1995: 157). Like Co-op Atlantic, at a certain level of consumer power can come the realization that producer interests are in the consumer's best interests; the rift begins to close.

In the Co-op Atlantic case, the cultural actors focus on reducing a kind of psychic distance between producers and consumers. This example illuminates the concept of relocalization. The distance cannot be imagined to be solely spatial. Relocalization prescriptions echo the environmental analyses that convert environmental problems into spatial metaphors — for instance, the ecological footprint analysis of Wackernagel and Rees (1996), which converts our level of energy and resource use into feet and acres of planet space.

It is important to remember, as Wackernagel and Rees do, that analytical metaphors represent a particular choice, a way of shaping the data, and may well avoid the light that could be shed by the use of other metaphors. The rejuvenation of local food production is doubtless a key to a better food world: to free ourselves from cheap (subsidized) imports; to re-emphasize a food economy that promotes the local and eliminates links in the food chain. The spatial metaphor emphasizes breathtaking and moving statistics: for instance, most North American meals travel an average of 2,500 kilometres. But what aspects of the problem are we sweeping under the rug when we focus on the physical distance between producers and consumers? To answer this question might also be to begin to respond to a dilemma about trade. What responsibility do we have to producers in the South when we abandon their products (originally planted under pressure from our governments) and turn instead to local food? This question led me to examine the analytical metaphors that we use and to wonder what our solutions would look like if we had chosen other analogies or places to focus our energies. What if the psychic distance between producer and consumer, and its resultant indifference to producers near and far, are more of a problem than the actual distance?[2] In other words, what if the physical distance between producer and consumer is only part of the problem? Is it possible that the physical distance derives from other more fundamental problems?

The distance between producer and consumer is at its core an intellectual and symbolic distance, only secondarily spatial. The economic mythology in itself (the relentless "X") has shaped how we situate our actors in the food system. The creation of distinctive and alienated consumer and producer identities through our economic culture has made possible radical physical and moral disjunctures between where our food is grown and where it gets eaten. The spatial distance is only one inevitable result of these disjunctures.

The problem of the separation of producers and consumers recalls the issue of identity construction. Again, too, this is an ethnographic and not just economic argument. The tenets of pure economic theory arrive in our culture like slightly scorched tablets, with obscure formulas and pronouncements that translate and manifest culturally in indeterminate ways. This process (from economic precepts to practice on the ground) is a key moment of the construction of the North American identity. Advertising, media, school curricula, administrative interactions (like getting a drivers' licence) all participate in a construction of identity that reflects the gospel of economic thought. Our relation to this process is complex; we do not just take the instruction manual as handed to us, but tend to taste it and, puppy-like, chew it over. It is a continuing process of construction and reconstruction.

The manifestation of the economic cross metaphor in everyday life reveals a complex work of identity construction. We have seen in Cuba, Brazil, and Maritime Canada that there is nothing natural or inevitable about the opposition between producers and consumers. How did we get to this odd place? How is that the opposed interests came to be so exclusively the cultural form, regulated by rules of business, reflected in Economics 101, naturalized in our cultural practices?

Historical Roots of the Producer-Consumer Split

The producer-consumer division is no new problem, but is deeply rooted in our cultural history. In the 1970s the writers of the People's Food Commission report, *The Land of Milk and Money*, were startled to find that, even when offered alternative perspectives, consumers and producers persisted in blaming each other for the failures of the food system rather than blaming the system itself. Consumers think farmers are making too much; farmers think consumers are trying to ruin them. Still, we can easily imagine another path. Shiva (1993: 85) argues, "In the self-provisioning economies of the Third World, producers are simultaneously consumers and conservers." *Atlantic Co-operator* (2002), the newspaper of the Maritimes co-operative movement, reported on the Grand Prix Award won by the Atlantic Tender Beef program: "Many people believe that deciding to support local producers means that they will have to sacrifice on other values such as quality or price. But careful planning and co-operation among groups can deliver goods that meet the standards of national and international competitors, and even exceed them." To abandon a central metaphor can cause cultural anxiety — we wonder (absurdly), if producers and consumers are not opposed, will food still be edible?

A number of historical factors have brought us to this sorry pass. Many critics point out that regulations benefit large farms disproportionately and encourage a kind of system in which producers and consumers are mutually ignorant. The farmer-activists Signe Waller and Jim Rose (1995) point out, "The distribution system is geared to introducing as many middlepeople as possible." Gorelick (2000: 35) suggests the need for policy changes, though even with other changes for the better, he says, "Farmers would still be battling against skewed regulatory frameworks, laws and rules drawn up for the benefit of large-scale producers, and a general presumption against small-scale rural production by most modern governments." Even in the organic industry the large farms are sufficiently powerful to dictate prices to everyone else (Hamilton 1997). Agricultural subsidies are wildly skewed towards destructive models of agribusiness. In the United Kingdom, Monbiot (1996b) reports, "Farmers need to be both rich and eccentric to respond to the hunger for organic food. While taxpayers contributed 3 billion pounds last year to the destruction of the environment and the poisoning of our produce, the Ministry of Agriculture, Fisheries and Food handed out just 270,000 pounds for organic production." I suspect that in Canada the number of dollars going to organic production is closer to zero. Most small-scale producers are systematically excluded from programs of government support simply by virtue of their size. Small-scale producers only appear on the radar during misty-eyed propaganda from politicians about the Canadian farm and the noble farmer.

North America has seen a historical shift in cultural emphasis from producers to consumers, and a corresponding shift in power from producers to invisible megacorporations such as Cargill and to retail giants such as Loblaw and Sobeys, entities that are imagined to represent consumer desires.[3] Friedmann (1993a: 52) argues that food policy has shifted towards urban issues, and from agriculture towards food. The history of the co-operative movement, in Atlantic Canada and elsewhere, reflects this shift. Co-op Atlantic was originally a group of producers collaborating to purchase the supplies they needed for production (such as grains from the Prairies). The consumer co-ops of Co-op Atlantic were formed later, piggybacking on the established organization. Co-op Atlantic is remarkable, however, in not following the swing of the pendulum the whole way. Despite the manifest power of the retail co-ops, the strategy its members are proudest of deliberately builds a coalition between producers and consumers based on mutual interest in the local economy.

The history of land use and the enclosure of common lands also enters into the equation. Monbiot (1996a) argues that development has continued the work of the eighteenth-century enclosure movement in wiping out the common lands of Britain, and he explores similar histories in other places around the world. He couples our loss of an agricultural identity with production disconnected from needs: "Features that persisted for thousands of years, that place us in our land, are destroyed in a matter of moments for the sake of crops that nobody wants." He credits this separation from shared rights in land with opening the way for the use of land for profit alone.

The idea of land for profit also hones the problem of food and agriculture down to one of startling and absurd simplicity, ignoring the complexities of relations between production and consumption, and ploughing ahead with one interest (profit) in mind. Annette Desmarais (2007: 51) points out that Garrett Hardin's influential "tragedy of the commons" (which argued that humans were incapable of using shared resources sustainably because one person would inevitably hog it all and push the others out) offered a profound misunderstanding of the commons. Hardin's view, as well as the widespread enclosure of the commons imposed on small farmers, helped to destroy the complex concept of locally managed and negotiated shared resources that is central to sustainable and ecological food and agriculture. Such a reconfiguration of our landscapes, manifested in our use of them and in our new relations to them, lays the groundwork for the elegant spareness and intellectual vacuity of economic supply and demand.

In *Earth Democracy* Shiva (2005: 3) argues that the process of enclosure of land has been extended by analogy to the commons in general, to the resources of the planet: "While these first enclosures stole only land, today all aspects of life are being enclosed — knowledge, culture, water, biodiversity, and public services such as health and education. Commons are the highest expression of economic democracy." Hardin's tragedy of the commons and the many works that have followed him down the path of tragedy erase the traditional complex and democratic processes that managed shared resources; they assume that "commons" means unregulated chaos and unfettered greed leading to depletion (which sounds more like the results of present-day capitalism than economic relations built on the commons). Their intellectual blindness has put the seal on the casket of a regulated and equitable commons, enclosing it as surely as English law had enclosed the land in earlier times. Now, at least in North America, so focused are we on private ownership that, although we continue to share resources to some extent (water, public spaces, air), people might be hard put to talk about the idea of sharing resources. The commons has become one of those unthinkable friendly monsters that we need, once again, to begin to think about. As Shiva (2005: 29) states:

> The transformation of commons into commodities has two implications. It deprives the politically weaker groups of their right to survival, which they had through access to commons, and it robs from nature its right to self-renewal and sustainability, by eliminating the social constraints on resource use that are the basis of common property management.

These historical developments provide a background to the deepening divisions between producer and consumer. However, it still seems not quite sufficient to explain a culture's development by the division of labour, the separation of production from the home, and the compartmentalizing of our positions in the general economy and the dislocation of people from

shared land. This is not to question the force of political change
the Industrial Revolution or Fordism, but the crucial question re
cultural analysis: how did this make sense to people, how did the
of this separation hold persuasive power? The historical move
brought us here is probably a result of complex interactions be
culture's way of seeing things (the "X") and the practice generate
metaphors: regulations, policies, and the distribution of power.

Once again, this is not to say that a great physical distance do
ist between agribusiness in the South and eaters in the North. I ar
arguing that these actual distances are in themselves the metaphor
of the way in which we choose to shape our economic terrain. Meta
are powerful. They intrude into everyday life. They are not necessaril
flective of an existing reality but are more like magic spells that reconfig
the landscape, turn food into gold, and shape our identities. If the distan
between producers and consumers is indeed a metaphor that has shape
some of the key institutions of our food systems, can we shift power from
these institutions by challenging and reinventing our metaphors (and our
narratives)?

Knowledge in Relocalization Initiatives

The construction of producer and consumer identity is accomplished through
the shifting relations of knowledge in the culture. The ideal consumer looks
in the culture's mirror and sees someone smart, who can't be deceived, might
even be a little devious. These consumers are definitely determined to get
what they know is best for themselves and their families. The producer sees
an empty vessel for the knowledge of science, a blank slate left by the depar-
ture of traditional knowledge; producers' power comes from the status of
scientific knowledge as they apply it, not from their hard-won knowledge of
their own fields. The consumer's identity is defined by an apparent wealth of
knowledge, while the producer is just the opposite, defined by the absence of
knowledge. How can these different positions in the hierarchies of knowledge
be reconciled to heal the rift between producer and consumer?

The concern with imparting knowledge to consumers, and conversely
with honouring the existing knowledge of rural producers, is vivid in the
relocalization literature. The mission of Toronto's Karma Co-op includes
establishing connections with producers ("foster a healthy connection to the
food we eat, the people who grow it, and the other organizations who share
our beliefs") and education ("co-operatively educate ourselves on environmental issues"). Co-op Atlantic directors and staff cited education over and
over again as an important future goal and a key to keeping the co-ops viable. Unlike supermarkets, co-ops and natural food stores depend on truly
knowledgeable and aware consumers; they struggle with a culture that soothes

e consumer with simplistic blandishments about how smart they are. To insert ourselves into this dire situation requires tact; co-operative educators must both honour students for their constant ability to learn and to change, and recognize their own ability to learn and to change as they teach.

Shiva (1993: 60) argues that monoculture is a way of seeing the world as well as an agricultural method. She argues that the solution is a different approach to knowledge. "Democratising of knowledge becomes a central precondition for human liberation because the contemporary knowledge system excludes the humane by its very structure." Jules Pretty (1995: 8) likewise argues that truly sustainable agriculture requires a different approach to knowledge, characterized by "greater use of local resources and knowledge."

As Foucault points out, the way in which a culture situates knowledge is indicative of the power relations in that culture. The cross of supply and demand is only made possible by distinctive relations to knowledge: the artificial construction of consumer knowledge, which pumps consumers up with a delusion of power; and the denigration of producer power and knowledge, which is eventually reflected in the chicken farmer who doesn't even own the chickens he raises, or doesn't have the right to make production decisions about the birds. At the same time the delusions of supply and demand are reinforced by secrets and ignorance: a general lack of knowledge about where food comes from, what is in that food, and who produced it, and an exclusive world of scientific (high-status) knowledge about the work of production.

To open up a space for dialogue and exchange between producers and consumers we have to alter these dominant patterns in the construction of identity. We are not single-minded, eminently rational actors. We must recognize that we work through a multiplicity of interests, weighing and negotiating those interests at every turn. In turn, when allowed to multiply, the interests will illuminate the place of coalition. They will then highlight the combined mutual and opposed interests of producers and consumers. As Shiva (1993: 147) argues, "Diversity as a pattern of production, not merely of conservation, ensures pluralism and decentralisation." We must recognize a new approach to learning through the acknowledgement of shared interests and complementary knowledges. Pretty (1995: 134) emphasizes, for instance: "The success of sustainable agriculture depends not just on the motivations, skills and knowledge of individual farmers, but on action taken by local groups or communities as a whole."

Localization movements sweep the globe, from chefs combing the woods and waters of Maine for what's in season to the Malawi government restoring health to local maize production by subsidizing local small farmers. Each moment of localization is unique to its region, rife with the particular.

Localization promises an escape from the infertile moonscape of globally uniform food — all tasting the same, bearing the same brand names, offering the same limited ingredients of sugar, salt, and corn. Local food movements bring us back to the particular and the everyday miracle of foods, to food that tells stories that are unique to the origin of food: where the food came from, how it got to your plate, how it interacted with locally shared weather patterns, how it left behind rich, fertile land that promises future harvests of things good to eat and narratives good to think.

Notes

1. Supermarkets can afford to benefit from this same brand of ethics. They can maintain natural and organic displays even while losing money on those particular products. For them, the display promotes a useful image of the corporation as a community and health promoter whether or not anyone is actually buying the products.

2. One issue obscured by the focus on distance turns out to be relative energy use in all aspects of the food chain. Recent studies in the United Kingdom have pointed out that fossil fuel use in refrigeration, chemical fertilization, deforestation, livestock operations, and domestic transportation actually exceeds that of long-distance transportation (Oliver 2008).

3. Despite an apparent focus on and celebration of consumers and consumption, the consumer has little real power in a centralized, homogenized system. The artificial split between producers and consumers seems to lead to the increased fictionalization of both terms.

Chapter 9

From Voices to Power
Food Democracy and the People's Economics

> If we were to dissolve the image that looms in the economic foreground, what shadowy economic forms might come forward? In these questions we can identify the broad outlines of our project: to discover or create a world of economic difference, and to populate the world with exotic creatures that become, upon inspection, quite local and familiar (not to mention familiar beings that are not what they seem). (Gibson-Graham 1996)

The structures of alternative economic relations contain a mix of complex consumer identities. They include the social or symbolic capital that knits these identities together, the strategies of food security aimed at restoring equity and redistributing power, and negotiated and multiple interests. The food movements and alternative paths reveal patterns of astonishing strength and resilience.

I have tried in these pages to avoid what I call the progressive or leftist conditional, a strange grammatical form that shows up in many texts that attempt to imagine a better future: a future in which, for instance, everyone "would eat," everyone "would enjoy a political voice," and local agriculture "would thrive." Although dreams are crucial for achieving change, in dreaming we sometimes miss the magic right at hand. A dominant ideology is inevitably haunted within and without by its contradictions and deviations. Thus, no matter how determinedly media and economic experts try to shore it up, the singular, neo-liberal approach to economics breaks up at the edges like a gigantic glacier, massive and seemingly immutable, yet constantly slipping and melting. As Pierre Bourdieu and Gibson-Graham point out, we have allowed capitalism to gain a capital "C," to be unassailable and inevitable (see also Whatmore and Thorne 1997). The process of hegemony has concealed all the rifts and irrationalities that score capitalism's face. Bourdieu (1998: 55) argues: "Collectively, in the mode of consensus... people utter a fatalistic discourse which consists of transforming economic tendencies into destiny. Now, social laws, economic laws and so on only take effect to the extent that people let them do so." The goal, according to Gibson-Graham (1996: 10), is "to tame" the notion of a singular capitalism: "hedge it with qualifications, rive it with contradictions, discipline it with contingencies of politics or culture; make it more 'realistic.'"

Democracy: The People's Food

Democratic faith is the decision to believe that a world of democratic trust is possible because we can see it in each person sometimes. It is the decision to believe in what people can be on the basis of what they sometimes are. It is the decision to believe that each polity and each person contains the possibility of a democratic version of itself. (Lummis 1996: 153)

The alternatives to conventional economics are not random. The question is not so much how we get to those alternatives, since they are all around us, but how to recognize and implement the inklings of difference and change that have already been set in place. We must both reclaim historical awareness and moments and recognize the overlap and potential for coalition among current movements. The work of coalition-building must be a thoughtful, focused process; no easy venture, it requires attendance to rules of dialogue, consensus, and negotiation. Coalition-building demands a conscious and attentive democracy. This final section explores the notions of food democracy, and what it might really mean to invoke the language of democracy. How do we in practice learn to work together?

Food democracy initiatives are changing the face of the global food system North and South. In the South, groups of landless peasants are occupying and eventually winning unused land back from wealthy and absentee landowners. These actions demand consensus decision-making and popular education, even during the occupations, when the very lives of the peasants are in danger. The international peasant movement Vía Campesina insists on democratic practice and allows only rural producers as members. It institutes equality of power among its thousands of participants. The city of Belo Horizonte in Brazil, with food declared a basic human right, provides an array of alternative and democratic approaches to food distribution. The network of co-ops in Atlantic Canada provides food, gas, funerals, forestry, and agricultural supplies for the local population. The Food Project in Boston insists on youth-driven community garden efforts based on two urban agriculture lots.

A Tapas Plate of Food Democracy

Food democracy is about citizens having the power to determine agro-food policies and practices locally, regionally, nationally, and globally. (Hassanein 2003)

Three principles are key to food democracy: 1) Everyone has an equal say in what happens; 2) all stakeholders participate in some way — food democracy is inclusive of producers, consumers, processors, policy analysts, government, and labour; 3) Food democracy works to put the power over decisions about the food system in the hands of the people.[1] Power is not delegated to people who are not accountable to the people's needs.

Neva Hassanein (2003: 83) points out that democracy is a process, not a structure or an organization, and that it specifically solves the problem of conflicting interests and values. "Food democracy is a method for making choices when values and interests come into conflict and when the consequences of decisions are uncertain." What does this look like in practice? Although the term is used frequently, a few initiatives in the North stand out in their work to democratize the food system here, including the Community Food Security Coalition in California, Sustain in the United Kingdom, the Food Project in Boston, and the B.C. Food Systems Network in Canada. Each of these provides a forum for all stakeholder voices equally, while emphasizing different aspects of the challenges of democracy. Each project relies on a thoughtful process to ensure that power remains in people's hands.

Getting Everyone to the Table

The Community Food Security Coalition in Venice, California, created and implemented a Community Food Assessment process that demonstrates food democracy in action. The Community Food Assessment project offers a tool for communities to assess local food needs and resources through a participatory process. So far communities in nine cities (including Austin, Detroit, Los Angeles, and San Francisco) across the United States have participated in the project, with excellent results and concrete follow-up actions. The communities — which are generally low-income and ignored by central governments — begin to see their local areas in terms of food, where to get it, what is unavailable, and what needs to change to create a more equitable and sustainable system. By identifying systematic gaps in food access, the communities can come together around economic issues (Community Food Security Coalition 2002).

Moving towards Action

The organization Sustain has conducted four unique community mapping projects that bring diverse people together around graphic representations of local food issues. The process identifies local food problems through an exploration of people's experiences. That step is followed by community-based solutions and actions to meet local people's needs. Sustain emphasizes that the process is more than consultation, that the process of participatory appraisal, already used with success in Nepal, India, and Ghana, ensures genuine participation. Projects start from local, everyday experience and analyze that experience to turn participation into action (Sustain 2002).

Keeping Everyone at the Table

The Food Project in Boston boasts two community gardens, one downtown and one in the suburbs. The same staff administers both locations, but the two communities have very different profiles. One neighbourhood is inner-city and low-income; the other is suburban and middle- to upper-income. The daily operation of the Food Project is extraordinary. The project is run by youth participants. The adult staff members provide facilitation training and support, but, processes, and operations are all decided in a participatory process by the youth participants. Not only do they have clear procedures for decision-making, but they work hard to achieve particular relations of trust, courage to speak, and ongoing evaluation of both themselves and others. All of these practices ensure the widest possible distribution of democratic power. As many co-ops have learned to their cost, it is not enough just to give people power or a voice. They have to have a reason to use that power or voice and to be convinced of the possibility of effectiveness in this use. Aside from producing wonderful organic produce sold in various places, the Food Project teaches young people how to speak and lead in groups, how to work with and respect others, and how to commit to each other in a complex project (Food Project 2002).

Creating Lasting Coalitions Based on Democratic Principles

The B.C. Food Systems Network came to life in 1999. Its first mission was to facilitate presentations from diverse representatives and stakeholders from all over the province at the hearings of the Select Standing Committee on Agriculture and Fisheries. As the hearings moved across the province, at each site the network helped to organize presentations from farmers, community kitchen organizers, community gardeners, community nutritionists, First Nations, and Good Food Box organizers. After the initial series of presentations to government witnesses, the Network continued with another gathering of the community-based food organizations in 2000. The meeting featured a careful democratic process of participation and resulted in an increased awareness of food policy and shared food insecurity issues (B.C. Food Systems Network 2002). In addition to the conscious application of principles of participation and direct democracy,[2] the B.C. Food Systems Network also represents ongoing coalition work based on education by and for the people.

These bare-bones descriptions tell the stories of the initiatives in the rhetoric of hope and inspiration. The challenge here is to delve deeper. For instance, when we stand in the field with the Boston Food Project youth, engaging in weeding or perhaps in one of their trust-building exercises, we need to ask: what has moved this initiative from voices to power? What are they doing in California, the United Kingdom, Boston, and British Columbia that sets the projects apart from more conventional notions of getting people's voices heard? How can we emulate these instances of strong democratic practice? Each initiative adds to and enriches the definition of democracy: how do we get people to the table, how do we arrive at action once we are there, and then what makes us stay at the table to once again speak and act? Finally, how do we learn to act and speak with others at other tables?

The Prices of Democracy

> Our objective is not only to invent responses but to invent a way of inventing responses. (Bourdieu 1998: 58)

In 2000 Toronto's biggest natural food store had empty shelves. Still, the store was thriving, as if the less its staff put up, the better they did. This paradox has something to say about alternative food economies; about the anti-GMO movement; and about democratic power. It also says something about that sacred tenet of conventional economics: the notion of equilibrium (see chapter 3).

Why were some shelves empty? As a worker co-op that has been in existence for decades, the Big Carrot has grown and expanded, outlasted its competitors, and easily fended off the aggressive encroachment of Canada's first Whole Foods Market. The store makes all of its major strategic decisions by achieving consensus, which can in itself be a complex process: it involves all of the workers, who are also the owners (although new workers go through a probationary period before they are admitted to membership status). The Big Carrot has a board and a staff hierarchy for its day to day operations, as well as various committees that can make recommendations to board and membership. At the time of the empty shelves, the store had over thirty worker-owners; and it had empty shelves because, after a long decision-making process, its staff had removed all foods containing genetically modified organisms.

The store's Standards Committee had brought the issue forward and did the research, education, and advocacy that went into the decision to withdraw all GMO foods. Over two years of discussion and even acrimonious argument, the thirty-odd member-owners had examined all the evidence and decided that, although the decision would hurt the bottom line, they were going to take action.

The Big Carrot contacted every single one of its hundreds of suppliers to request a letter stating the GMO status of the products being supplied. After numerous requests, if a letter was not forthcoming, or if the letter was vague, the item was marked for removal. The day that the Big Carrot opened without GMOs, the shelves showed large gaps and some favourite items were missing (especially in the chip and snack aisle). Small signs explained that the item had been removed due to its GMO content or because the GMO content had not been or could not be verified by the manufacturer.

The reaction from the natural food industry ranged from puzzlement to horror. The industry (suppliers, salespeople, distributors) was slow to see the transformative nature of the GMO issue and tended to view it indulgently, like the latest diet craze. The idea that a major store would remove top-selling items — and leave gaping holes! — went against everything that many people thought about retail and the market.

It is a sacred precept of retail economics that you do not under any circumstances leave shelves empty. Supersized supermarkets go to great lengths to figure out ways of eliminating staff while still keeping the shelves stocked; this has led to new habits of design for the store shelves and new ways of managing inventory. The empty spaces or holes are dangerous because they might give the consumer ideas: instead of trying to choose between this or that bag of chips, a customer might see that empty space and choose to buy nothing at all. The consumers, trapped like rats in the supermarket maze, shopping until they drop, might be jolted out of the hypnosis of consumption and travel to a new place that the supermarket definitely does not want them to see.

Tradespeople did predict a significant drop in sales. The Big Carrot worker-owners also believed that it would hurt their bottom line, but they went ahead anyway. As it turned out, the store's sales increased considerably, and it became busier than ever — although that result does not explain what happened.

The Big Carrot story provides a fascinating counterpoint to consumer theory, to the willingness to pay theory and the idea that sales occur at an equilibrium point of demand and supply. In this case the Big Carrot was better off because the staff did not respond to demand. Most of the store's customers were willing to continue to purchase the genetically modified potato chips — that is, they were willing to pay. Instead the Big Carrot offered information. The staff used the store as a giant blackboard to teach people about the omnipresence of GMOs in their food, even in so-called "natural" food. The worker-owners were surprised at the increase in sales, as well as an onslaught of media attention brought on by the policy.

It is an inevitable part of the workings of a natural food store or co-op that the people involved all fight over the issue of standards. Do you provide everything the customers want, and then try to teach them about food politics so they will make better choices, or do you refuse to stock certain items? The usual foods slated for removal are refined sugars, preservatives, meat, stimulants like coffee and chocolate, and alcohol. The Big Carrot just took this practice a little farther by removing something so ubiquitous that it left gaps on the shelves (although the staff members were surprised at how quickly they were able to fill these gaps — organic chips coincidentally appeared on the market at about the same time).

Patience and the Democratic Process

What brought the Big Carrot to take this step, which represented such a great break with standard economic theory and in particular the much-vaunted theory of equilibrium? As a co-op, what the Big Carrot did, essentially, was engage in an intensive process of democratic decision-making. In its co-op structure, all voting members must agree on strategic decisions. As various staff members told me, there was no agreement on this particular step at the beginning. The idea of dropping GMOs was brought forward by new members, not the founders (many of whom are still around), but young and (as a founder said) enthusiastic new worker-owners. There was resistance to the idea. Many people were worried that eliminating GMOs would hurt the store. One person commented that people were scared. Members initially agreed only on doing research on the issue, and the research was followed by numerous presentations at staff meetings. Eventually, still with some disagreement, even shouting, the co-op came to a consensus, and the Big Carrot became the first store in North America to drop GMOs.

Many co-op observers, even supporters, like to point out that it can take co-ops a long time to make decisions. As Heather Barckley, the Big Carrot's board president, told me, "The reality of trying to get forty-five people to agree on something can be like pulling teeth." Barckley, whose task it is to facilitate staff meetings, said it can take half an hour to decide on one issue that seems like it should take a few minutes. It's like "tugging and pulling backwards and forwards." On some issues the membership tends to be conservative; on other issues it might be ready to take risks. "It's a constant backwards and forwards but that's the way it's supposed to be."

Achieving agreement, change, and collaboration in a co-operative system requires patience, careful listening, and time. Many people will complain that democracy, especially in business, simply takes too long. Yet the fruit of the process can be the building of strong bonds and a community-wide commitment that can weather great challenges and the vicissitudes of poverty and economic downturns in a way that far surpasses the abilities of non-democratic structures. In an interview George LaBelle, who helped to organize the United Maritime Fishermen (UMF), described the time-consuming co-operative work that he had experienced in working to amalgamate three fisheries co-ops on Prince Edward Island.

> I set a goal of getting the fisheries co-ops into membership with the United Maritime Fishermen and getting amalgamation between

three on the north point of the island. We had had short courses the last couple of days, a credit union session and sessions in the store and square dancing. Some of [the co-ops] thought this was right so they made the decision to [amalgamate and join the UMF]. Down at another place, the manager there, he ran that thing himself. And I go in there and tried to talk to him and I wasn't getting anywhere so I just went after that and I'd say "hello" and "what's going on" and go down and throw some stones in the water.

LaBelle explained that one day the manager followed him to the water and finally started to talk; he had been selling to the corporate middlemen, who had suddenly dumped him without warning, refusing to buy his fish. He was finally ready to sign up with the UMF and work with others to sell their fish co-operatively. LaBelle's patience is the essence of economic democracy; it is not enough just to put forward your ideas about an important project — you have to give others time to listen and to speak.

As the Co-op Atlantic co-operators reminded me, throughout the dialogic process of decision-making they will fight for their own point of view. The opportunity to discuss the problems means that once a decision is made the participants will know why it was made and can feel they were heard. The support for the action becomes correspondingly richer and deeper. The Big Carrot's Asa Copithorne explained, "Even if the individual doesn't agree with it, just the fact that they took part in some of the debates or even just that they were in the room at the time, that they were aware that it has been discussed, that they had the opportunity to voice their opinion, that helps people to accept decisions that are made that they don't necessarily agree with." At first he called this process "informal," but later concluded that it was democracy.

It has always puzzled me when people complain about the endless meetings that are an inevitable part of a smoothly functioning co-op. Would people really prefer to have a CEO, with interests quite other from theirs, make all the decisions for them? Democracy is hard work, even ugly at times but it is made harder and uglier by the barren notions we have about democratic process. All of us have been in meetings that digress, that go on too long about nothing, that are monopolized by the same person who drones on for minutes at a time. These problems, however, are not innate in democracy, but in the widespread lack of training in facilitation and democratic practice.

An ethnographer from Mars would find it odd that we in North America are so proud (even aggressive) about an institution that we know so little about — democracy. The Big Carrot board president, who performed the extraordinary feat of facilitating thirty-odd stubborn and opinionated people through this important decision, remarked to me that new worker-members have to be taught how democracy works. Like many new co-operators, they believe that being in a co-op means that they finally have a voice, and it's a voice they want to exercise at all times. Barckley pointed out that all the member-owners start out as clerks in the store. Given the Big Carrot's hierarchical staff structure, when they are working on the floor they have a manager or several managers to answer to. In addition, they have no say in the operations of other departments — they should not wander over to the deli and harangue the manager there for using, say, soy sauce instead of tamari. But in staff meetings they have an equal say, and (harder to remember) an equal right to listen carefully to everyone else.

Successful democratic dialogue requires this ability to make decisions in regulated moments of equalized power. The Big Carrot members were not expected at the beginning to know enough to make a strategic decision about the issue of GMOs. The decision came only after two years of research and knowledge transfer; and it was by no means a foregone conclusion. The decision was made in the context of power equity — in staff meetings where all members assembled as equal owners of the co-op.

The importance of knowledge in an economic democracy spilled over from the Big Carrot's staff meetings to later developments. The empty shelves with the explanatory tags meant that the staff assumed that the customers would also grow and change, learn and possibly shift their opinions, and that they would derive a benefit from knowledge. Beyond the doors of the Big Carrot, the store took the extraordinary step of freely offering all of its hard-won research information to any other independent store that wanted to consider going GMO-free. For years, though, despite the widespread interest among natural food stores, no other operation took up the challenge — in some ways, the Big Carrot's very different approach to knowledge circulation may have seemed too radical. Only much later did another Toronto store, Karma Co-op, follow up on the offer.

When I interviewed her Barckley was already looking ahead to the next big decision. The Big Carrot, she said, cannot stand still; it must constantly change to survive, and that means more democratic dialogue. More shouting. She seemed to feel a fair degree of equanimity when she contemplated this future. "We're always arguing here about what we sell. We always will." She added that "sometimes" the arguing "upsets some of the members who aren't used to it, but it's all part of the process. You can't get forty-five people in a room and have them all agree. It's just not going to happen, and they will argue, but as long as they keep it on a reasonable level I think it's better. I'd rather they do that than sit there (sometimes as they are wont to do) and not say a word." In the rapid growth sector that is natural food, change is much more of an issue than is stability or equilibrium. The failure to recognize this issue has hurt many natural food businesses, as they try to keep doing what they were doing before, maintaining a status quo, as the business bulges beneath them, making staff, capital, and space demands that they don't notice until it is too late.

I have worked recently in renewable energy co-ops and find a key metaphor for democracy in that sector. When you install your solar panels to produce energy, you will produce one level of power (voltage). However, in order for your new watts to be shared in a publicly owned system, the locally produced power has to be "stepped up" or "transformed" to be able to feed into the electric grid (which has higher volts). If you attempt to create a circuit from the lower voltage solar panels directly to the higher voltage transmission lines you get an explosion, and a sound like frying bacon. Likewise, our society seems these days to be locked into systems where small-load wires are connected to big-load wires without any intermediate transformation. The result is not healthy (democratic) exchange, but explosions and fried circuits.

As North American nations struggle to convince people to bother to go to the polls at all, we must find a transformative exchange to rejuvenate our inadequate (and potentially explosive) democracies. Francesca Polletta, in *Freedom Is an Endless Meeting*, quotes the Port Huron Statement (issued by activist movements in the 1960s) to define participatory democracy:

> In a participatory democracy, the political life would be based on several root principles: that decision-making of basic social consequence be carried on by public groups; that politics be seen positively, as the art of collectively creating an acceptable pattern of social relations; that politics has the function of bringing people out of isolation and into community. (Polletta 2002: 126)

The work of participatory social or economic democracy insists on consensus, and a shift in our attitude to decision-making, our power relations, and the negotiation of interests. Consensus as defined by economic democracy is just the kind of monster, a multi-headed hydra, that we might need instead of equilibrium.

Democratic organizations, including co-operatives, used the concept of consensus deliberately and often quite formally. "Consensus" means more than agreement. It can also, according to the *Oxford English Dictionary*, be a "feeling, thinking or judging together," a harmonizing. Thus consensus is not reached by voting alone, although voting may be involved. Polletta (2002: 210) states: "Decision-making that is deliberative may end in a vote, probably one requiring a supermajority. But what distinguishes it from majoritarian voting in an adversary system is its emphasis on having participants make their reasoning accessible and legitimate to each other."

Consensus offers participants a rich panoply of positions and strategies beside which the anemic process of voting used by most state democracies pales by comparison. Participants can agree with reservations (which they present). They can agree not to block the action, though they might disagree with the decision. They can choose to block or veto, and discussion can either continue or the issue can be dropped at that point. They can also abstain from participation in the voting, as long as they clarify why they are abstaining.

Quaker meetings base decisions on consensus; deliberations can take months, as all of the participants express and discuss their thoughts, interests, and reservations. In this way, however, they are able to reach difficult and even dangerous positions — the kind of decisions that found them, for instance, on the front lines of the 1960s anti-war movement (in non-violent protests). The difference in strategic decision-making offered by economic democracies is both small and monumental. It is like the difference between a Western orchestra and a Javanese gamelan ensemble. The Western orchestra tunes to the oboe's or concertmaster's A. The gamelan players tune to each other, so that each ensemble has its unique tuning and its unique sound. Likewise, each moment of economic democracy is wildly, deliciously different, and yet, just as we recognize the beauty of gamelan music, we can recognize each of those moments as an expression of true democracy. An economic culture can attain an ability to transform and change by building consensus rather than reaching for equilibrium.

As Polletta (2002: 183) points out, the work of consensus offers a transformative view of interests that opposes and humanizes the notion of interest or self-interest: "Interests are seen as developing in and through relationships with others. Self-interest is also seen as encompassing more than material concerns." Willingness to pay theory assumes that the self-interest of consumers is transparent and unchanging, and needs only to be unveiled by the relentless auction of price between buyer and seller. Consensus work assumes that interests are generated through the decision-making process itself. "The alternative... is that both individual and common interests may emerge from discussion and deliberation — not through a process of negotiation (which assumes that interests are fixed) but through a process of self and collective discovery" (2002: 187).

The insistence of the Big Carrot and other economic democracy groups on consensus is not idealistic, but posits an essential alternative to conventional economic practice. It insists on the dynamics of the negotiation of interest; it values conflict and conflict resolution; it assumes regulated moments of equalized (transformed) power; it assumes change, both personal and social, that can be reached only through the dialogical exchange of views and a genuine, transformative education that is expected to leave everyone, educators and educated alike, in new positions as the process unfolds. "Democracy in social movements does not produce dutiful citizens," Polletta (2002: 230) argues. "It produces people who question the conventional categories and responsibilities of citizenship — and who question the boundaries of the political, the limits of equality, and the line between people and their representatives."

The Big Carrot's relation to decision-making, democratic change, and knowledge is indeed transformative. The Big Carrot, though by no means an isolated example, is of significant influence in the region. It is one of the largest and most successful natural food stores in Canada. Its structure is an asset, not a hindrance. It also has a unique relation to surrounding businesses; its premises are located on a small "commons," of which the store was given a third-ownership by the forward-thinking landowner. The profits of the land ownership in the commons must be invested, with one-third to go to a community economic development fund (focused on food initiatives); the other two-thirds go to reinvestment in the store. The businesses the store shares space with are, to a degree, like-minded: an environmental goods store, an independent book-seller, and massage therapists. The Big Carrot also believes that the circulation of knowledge — its symbolic capital — will benefit everyone, growing in value (see Mauss 1967). In the spirit of the gift economy, they offered the results of their two years of painstaking research to the natural food community. This is an alternative economic enterprise that is loudly visible and powerful in the progress of a volatile sector. It threatens to transform economic practice beyond the bounds of its front doors.

From Voices to Power

> The Vía Campesina works in an environment of constant tension and reaffirmation.... It is a movement in which participants from around the world seek not only to provide an alternative voice in international forums, but also to use the connections among themselves to build a solid foundation for their lives. (Desmarais 2007: 198–99)

From the work of the PFC to the push to relocalization, then, the step from principles to action is by no means an obvious one. Once voices begin to sound together, to speak about food (and economics), how are these disparate words to come together in practice and change? The authors of *The Land of Milk and Money*, the PFC report, struggled with how to explain the dilemmas posed by the hearings, and the tendency of consumers and producers to blame each other for the problems of the food system. They wondered how to get people to recognize mutual interests and focus on structural problems rather than blaming each other in a fruitless and angry babble.

One reason the step from voices, or witnessing, to action is non-obvious is because knowledge alone is not enough to change people's minds. The way in which information is offered up is at least as important as what is actually said. Corporate spin-doctors are well aware of this lesson. The truthfulness of utterances resonates with the trustworthiness of the speaker and the process of conviction and belief that is cultural and not inevitable (see Austin 1975).

Sociologists have demonstrated, for instance, that a knowledge of impending environmental crisis — a knowledge now held by the majority of people in the United States and Canada — is not enough to cause them to act. Thus, it may be naive to think that all we have to do is to inform consumers about the issues (of unsustainable food practices, or agricultural workers forced to work with pesticides without protection, or dangerous food products, or global warming) and they will change their purchase decisions. Obviously, if that were true, there would be a very different food system in place. Then, too, sociologists disagree about what makes people act. For people wanting to change the food system, this is the million-dollar question: how do we tell everyone about the problems in such a way that people move from speaking and hearing to action? How do we get from knowledge to action?

The Roots of Popular Education in Canada

> Discussions about the quality and distribution of food leave most of us feeling overwhelmed and depressed. We are told that one food causes cancer, and another raises blood cholesterol. We need this vitamin to counteract the effects of that poison. We listen to endless debates between vegetarians, meateaters, and other nutritional theorists. We are confronted with the undeniable facts of worldwide malnutrition and the exploitation of third world countries.... Unfortunately, most solutions to these problems are phrased in terms of individual responsibility. ("Women Helping Women," People's Food Commission 1979)

At the root of democratic practice lies an elaborated process of listening and speaking, a relation to other people's voices and their knowledge. This practice can lead to real change. Such a participatory and dialogic process is embodied in many instances of food activism. The notion of democratic dialogue is integral to a radical approach to education. It is no coincidence that the Big Carrot's significantly different attitude to knowledge and education is echoed in important education movements that have been part of democratic and dialogic work for change. The People's Food Commission and the Coady movement for co-op development in Atlantic Canada predate but may herald popular education initiatives in Canada. As Denise Nadeau (1996:

4) describes it: "Popular education brings ongoing 'consciousness-raising' to organizing. It shifts the emphasis from organizing for single events to organizing a group of isolated individuals into a collective of people committed to acting together for justice." This kind of education seeks not just moments of democracy, but a time for democracy, perhaps even a whole history.

Popular education focuses on the link between education and (democratic) action. Popular education makes this link through an analysis of power: who has it, who doesn't; what kind of power each person or group has; and who constitutes their allies. C. Douglas Lummis (1996: 43) states: "Democracy presents us with a dilemma. On the one hand, the people are free and to be respected: they should be left as they are. On the other hand, if the people are to hold power they must form themselves into a body by which power in principle can be held." The principles of a popular education are key to the movement for food democracy, providing a tried and true process for moving from experience to action.

Some of the most interesting movements for social change around food, which echo these principles of democracy even if they do not use the word, incorporate popular education initiatives. The Landless Workers' Movement (MST) for land reform and indigenous agriculture in the South (mostly Brazil, but inspiring movements elsewhere as well) insists on education among the people occupying land. The land parcels that they occupy usually lie disused and are part of giant estates amassed by the powerful. Extensive land grabs removed the land from access to people who need food and are willing to grow it. Sue Branford and Jan Rocha (2002: 112) write about the movement: "Wherever there is an MST occupation, camp or settlement, there is a school.... The struggle for land has also become a struggle for education, for schools, for the right to know." The learners are peasants and their families are occupying land in order to farm it. They are under constant threat of violent eviction, although if they manage to stay long enough they can win legal rights to the land. These learning venues occur despite the dangerous and oppressive context. According to Branford and Rocha (2002: 125), "For the sem-terra [landless], true education not only teaches you how to read and write but also instills in you the courage to rebel." Radical education thus occurs while the landless work to redress the unequal distribution of power.

Farmer movements such as Brazil's landless movement and other serious campaigns to return power to the rural producers, many of which collaborate through the international Vía Campesina movement, are determined to maintain the movements as peasant and rural producer-based movements. La Vía Campesina bans sympathetic NGOs from its membership based on the principle that even if the organizations have the best intentions in the world, the uneven distribution of power and access to resources would inevitably distort the power of the non-farmers in the movement (Desmarais 2007).

La Vía Campesina grows and thrives despite daunting obstacles from the power of the World Trade Organization and its associated transnationals. The coalition continues to put pressure on the international powerbrokers of food, protesting to save its members' livelihoods wherever the powermongers gather. La Vía Campesina has been instrumental in the breakdown of international trade talks and initiating vigorous citizen protest, from Seattle to Hong Kong. Annette Desmarais (2007: 27) writes, "Through solidarity and unity, the Vía Campesina has consolidated a collective peasant identity as 'people of the land,' mounted radical opposition to multilateral institutions, defined alternative policies on key issues of concern to rural communities, and engaged in collective action in efforts to build food sovereignty."

The work of land reform and development of sustainable, locally based agriculture (that is, farming first and foremost for subsistence and local markets) has given rise to the Farmer Field School (FFS) movement. These venues for peer exchange and education provide the tools for a revival of indigenous agriculture, focused on food provision and attuned to the local habitat, indigenous varieties and limited means of peasant farmers. The movement arose first in Indonesia, then spread across Asia and Southeast Asia.

Michel Pimbert (2002: 3) argues that the pedagogical approach of the Farmer Field School reflects the kind of philosophy inherent in sustainable agriculture: "The kind of social learning, negotiation and collective action associated with community based FFS lends itself to a mode of decision making needed for the local adaptive management of ecosystems, landscapes and the ecological services they provide." Indigenous farmers have shown a great interest in agro-ecology, the movement for sustainable agriculture that incorporates the health of the community, the planet, and the people who farm and eat (see Wright and Wolford 2003). The Farmer Field schools also lead to an increased commitment to participatory democracy: "Many FFS alumni have grown stronger in the belief that democracy without citizen participation and discussion is ultimately an empty and meaningless concept" (Pimbert 2002: 7; see also Pontius, Dilts, and Bartlett 2002).

The educational work in farmers' movements around the world recalls the Coady movement and the Farm Radio forums in Canada from 1941 to 1965. The National Farm Radio was organized jointly by the Canadian Broadcasting Corporation (public radio), the Canadian Association for Adult Education, and the Canadian Federation of Agriculture. The forums featured educational radio programs with accompanying study guides for farmers, who would gather in someone's home to listen to and discuss the program together. The show's motto was "Read. Listen. Discuss. Act" (CBC 2008).

Education was also central to the Coady movement in the Maritimes, with its focus on economics and literacy education for fishermen and farmers. The co-operatives were seen as a practical goal in the larger education mission.

A Fractious Democracy

> If there are contradictions or differences, this is normal. What we need to do in the Via Campesina is to ensure that we always have the capacity to listen to each other and always act with deep respect for the way of thinking of each of the organizations and to always discuss in an open and transparent way and then move forward. (Rafael Alegría, Operational Secretariat, 1996–2004, quoted in Desmarais 2007: 38)

The resuscitation of direct/participant/radical democracy in our era of job and food insecurity, loss of shelter, hunger, and deepening poverty in countries like Canada represents an exciting trend towards rethinking our political relations with each other. What characterizes direct or participatory democracy? As Lummis (1996: 138) puts it, "Participatory democracy means the right to participate in the making of decisions that affect one's life." The PFC in the late 1970s and La Vía Campesina today promote a process that is revisited and theorized in work such as Lummis's *Radical Democracy* and Judy Rebick's *Imagine Democracy* (2000).

Lummis argues that radical democracy (which only appears for Lummis in certain historical moments) is not inherent in the institutions of democratic societies, but is a state of mind, a way of relating to others, which stands aside from a state or any other institution and can in fact have unpredictable effects on institutions. Lummis (1996: 139) states: "It is the basic idea of democracy that the people are sovereign: their power is prior to the power of the state." Rebick (2000: 9) draws inspiration from Thomas Paine's definitions of democracy: "Democracy should be designed, argued Paine, to bring out that genius in everyday people because society would benefit tremendously from unleashing so much energy and creativity." Democracy movements across the world make a careful distinction between the kind of democracy practised by the United States or Canada and so-called strong democracy, in which people's voices are made effective by a combination of equity, equal access to power, participation, and proportional representation (see Swift 2002).

Food democracy initiatives reflect a global climate of change and the search for strong democracy. Tim Lang (1999: 218) writes, "I use the expression food democracy to refer to the demand for greater access and collective benefit from the food system.... Ultimately, food is both a symptom and a symbol of how we organize ourselves and our societies.... From the political perspective, it makes sense to see the dynamics of the food system as a titanic struggle between the forces of control and the pressure to democratize." The challenges and struggle to achieve democracy may be embodied in the workings of the food system.

The Meeting Went on for Hours...

Democratic politics must accept division and conflict as unavoidable, and the reconciliation of rival claims and conflicting interests can only be partial and provisional. (Mouffe 1996: 24).

Conflict is an aspect of democracy that is often buried and therefore misused. It represents, among other things, a thoughtful engagement and negotiation of conflict that distinguishes strong democratic functioning. As Neva Hassanein (2003: 79) points out, "Conflict is not something to shy away from; conflict leads to change."

When you have, for instance, a roomful of Atlantic co-operators who sit on various different boards and for decades have been part of million-dollar decisions, you would not expect them to give up their positions without a fight. The co-op history of Canada tends to focus on this conflict and on the contradictions of co-ops, on ideals vs. practice, for instance. Indeed, the literature on co-ops can make you wonder how co-ops ever get anything done. But that particularly discouraging view comes from applying a static time frame to a dynamic situation. Within that snapshot view, it is quite likely that at any given moment various groups within a co-op or organization will be at loggerheads; that still moment can also represent what is in fact an ongoing process of negotiation, compromise, and innovative solution. When we succeed in capturing co-op operations as a process, not a structure, we have succeeded in glimpsing food democracy.

Co-ops are charged not only with making a complex process (democracy) happen but also with teaching people how to carry out that work and why it is valuable and possibly essential. In addition, in the most common form of food co-ops for many people, consumer co-ops (owned by the customers), the power of the staff (non-member/owners) is unclear and not mandated by the structure. That is, a key category of interest or stake in the business — that of the workers — is not represented, which reduces the democratic quality. When interests and their companion knowledges are not brought to the table, democracy falters and decision-making is distorted. This problem finds interesting solutions in multi-stakeholder co-ops or the even more innovative new form in Quebec called solidarity co-ops (*coopérative de solidarité*). Solidarity co-op owner/members include workers and users of the co-op (members, clients) as well as community supporters (Coopérative de Développement Régional Montréal-Laval 2007).

The concept of food democracy has roared into food activism, becoming a term bruited from title pages and appearing in resounding conclusions. It encapsulates a yearning felt in food change work, for more participation, for more distributed power, for a sense of control over our means of survival. Democracy is in danger of being naturalized by right and left alike as the only way to go to create fair and equitable politics — with a sense of inevitability that, given its short and place-specific history, would certainly bear further examination. This is not to say that peoples around the world have not yearned, and died, for democratic concepts — the right to self-determination, the right to vote for representatives, the right to participate in political dialogue, and various freedoms associated with democratic process — but that in North America the word itself has become reified, an anthem, a call to arms for right and left. Particularly in North America, though, it is also a cultural concept, with an important ability to move people to action and to stir their hearts.

The concept of food democracy may well be a key to changing an inequitable food system that is failing so many of us. As well as the emphasis on participation, the witnessing of voices, and the movement from voice to action, in food democracies the resurrection of conflict as a positive force in social relations presents one of the greatest challenge to conventional food economics. The notion of constructive conflict can subvert the standard opposition of producer and consumer. This was the case for John Harvie's Co-op Atlantic beef producers and their co-op retailer counterparts. "We began to work together," Harvie said, "realized we weren't so bad after all." He spoke of how they had "a barbecue with producers and retailers laughing it up, it's quite a thing: it's quite significant."

Food democracy, by assuming the value of ongoing negotiation, disagreement, and change, assumes a culture built on economic relations that are constantly in flux; just as symbolic capital determines the flavour and the success of alternative economic relations by circulating, so too must an economic system built on democracy be adept at change. The success of food democracy, or any democratic system, may lie in a yearning for equilibrium and for a resolution of all conflict that is never quite realized but impels ongoing action — witnessing, speaking, participating — in other words, change driven by hope. The work of food democracy, like that of ecology, does not discard equilibrium but reimagines equilibrium. Food democracy allows participants to depart from a search for a perfect balance point and to focus instead on the negotiation of duelling and overlapping interests.

People sometimes complain about how a co-op closed down, and they conclude from this that the form must be inadequate or that it leads only to impermanent economic experiments. But not only do co-ops survive better than conventional businesses, but also such alternative economic formations are in place to fill everyone's needs rather than to persist and rack up profits at the expense of everything else. A co-op may fill that role successfully for a decade or more, after which the community might have other needs and move on. Sometimes the co-op will move with them; at other times new alternative economic relations will be constructed. Aside from real crises and business failures, which are statistically a great deal fewer than most people imagine, this responsiveness is the strength of such alternatives, not their weakness, just as a strong democracy knows to heave out incumbent officials who are no longer filling the needs of the nation's people.

The Aroma of Change

We have detected the aromas of an alternative economics wafting deliciously from the tales of organic agriculture, anti-GMO initiatives, co-ops, fair trade movements, and food sovereignty actions. Taken together, this edible action has challenged conventional consumer theory, as well as the mouldy doctrines of capital, supply and demand, and equilibrium. We are not exactly imagining a better world, although that is important as well. We are merely opening our eyes to the tools that lie close to hand all around, the resistance that breaks down hegemony, and which that hegemony cannot help but engender in its headlong course.

What kind of economic relations are driven by this dialogic, conflictual, participatory process? They are economic relations that are above all amenable to change, that embrace the process of conflict, dialogue, and negotiation as a necessary part of economic exchange. This type of change is quite different from the kind heralded by corporate action: mergers, downsizing, elimination of the workforce, reduction of environmental responsibility. CEOs are proud of being able to make such decisions with cold calculation in order to maximize shareholder equity. Such change is, when you come right down to it, astonishingly uniform and witheringly lacking in innovation. One can easily predict what a corporation will do next, for in fact it has a limited number of options. In the case of our alternative economics, the process of dispute and consensus guarantees a kind of flexibility and creative thinking that is unavailable to the corporate model. The ability to change and innovate is precisely the strength of a democratic enterprise.[3]

Across the landscape that we have traversed, we can see the glow of alternatives that sparkle with difference and particularity. It is there that we find sheep farmers dismantling McDonald's; consumers demanding access to computers with their weekly box of produce; workers occupying and eventually owning bankrupt factories in Argentina; nations refusing to participate in the IMF and WTO (despite lucrative financial offers coupled with threats of violence), and a foreign state-owned oil company offering discounted oil to low-income Americans. In the movements of economic democracy, sustainable agriculture, and food sovereignty, we find new definitions of equity. Such initiatives wrest equity from the tiny text of corporate annual reports, where an investor's share of equity determines not equality but power over others — the more equity, the more votes. Equity in alternative food economies is restored and rehabilitated with commitments to fairness, equitability, and trust. As with all the economic terms redefined by the alternatives, we must decide which kind of equity we prefer.

Potatoes That Tell Stories

In other words, we are talking about a whole way of life when we talk about the food we eat, where we live, about marketing, economics and legal systems, and changing tax structures. (Ecology Action Centre, People's Food Commission, Halifax, 1979)

The questions I have raised throughout this book have investigated food innovations in order to study a culture of change. The key question is not so much what makes people change or act but what paths do people follow as they change the food system, and which paths will actually get us where we would like to be. The answers to the search for a new food economics, which already exists all around us, lie not in the nouns but in the verbs: we need not just to emphasize multiple interests, equity, and social capital, but also to focus specifically on *how* people negotiate and move among multiple interests, *how* they redefine consumer action, and *how* social capital is traded and exchanged to strengthen economic systems. These economic practices (negotiating, redefining, moving, trading, exchanging) are embedded in democracy. Where the conventional economic images would have the shuffling of the market come to rest at price, the workings of economic and food democracy talk about value. As Hassanein (2003: 85) puts it, "Food democracy is a method for making choices when values come into conflict and when the consequences of decisions are uncertain."

Although conventional economics often uses the concept of value interchangeably with price, the word necessarily drags in additional meanings of quality and ethics. Thus we can value both a friendship or a banana, but would avoid putting a price on the friendship. As goods move around through economic relations, the value that defines them orchestrates social and symbolic relations, histories of exchange, and the dialogic quality of shared accounting. Value is a result of people talking together about their commitments, trusts, and beliefs; it is a recognition of the shared quality of the goods that are exchanged. Harvie explained to me that the Atlantic-grown initiative (agri-food strategy) produces products that are not just commodities (to be priced in the teeter-tottering of an "efficient" market). He pointed out that the products have "some meaning, some value." Then in a rhetorical move echoed in another interview with the vice-president of Agriculture at Co-op Atlantic, he equated the "value" with a narrative: "We think if we can tell you where your potatoes were grown and by whom and why and for whom and deliver a superior quality product... we have a story to tell, instead of just selling a commodity."

For this co-op, economic goods are not just equivalent to cash; unlike money, these goods want to talk to us. They come to us trailing stories of where they have been, how they grew, who was part of their history. The narrative quality of everyday things, encapsulated in "value," opens goods up to the movement of ethics and history. They become part of a dialogue about who we are and where we want to be next. Value is necessarily negotiated between self and others. It is dialogic, even conflictual, an expression of an ongoing process of talking together, telling stories and taking multiple positions. Like a huge game of Twister, we get all mixed up ("whose leg is that anyway?"), and the resulting tangle is fruitful for society.

Hilary Wainwright (2003: 142) writes: "The most fundamental learning, or relearning, will have to go on in the public bodies: especially learning the ability to work with the unpredictability and initial chaos — generally organized chaos — of genuine democracy." Again, as Lévi-Strauss said, food is good to think with, and what we think about with food is economics, especially different kinds of economics. As with Lévi-Strauss's endlessly proliferating tomes about symbols, a "thick description" (as anthropologist Clifford Geertz calls it) of food in the world brings us back to a joyful and patterned chaos of specificity. This thinking may lead us to new, more people-oriented economies, but our alternative systems will always preserve the dynamic qualities of consensus and of difference. Food democracy, relocalization, and co-ops can change the way in which we "relate," that is, not only how we take shape around each other's needs, demands, and particularities, but also how we tell stories, as in "to relate a history." The narrative quality of "relations," whether economic or symbolic, must inform the direction we take to heal the rifts in our society.

To challenge the image of an impenetrable and monolithic capitalist economy, we must pursue alternatives that hover both within and without the dominant system. Following Gibson-Graham and other non-orthodox economists, I have argued that capitalism is, beneath its towering and hegemonic status in our society, riven with alternatives, and already fragmented by alternative patterns of economic exchange. The resistance and alternatives are both challenging and well-embedded in the workings of our economy. The cases range from movements for better food through food security initiatives and social movements that deliberately seek to change or to work outside market economics to the innovations of alternative economic organizations such as co-operatives. The alternatives emphasize and resolve different food problems, but they come together in a reverberating pattern of change. The paths lead over and over again towards democratic process. Once our ears are attuned to recognize this pattern as it comes to us over the jack-hammer clamour of the market economy, we can begin to see the alternatives and their successes everywhere.

Two people were walking down a busy city street. Cars bumped over potholes and blew their horns in frustration with each other. All around them, people rushed from one place to another, talking to one another, calling out to friends. One of the walkers paused and lifted a finger: "Did you hear that cricket?" she asked. Her friend was astonished. "How could you hear a cricket with all this noise around?" he asked. She pulled a handful of coins from her pocket and tossed them on the sidewalk where they clinked and rolled away. Everyone around them stopped to listen. "You see," she said, "it depends on what you are listening for." The practices of food action demand that we begin to listen: for democracy, for real education, and for social change.

Notes

1. I developed these principles originally for a section of food democracy on the website of FoodShare, for which I also researched the case studies cited here.
2. One key organizer for the B.C. Food Systems Network, Cathleen Kneen, was also an organizer with the People's Food Commission. When I remarked in the interview that I wanted to talk to her because of the similarity of the two projects, she said that the resemblance was intentional.
3. Likewise ecologists, in moving on from equilibrium and looking at dynamic and changing systems, were forced to develop the technical concept of "surprise" to describe the uneven and sometimes sudden changes that an ecosystem can undergo.

References

Ahn, Christine. 2003. "Death at the WTO." *Common Dreams*. September 12. Available at <http://www.commondreams.org/views03/0912-01.htm>, accessed July 2008.

Allen, Patricia. 1999. "Reweaving the Food Security Safety Net: Mediating Entitlement and Entrepreneurship." *Agriculture and Human Values* 16. Netherlands: Kluwer Academic Publishers.

Allen, Patricia, and Martin Kovach. 2000. "The Capitalist Composition of Organic: The Potential of Markets in Fulfilling the Promise of Organic Agriculture." *Agriculture and Human Values* 17. Netherlands: Kluwer Academic Publishers.

Altieri, Miguel. 1998. "Ecological Impacts of Industrial Agriculture and the Possibilities for Truly Sustainable Farming." *Hungry for Profit: Agriculture, Food, and Ecology*. Monthly Review 50, 3 (July/August).

Altieri, Miguel (ed.). 1998. "Hungry for Profit: Agriculture, Food, and Ecology." *Monthly Review* 50, 3 (July/August). Republished in Fred Magdoff (ed.), *Hungry for Profit*. New York: Monthly Review Press (2000).

Aranha, Adriana Veiga. (unpublished). "Food Security, Public Management and Citizenship: The Experience of Belo Horizonte 1993/2003." Presentation for workshop "Community Food Security," Ryerson University, Toronto, Canada, July 2003.

Aronowitz, Stanley. 1996. "Towards Radicalism." In David Trend (ed.) *Radical Democracy*. New York: Routledge.

Atlantic Co-operator. 2002. "Bringing Atlantic Farmers and Consumers Together." Available at <www.theatlanticco-operator.coop>, accessed December 2003.

Ausubel, Kenny. 1994. *Seeds of Change: The Living Treasure*. New York: Harper Collins.

Austin, John Langshaw. 1975. *How To Do Things With Words*. J.O. Urmson and Marina Sbisa (eds.). Cambridge, MA: Harvard University Press.

Ayala, Lucy (ed.). 2004. *II National Conference on Food and Nutritional Security*. Olinda, Brazil.

B.C. Food Systems Network. 2002. Website at <www.fooddemocracy.org/>.

Baker, Lauren. 2003. "Seeds of Our City: Case Studies from 8 Diverse Gardens in Toronto." Toronto: FoodShare.

Bakhtin, Mikhail Mikhailovich. 1981. *The Dialogic Imagination: Four Essays*. Trans. by Caryl Emerson and Michael Holquist. Austin: University of Texas Press.

Barboza, David. 2000. "Modified Foods Put Companies in a Quandary." *The New York Times*, June 3.

Barbolet, Herb, and R. Kneen. 1998. "FarmFolk/CityFolk: How a Coalition of Urban and Rural Organizations Is Empowering Local Groups and Increasing Activism." *Briarpatch* March, 27, 6–8.

Barndt, Deborah. 2002. *Tangled Routes: Women, Work and Globalization on the Tomato*

Trail. Aurora: Garamond Press.

Barnes, Alan. 1999. "Ideas Make the Difference." *Toronto Star.* November 20.

Barthes, Roland. 1957. *Mythologies.* New York: Noonday Press.

Beardsworth, Alan, and Theresa Keil. 1997. *Sociology on the Menu: An Invitation to the Study of Food and Society.* New York: Routledge.

Bebb, Adrian. 2004. "Genetically Modified Foods in Europe: Politicians Say Yes — Public Says No! Friends of the Earth." Press Release, May 19.

Beck, Ulrich. 1992. *Risk Society: Towards a New Modernity.* London: Sage.

_____. 1994. "The Reinvention of Politics: Towards a Theory of Reflexive Modernization." In U. Beck, A. Giddens and S. Lash (eds.), *Reflexive Modernization: Politics, Tradition and Aesthetics in the Modern Social Order.* Stanford: Stanford University Press.

Berry, Connie. 2003. "Juan Valdez, Meet Jane Walden: All Our Food Should Be 'Fair Trade' — in the North and South." *Alternatives Journal* 29: 26–27.

Berryman, Phillip. 1987. *Liberation Theology: The Essential Facts About the Revolutionary Movement in Latin America and Beyond.* London: I.B. Tauris and Co.

Bilger, Burkhard. 2004. "The Height Gap." *The New Yorker.* April 5.

Black, Maggie. 1992. *A Cause for Our Times: Oxfam, the First 50 Years.* Toronto: Oxford University Press.

Bourdieu, Pierre. 1977. *Outline of a Theory of Practice.* New York: Cambridge University Press.

_____. 1998. *Acts of Resistance: Against the Tyranny of the Market.* Trans. by Richard Nice. New York: New York Press.

Branford, Sue, and Jan Rocha. 2002. *Cutting the Wire: The Story of the Landless Movement in Brazil.* London: Latin American Bureau.

Bread for the World Institute. 2008. Available at <www.bread.org/learn/hunger-basics/hunger-facts-domestic.html> accessed July 2008.

Brown, Paul. 2001. "Genetically Engineered Rice Promoters 'Have Gone Too Far.'" *The Guardian.* Available at <wwww.theguardian.co.uk> accessed February 10, 2001.

_____. 2005. "Scientists Warn of Superweed Risk." *Guardian Unlimited* August 18.

Butler, C.T., and Keith McHenry. 1992. *Food Not Bombs.* Tucson: See Sharp Press.

Campaign for Ethical Marketing. 2004. Baby Milk Action campaign. Available at <www.babymilkaction.org> accessed July 2008.

Canadian Broadcasting Corporation (CBC). 2008. "National Farm Radio Forum." CBC Digital Archives. Available at <http://archives.cbc.ca/programs/508/> accessed July 2008.

Canadian Co-operative Association. 2003. Website at <http://www.coopscanada.coop/>.

Canadian Co-operative Association. 2005. *The Power of Co-operation.* Available at <http://www.coopscanada.coop/aboutcoop/coopweek/2005coopweek/index.cfm> accessed July 2008.

Canadian Organic Growers. 2007. Website at <www.cog.ca/organicstatistics.htm> accessed July 2008.

Carlsen, Laura. 2004. "The People of Corn." *New Internationalist* 374, December.

Carson, Rachel. 1962. *Silent Spring.* Boston: Houghton Mifflin.

Castleman, Amanda. 2003. "Food Fight Europe and America Gear Up for a

Confrontation at the WTO." *In These Times* May.

Centre for the Study of Cooperatives. 1992. *Co-operatives in Principle and Practice.* Occasional Paper #92-01, March 1992, Saskatoon: Centre for the Study of Co-operatives.

Charman, Karen. 2003. "Down on the BioPharm." *In These Times* February.

Chiasson, Joe Braemore. 1989. "Braemore Co-operative 1964–1989." Store pamphlet.

Civic Economics. 2004. "The Andersonville Study of Retail Economics." Available at <www.AndersonvilleStudy.com> accessed October, 2004.

Community Food Security Coalition. 2002. Website at <www.foodsecurity.org/index. html> accessed July 2008.

Consumer Reports. 2000. "Produce Safety: New Data on Pesticide Levels." September. Website at <www.consumerreports.org>. Article reprinted at <http://archives. foodsafety.ksu.edu/agnet/2000/10-2000/ag-10-23-00-01.txt> accessed July 2008.

Co-op Atlantic. 2003. Website at <www.co-opsonline.com> accessed July 2008.

Co-operative College of Canada. 1982. *Patterns and Trends of Canadian Co-operative Development.* Saskatoon: Co-operative College of Canada.

Coopérative de Développement Régional Montréal Laval. 2004. Website at <www. cdr.coop/> accessed July 2008.

Cooperative Grocer. 2003. Website at <www.cooperativegrocer.coop>.

Co-operative Union of Canada. 1981. *Cooperatives Canada.* Ottawa: Co-operatives Union of Canada.

Cox, Craig. 1994. *Storefront Revolution.* New Brunswick, NJ: Rutgers University Press.

Cummins, Ronnie (ed.). 1998. "Cover-up Alleged at Health Canada: Were Pushed to Approve Drug, Scientists Say." *The Globe and Mail* (Canada)/*The Toronto Star,* September 17. Available at <http://www.mindfully.org/GE/rBST-Coverup-Canada.htm> accessed July 2008.

Davis, Mike. 1998. *The Ecology of Fear: Los Angeles and the Imagination of Disaster.* New York: Metropolitan Books (Henry Holt and Company).

De Certeau, Michel. 1988. *The Practice of Everyday Life.* Trans. by S. Rendall. Berkeley: University of California Press.

Desmarais, Annette Aurélie. 2007. *La Vía Campesina: Globalization and the Power of Peasants.* Halifax: Fernwood Publishing.

Dicum, Gregory. 2006. "Fair to the Last Drop?" *Boston Globe.* Available at <http:// www.boston.com/news/globe/ideas/articles/2006/10/22/headline_fair_to_ the_last_drop/> accessed October 22, 2006.

Douglas, Mary. 1982. *In The Active Voice.* London: Routledge and Kegan Paul.

Douthwaite, Richard. 1992. *The Growth Illusion.* Tulsa: Council Oak Books.

_____. 1996. *Short Circuit: Strengthening Local Economics for Security in an Unstable World.* Devon, England: Green Books.

_____. 1996a. Reclaiming Community: Steps to Building a Healthy Local Economy. *New Internationalist* 278: 26–27.

Ecologist (editor). 2001. "You Dig?" 31, 2 (March).

ETC Group. 2003. "Oligopoly, Inc.: Concentration in Corporate Power: 2003." Available at <http://www.etcgroup.org/en/materials/publications.html?pub_

id=136> accessed July 2008.

_____. 2005. "Oligopoly, Inc. 2005: Concentration in Corporate Power." Available at <http://www.etcgroup.org/en/materials/publications.html?pub_id=42> accessed July 2008.

Fair Trade Toronto. 2007. Website at <www.fairtradetoronto.com> accessed July 2008.

Fairholm, Jacinda. 2002. "Growing New Farmers." Report of Major Project for Masters Degree submitted to the Faculty of Environmental Studies at York University.

Fallon, Sally. 2000. "Sausages, Sauerkraut and Cheese." *The Ecologist* 30, 4: 41.

Farm Folk/City Folk. 2003. Website at <www.ffcf.bc.ca> accessed July 2008.

Federated Co-operatives Ltd. 2008. Website at <www.fcl.ca> accessed July 2008.

Field, D., and A. Mendiratta. 1999. *Food 2002: Phase 2 Multisectoral Policy Recommendations.* Toronto: FoodShare.

Fiske, John. 1993. *Power Plays, Power Works.* New York: Verso.

Folbre, Nancy. 1994. *Who Pays For the Kids: Gender and the Structures of Constraint.* New York: Routledge Press.

Food and Agriculture Organization. 2004. "World Food Summit: Five Years Later Reaffirms Pledge to Reduce Hunger." Available at <http://www.fao.org/world-foodsummit/english/newsroom/news/8580-en.html> accessed July 2008.

Food and Agriculture Organization. 2008. Website at <http://www.fao.org> accessed July 2008.

Food Project (Boston). 2002. Website at <www.thefoodproject.org/> accessed July 2008.

FoodShare. 1999. "Food 2002 Report." Available at <http://www.foodshare.net/foodpolicy02.htm> accessed July 2008.

_____. 2007. "Program Overview 2007." Available at <foodshare.net/download/Overview2007.pdf> accessed July 2008.

Forgacs, David (ed.). 2000. *An Antonio Gramsci Reader: Selected Writings 1916–1935.* New York: Schocken Books.

Foucault, Michel. 2002. *The Order of Things: An Archaeology of the Human Sciences.* New York: Routledge.

Frank, Thomas. 2001. *One Market Under God.* New York: Anchor Books.

Freire, Paulo. 1988. *Pedagogy of the Oppressed.* New York: Continuum Publishing.

Friedmann, Harriet. 1993a. "After Midas' Feast: Alternative Food Regimes for the Future." In P. Allen (ed.), *Food for the Future: Conditions and Contradictions of Sustainability.* John Wiley and Sons.

_____. 1993b. "The Political Economy of Food: A Global Crisis." *New Left Review* 197, January–February.

Funes, Fernando, Luis García, Martin Bourque, Nilda Pérez, and Peter Rosset. 2003. *Sustainable Agriculture and Resistance: Transforming Food Production in Cuba.* Oakland, CA: Food First Books.

Geertz, Clifford. 1973. *The Interpretations of Cultures.* New York: Basic Books.

George, Susan. 1990. *Ill Fares the Land.* London: Penguin.

Gibson-Graham, J.K. 1996. *The End of Capitalism (As We Knew It): A Feminist Critique of Political Economy.* Malden, MA: Blackwell.

Gillam, Carey. 2003. "Monsanto Stock Slips on Pharmacia-Pfizer Deal." *Reuters*

Company News. Available at <http://www.organicconsumers.org/Monsanto/Shareholder0702.cfm> accessed July 2008.

Gillard, Michael Sean, Laurie Flynn, and Andy Rowell. 1999. "UK: International Scientists Back Shock Findings of Suppressed Research into Modified Food." *The Guardian* February 12.

Glasbeek, Harry. 2002. *Wealth by Stealth: Corporate Crime, Corporate Law, and the Perversion of Democracy*. Toronto: Between the Lines.

Goodman, David, and Michael Redclift. 1991. *Refashioning Nature: Food, Ecology and Culture*. London: Routledge.

Gorelick, Steven. 2000. "Solutions for a Farming Future." *The Ecologist* 30, June: 34–35.

Gunderson, Lance H., and C.S. Holling (eds.). 2002. *Panarchy: Understanding Transformations in Human and Natural Systems*. Washington: Island Press.

Guthman, Julie. 1998. "Regulating Meaning, Appropriating Nature: The Codification of California Organic Agriculture." *Antipode* 30, 2. Malden, MA: Blackwell.

Halpern, Sue. 1999. "Garden-Variety Politics." *Mother Jones* September/October.

Halweil, Brian. 2000. "Where Have All the Farmers Gone?" *WorldWatch* September/October.

Hamilton, Lisa. 1997. "Diamonds in the Dirt?" *Z Magazine*. Available at <http://www.zmag.org/zmag/viewArticle/13374> accessed July 2008.

Hannigan, John. 1995. "Social Construction of Environmental Problems." In *Environmental Sociology: A Social Constructionist Perspective*. New York: Routledge.

Hansen, Michael. 2000. "Genetic Engineering Is not an Extension of Conventional Plant Breeding." Consumer Policy Institute, January. Available at <http://www.consumersunion.org/food/widecpi200.htm> accessed July 2008.

Hassanein, Neva. 2003. "Practicing Food Democracy: A Pragmatic Politics of Transformation." *Journal of Rural Studies* 19, 1 (Jan.): 77–86.

Henderson, Hazel. 1996. *Creating Alternative Futures: The End of Economics*. Bloomfield, CT: Kumarian Press.

Henderson, Hazel. 1991. *Paradigms in Progress*. Indianapolis: Knowledge Systems.

Hines, Colin. 2001. "The New Protectionism." *The Ecologist* 31, March: 44–45.

Holling, C.S. 1973. "Resilience and Stability of Ecological Systems." *Annual Review of Ecology and Systematics* 4: 1–24.

hooks, bell. 1996. "Representation and Democracy: An Interview." In David Trend (ed.), *Radical Democracy: Identity, Citizenship and the State*. New York: Routledge.

Howard, Phil. 2007. "Organic Industry Structure." Available at <www.msu.edu/%7Ehowardp/organicindustry.html>.

Husbands, Winston. 1999. "Hungry for a Home: Housing, Hunger and Food Assistance in the Greater Toronto Area." Toronto: Daily Bread Food Bank.

International Co-operative Alliance. 2008. Website at <www.ica.coop> accessed July 2008.

Jones, Lucy. 2004. "How Fair Trade Hit the Mainstream." *BBC News Online*. March 2. Available at <http://news.bbc.co.uk/2/hi/business/3522059.stm> accessed July 2008.

Karma Co-op. 2003. Website at <www.karmacoop.org> accessed July 2008.

Kaskey, Jack. 2007. "Monsanto Loss Widens; 2008 Forecast Trails Estimates." *Bloomberg.* October 10. Available at <http://www.bloomberg.com/apps/news

?pid=20601087&sid=aYwErrIVTzWo&refer=home> accessed July 2008.

Keen, Steve. 2001. *Debunking Economics: The Naked Emperor of the Social Sciences*. New York: Zed Books.

Kelly, Marjorie. 2000. "The Divine Right of Capital: Stockholders as the New Aristocracy." *Tikkun*. July/August.

Kirby, Alex. 2003. "'Mirage' of GMs' Golden Promise." *BBC News Online*. September 24. Available at <http://news.bbc.co.uk/2/hi/science/nature/3122923.stm> accessed July 2008.

Klonsky, Karen. 2000. "Forces Impacting the Production of Organic Foods." *Agriculture and Human Values* 17. Netherlands: Kluwer Academic Publishers.

Kneen, Brewster. 1993. *From Land to Mouth*. Toronto: New Canada Publications.

_____. 1995. *Invisible Giant: Cargill and Its Transnational Strategies*. Halifax, NS: Fernwood Publishing.

_____. 1999. *Farmageddon: Food and the Culture of Biotechnology*. Gabriola Island, BC: New Society Publishers.

Koc, Mustafa, Rod MacRae, and Luc Mougeot (eds.). 1999. *For Hunger-Proof Cities: Sustainable Urban Food Systems*. Ottawa: International Development Centre.

Korten, David. 2001. *When Corporations Rule the World*. Bloomfield, CT: Kumarian Press.

Kovel, Joel. 2002. *The Enemy of Nature*. Halifax, NS: Fernwood Publishing.

Krugman, Paul. 2005. "Girth of a Nation." *The Agribusiness Examiner*. July 5. Available at <http://soundingcircle.com/newslog2.php/__show_article/_a000195-000779.htm> accessed July 2008.

Lang, Tim. 1999. "Food Policy for the 21st Century: Can It Be Both Radical and Reasonable?" In Mustafa Koc, Rod MacRae and Luc Mougeot (eds.), *For Hunger Proof Cities: Sustainable Urban Food Systems*. Ottawa: International Development Centre.

Langevin, Mark S., and Peter Rosset. 1997. "From *Food First Backgrounder*, Fall 1997." In Douglas H. Boucher (ed.), *The Paradox of Plenty: Hunger in a Bountiful World*. San Francisco: Food First.

Lawn, C.R. 2003. "Where Have All the Co-ops Gone?" *Fedco Seeds*. Fall. Available at <http://www.fedcoseeds.com/seeds/co_ops.htm> accessed July 2008.

Lévi-Strauss, Claude. 1962. *Totemism*. Trans. by R. Needham. Boston: Beacon Press.

_____. 1966. *The Savage Mind*. Chicago: University of Chicago Press.

Library and Archives of Canada. 1977–1980. People's Food Commission fonds. Archival number R3198-0-1-E. (PFC).

Lilliston, Ben, and Ronnie Cummins.1998. "Organic Versus 'Organic': The Corruption of Label." *The Ecologist* July August.

Lummis, C. Douglas. 1996. *Radical Democracy*. Ithaca: Cornell University Press

Lutz, Mark. 1999. *Economics for the Common Good*. London: Routledge.

MacLeod, Greg. 1997. *From Mondragon to America: Experiments in Community Economic Development*. Sydney: University College of Cape Breton Press.

MacPherson, Ian. 1999. "Of Spheres, Perspectives, Cultures, and Stages: The Consumer Co-operative Movement in English-Speaking Canada, 1830–1980." In Ellen Furlough and Carl Strikwerda (eds.), *Consumers Against Capitalism? Consumer Cooperation in Europe, North America, and Japan, 1840–1990*. New York: Rowman and Littlefield.

MacRae, Rod. 1990. "A History of Sustainable Agriculture." *Ecological Agriculture Projects*. Available at <http://eap.mcgill.ca/AASA_1.htm> accessed July 2008.

Madeley, John. 2002. *Food for All: The Need for a New Agriculture*. Halifax, NS: Fernwood Publishing.

Manning, Richard. 2004. *Against the Grain*. New York: North Point Press, a Division of Farrar, Straus and Giroux.

Mauss, Marcel. 1967. *The Gift: Forms and Functions of Exchange in Archaic Societies*. Trans. by Ian Cunnison. New York: Norton.

McMurty, John. 1998. *Unequal Freedoms: The Global Market as an Ethical System*. Toronto: Garamond Press.

Monaghan, Peter. 2003. "Taking on Rational Man." *Chronicle of Higher Education* January 24.

Monbiot, George. 1996a. "The Land Is Ours." *Schumacher Lectures*. Bristol (UK).

_____. 1996b. "Breaking the Foodchain." *The Guardian* November 5.

_____. 1997. "Social Engineering." *The Guardia*. September 17.

_____. 2001. "The War Against Small Farms." *The Guardian* August 7.

Mondragon Corporacion Cooperativa. 2004. Website at <www.mcc.es/ing/index.asp> accessed July 2008.

Montague, Peter. 1997. "The True Story of Alar — Part 2." *Rachel's Health and Environment Weekly* 531, January 30.

Moore, Michael. 2003. *Dude, Where's My Country?* New York: Warner Books.

Mouffe, Chantal. 1996. "Radical Democracy or Liberal Democracy?" In David Trend (ed.), *Radical Democracy*. New York: Routledge.

Nace, Ted. 2006. "Breadbasket of Democracy." *Orion Magazine* May/June.

Nachman-Hunt, Nancy. 2003. "Will Fair Trade Become the Next Growth Wave?" *The Natural Foods Merchandiser* September 1.

Nadeau, Denise. 1996. *Counting Our Victories: Popular Education and Organising*. BC: Repeal the Deal Productions.

National Co-operative Business Association. 2008. Website at <www.ncba.coop> accessed July 2008.

National Farmers Union (Canada). 2003. "The Farm Crisis, Bigger Farms and the Myths of 'Competition' and 'Efficiency.'" Saskatoon, November 20.

Nelson, Robert. 2001. *Economics as Religion: from Samuelson to Chicago and Beyond*. University Park: Pennsylvania State University Press.

Nestle, Marion. 2003. *Safe Food: Bacteria, Biotechnology and Bioterrorism*. Berkeley and Los Angeles: University of California Press.

Nystrom, Lorne (ed.). 1999. *Just Making Change*. Ottawa: Golden Dog Press.

Olewiler, Nancy, and Barry Field. 1995. *Environmental Economics*. Second Canadian edition. Toronto: McGraw-Hill Ryerson.

Oliver, Rachel. 2008. "All About: Food and Fossil Fuels." *CNN online*. March 17. Available at <http://edition.cnn.com/2008/WORLD/asiapcf/03/16/eco.food.miles/> accessed July 2008.

O'Neill, Brian. 2001. "What's Eating Us?" *Oxfam News*. Website at <www.Oxfam.ca/news/>.

Organic Consumers Association. Website at <www.organicconsumers.org> accessed July 2008.

_____. 2003a. "UK Supermarket Giants Say No to GMO." *Reuters News Service*. July

17. Available at <http://www.organicconsumers.org/supermarket/uk_super-market_gmos.cfm> accessed July 2008.

_____. 2003b. "1 out of 10 for Starbucks Effort." Media Release. April 24. Available at <http://www.organicconsumers.org/Starbucks/042403_fair_trade_starbucks.htm> accessed July 2008.

Organic Trade Association. 2007. Website at <www.ota.com> accessed July 2008.

Ottawa Food Security Council. 2003. "Timeline." Website at <www.spcottawa.on.ca/ofsc/>.

Oxfam Québec and Argus Films (producers). n.d. *Coffee with a Taste of Fairness* (videotape). Ecooconic and Aseed.

Oxford English Dictionary. 1991. Second Edition. Oxford: Clarendon Press.

Patel, Raj. 2007. *Stuffed and Starved: Markets, Power and the Hidden Battle for the World's Food System*. Toronto, ON: HarperCollins.

Peace and Environment Resource Centre. 2004. "Community Economic Development." Website at <http://perc.ca>.

Pegg, Shawn. 2007. *Hunger Count 2007*. Toronto: Canadian Association of Food Banks.

People's Food Commission (PFC). 1980. *The Land of Milk and Money: The National Report of the People's Food Commission*. Toronto: Between the Lines.

_____. Archives, National Archives, Ottawa.

_____. Local Working Group Kit. Unpublished.

Petrini, Carlo. 2001. *Slow Food: The Case for Taste*. Trans. by William McCuaig. New York: Columbia University Press.

Pimbert, Michel P. 2002. "Social Learning for Ecological Literacy and Democracy: Emerging Issues and Challenges." Paper for *International Learning Workshop on Farmer Field Schools*. Indonesia, October.

Polanyi, Karl. 1944. *The Great Transformation*. Boston: Beacon Press.

Pollan, Michael. 2001. "Behind the Organic-Industrial Complex." *New York Times* May 13.

Polletta, Francesca. 2002. *Freedom Is an Endless Meeting: Democracy in American Social Movements*. Chicago: University of Chicago Press.

Pontius, John, R. Dilts, and A. Bartlett (eds.). 2002. *From Farmer Field School to Community IPM: Ten Years of IPM Training in Asia*. Thailand: FAO.

Porter, Catherine. 2007. "Food Growers Target Customers with a Conscience." *Toronto Star* October 3.

Pottier, Johan. 1999. *Anthropology of Food: The Social Dynamics of Food Security*. Malden, MA: Blackwell.

Pretty, Jules N. 1995. *Regenerating Agriculture: Policies and Practice for Sustainability and Self-Reliance*. Washington, DC: Joseph Henry Press.

Putnam, Robert D. 1995. "Bowling Alone: America's Declining Social Capital." *Journal of Democracy* 6, 1.

Qualman, Darrin, and Nettie Wiebe. 2002. "The Structural Adjustment of Canadian Agriculture." *Canadian Council for Policy Alternatives*. CCPA Publication. November.

Race, Matthew. 1999. *Jobs of Our Own: Alternatives to the Market and the State*. London: Comerford and Miller.

Raffensperger, Lisa. 2007. "Brazil Upholds Right to Food for Millions." *Earth Trends*

World Resources Institute online. October 16.

Ransom, David. 2001. *No-Nonsense Guide to Fair Trade*. Toronto: New Internationalist Publications and Between the Lines.

Rebick, Judy. 2000. *Imagine Democracy*. Toronto: Stoddart Publishing.

Roberts, Wayne. 2003. "Beyond Organics: Third World Farmers Tell Us Why Banning Pesticides is Not Enough." *NOW Magazine* January 30–February 5.

Rocha, Cecilia. 2000. "An Integrated Program for Urban Food Security: The Case of Belo Horizonte, Brazil."

Roosevelt, Margot. 2004. "The Coffee Clash." *Time Magazine* March 1.

Rosser, J. Barkley Jr. 1992. "The Dialogue Between the Economic and Ecologic Theories of Evolution." *Journal of Economic Behavior and Organization* 17: 195– 215.

Rosset, Peter. 1999. "Afterword." In Douglas H. Boucher (ed.), *Paradox of Plenty: Hunger in A Bountiful World*. Oakland, CA: Food First Books.

_____. 2000. "Small-Scale Farming." *The Ecologist* 30, June: 36.

Roy, Arundhati. 1999. *The Cost of Living*. New York: Modern Library (Random House).

Ruiz-Marrero, Carmelo. 2004. "Is Organic Farming Becoming a Victim of its own Success?" *Corpwatch*. November 25. Available at <http://www.corpwatch.org/article.php?id=11712> accessed July 2008.

Sanders. 2004. "Lessons from the Land Institute." *Audubon Magazine* March.

Schlosser, Eric. 2002. *Fast Food Nation*. New York: Harper Collins.

Schumpeter, Joseph A. (ed. from manuscript by Elizabeth Boody Schumpeter.) 1954. *History of Economic Analysis*. New York: Oxford University Press.

SEJUP (Servico Brasileiro de Justica e Paz). 2004. No. 503, January 2.

Shiva, Vandana. 1993. *Monocultures of the Mind*. London: Zed Books.

_____. 2000. "Global Perspective." *The Ecologist* 30, June: 37.

_____. 2005. *Earth Democracy: Justice, Sustainability and Peace*. Cambridge, MA: South End Press.

Shuman, Michael. 2000. *Going Local: Creating Self-reliant Communities in a Global Age*. New York: Routledge.

Shutkin, William A. 2000. *The Land That Could Be: Environmentalism and Democracy in the Twenty-First Century*. Cambridge, MA: MIT Press.

Sierra Club. 1998. Press Release. Sept. 16. Available at <http://www.sierraclub.ca/national/media/scc-nfu-coc-se98.htm> accessed July 2008.

Sligh, Michael, and C. Christman. 2003. "Who Owns Organic? The Global Status, Prospects, and Challenges of a Changing Organic Market." Pittsboro, NC: Rural Advancement Foundation International (RAFI).

South Central Farmers. 2008. "For South Central Farmers, a New Setting for Their Plots." April 28. Available at <http://www.southcentralfarmers.com/index.php?option=com_content&task=view&id=323&Itemid=47> accessed July 2008.

Stanford, Jim. 1999. *Paper Boom: Why Real Prosperity Requires a New Approach to Canada's Economy*. Ottawa: Canadian Centre for Policy Alternatives and Toronto: James Lorimer.

Stille, Alexander. 2002. "Slow Food's Pleasure Principles." *Utne Reader* May/June.

Stop Communtiy Food Centre, The. 2007. Website at <www.thestop.org> accessed July 2008.

Sustain (U.K.). 2002. Website at < http://www.sustainweb.org/index.php> accessed July 2008.

Suzuki, David. 2004. "A Geneticist's Personal Perspective." Available at <http://www.davidsuzuki.org/files/General/DTSbiotech.pdf> accessed July 2008.

Swift, Richard. 2002. *The No Nonsense Guide to Democracy*. Oxford: New Internationalist Publications and London: Verso.

TransFair Canada. 2007. Website at <www.transfair.ca> accessed July 2008.

TransFair USA. 2007. Website at <www.TransFairusa.org> accessed July 2008.

TransFair. 2004a. "Fair Trade Market Achieves Record Growth in 2003." Available at <http://www.transfairusa.org/content/about/archives_pr/pr_040329.php> accessed July 2008.

TransFair. 2004b. "TransFair USA Announces Fresh Fruit as Newest Fair Trade Certified Product." Available at <http://www.transfairusa.org/content/about/archives_pr/pr_040122.php> accessed July 2008.

Trend, David (ed.). 1996. *Radical Democracy: Identity, Citizenship, and the State*. New York: Routledge.

United Northeast. 2004. "A Brief History of United Northeast." Website at <www.unitednortheast.com/>.

United States Department of Agriculture (USDA). 2004. "Organic Production." Available at <www.ers.USDA.gov/Data/Organic/> accessed July 2008.

_____. 2005. "U.S. Market Profile for Organic Food Products." February 22.

Wackernagel, Mathis, and William Rees. 1996. *Our Ecological Footprint: Reducing Human Impact on the Earth*. Gabriola Island, BC: New Society Publishers.

Wainwright, Hilary. 2003. *Reclaim the State: Experiments in Popular Democracy*. London, New York: Verso.

Wale, Michael. 2001. "Digging for Victory." *The Ecologist* 31, March: 54–55.

Waller, Signe, and Jim Rose. 1995. "A Conversation About our Food System." *Z Magazine* February.

Waridel, Laure. 1997. *Coffee With A Cause*. Montreal: Les Editions Intouchables.

Webber, Marlene. 1992. *Food for Thought: How Our Dollar Democracy Drove 2 Million Canadians into Food Banks to Collect Private Charity in Place of Public Justice*. Toronto: Coach House Press.

Welsh Galluzzo, Teresa. 2005. "Small Packages, Big Benefits: Economic Advantages of Local Wind Projects." Iowa Policy Project.

Whatmore, S. and L. Thorne. 1997. "Nourishing Networks: Alternative Geographies of Food." In D. Goodman and M. Watts (eds.), *Globalising Food: Agrarian Questions and Global Restructuring*. London: Routledge.

Wheeler, Glenn. 2002. "Bitter Over Beans: Starbucks Deal with Oxfam Percolates Angst." *NOW Magazine* August 22–28.

Wilson, Patricia. 1997. "Building Social Capital: A Learning Agenda for the Twenty-first Century." Vol. 34, nos. 5-6.

Wright, Angus, and W. Wolford. 2003. *To Inherit the Earth: the Landless Movement and the Struggle for a New Brazil*. Oakland, CA: Food First Books.

Wu, Jianguo. 1995. "From Balance of Nature to Hierarchical Patch Dynamics: A Paradigm Shift in Ecology." *The Quarterly Review of Biology* 70, 4 (December).

Yalnizyan, Armine. 1998. *The Growing Gap: A Report on the Growing Inequality Between the Rich and Poor in Canada*. Toronto: Centre for Social Justice.